PERGAMON INTERNATIONAL LIBRARY
of Science, Technology, Engineering and Social Studies

*The 1000-volume original paperback library in aid of education,
industrial training and the enjoyment of leisure*

Publisher: Robert Maxwell, M.C.

Planning U.S. Security

Pergamon Titles of Related Interest

Related Journals*

PERGAMON POLICY STUDIES ON SECURITY AFFAIRS

Planning U.S. Security
Defense Policy in the Eighties

Edited by
Philip S. Kronenberg

A Study Developed at the National Defense University

Pergamon Press
NEW YORK • OXFORD • TORONTO • SYDNEY • PARIS • FRANKFURT

Pergamon Press Offices:

U.S.A.   Pergamon Press Inc., Maxwell House, Fairview Park,
                     Elmsford, New York 10523, U.S.A.

U.K.   Pergamon Press Ltd., Headington Hill Hall,
                     Oxford OX3 0BW, England

CANADA   Pergamon Press Canada Ltd., Suite 104, 150 Consumers Road,
                     Willowdale, Ontario M2J 1P9, Canada

AUSTRALIA   Pergamon Press (Aust.) Pty. Ltd., P.O. Box 544,
                     Potts Point, NSW 2011, Australia

FRANCE   Pergamon Press SARL, 24 rue des Ecoles,
                     75240 Paris, Cedex 05, France

FEDERAL REPUBLIC Pergamon Press GmbH, Hammerweg 6,
OF GERMANY   6242 Kronberg/Taunus, Federal Republic of Germany

Library of Congress Cataloging in Publication Data
Main entry under title:

Planning U.S. Security.

   (Pergamon policy studies on security affairs)
   Bibliography: p.
   Includes index.
   1. United States--Military policy. 2. United
States--National security. I. Kronenberg,
Philip S. II. National Defense University.
III. Series.
UA23.P54   1981   355'.0335'73   81-13791
ISBN 0-08-028082-X   AACR2
ISBN 0-08-028081-1 (pbk.)

Opinions, conclusions, and recommendations expressed or implied within are solely those of the authors, and do not necessarily represent the views of the National Defense University, the Department of Defense, or any other US Government agency or private organization.

Printed in the United States of America

To Shafer, Gigi, and Grant . . . and all the other children who rely on planners, warriors, practitioners of statecraft, scholars, and other superheroes to provide a safe and decent world.

CONTENTS

FIGURES

FOREWORD

There are increasingly complex challenges to free world values and institutions and, thus, to US national security interests and objectives. To be optimally prepared to meet these challenges rationally, the United States must have a coherent national security planning process that reflects a future-oriented concept of US interests and objectives, permitting us to orchestrate all elements of the nation's power in behalf of those objectives. These realities have been recognized by our senior military leader, the Chairman of the Joint Chiefs of Staff, General David C. Jones, USAF. It was in response to the expressed concerns of General Jones that the National Security Affairs Institute of this University cosponsored a series of seminars with the Under Secretary of Defense for Policy during the fall and winter of 1980-81.

The seminar participants were distinguished members of government, the military, academe, and other civilian sectors, with relevant expertise in the areas of long-range national security policy and strategy development. They conducted a far-ranging dialogue on the multiple aspects of planning US security and specifically examined the complex institutional and structural constraints on long-range planning while they sought to identify principles that should underlie the security planning process.

It was agreed that the diffusion of power and responsibility designed into our political system is reflected in the US security planning process. No one governmental institution monopolizes this process; instead, it is characterized by many actors in a plurality of organizations having diverse, sometimes conflicting, priorities on security issues. If there is no locus for managing the priority setting of these actors, and for integrating diverse priorities into a coherent, long-range strategic framework, the result is ambiguity in policy and strategy and a planning product that is less than optimally suited for a consistent, proactive US role in safeguarding national interests in a changing global environment. Although the seminars did not seek consensus on solutions, they did generate, as reflected in this volume, a clearer perspective of our security planning process, some provocative and creative suggestions for improving that process, and some tentative principles to guide US national security planning.

As the new President of this unique University, I will seek to foster a climate that encourages and rewards original thinking and innovative approaches to national security. It is, therefore, with pleasure that I introduce this volume to national security policymakers and other thoughtful readers who may find much in this volume to stimulate further dialogue and ideas on the critical task of planning for US security in a turbulent world.

JOHN S. PUSTAY
Lieutenant General, USAF
President

PREFACE

This volume addresses the concept of national security planning and several dimensions of the planning process including its politics and strategy, the societal context, organizational issues, the relationship between planning and the intelligence function, and measures needed to improve planning. The book is intended to interest and challenge the experienced practitioner or student of defense policy, while at the same time informing the knowledgeable lay reader.

The book grows out of the six monthly sessions of the 1980-81 Dinner Seminar Series on National Security Affairs. These sessions represent the fourth in an annual seminar series convened by the National Security Affairs Institute of the National Defense University. The University is the parent organization of the National War College and the Industrial College of the Armed Forces.

The Institute was established to respond to the mission of the National Defense University (NDU) to provide creative new approaches to the major national security policy issues facing the United States Government. The Institute complements other NDU research programs that develop studies of national security policy and strategy issues and draws on the distinctive capabilities of the student bodies, faculties, and associated Senior Research Fellows of the National Defense University.

The Institute is in a unique position in that much of its research efforts have been related to the policy research programs of the Office of the Under Secretary of Defense for Policy. Cosponsorship by this government agency insures that policymakers will profit directly by joining in Institute seminars and will have available to them the products of these discussions, incorporated in such works as this volume. In cosponsorship with the Under Secretary for Policy, the National Security Affairs Institute organizes conferences, symposia, and other forums in which senior civilian and military policymakers from the executive and legislative branches can join in candid, informal discussions with experts from the academic community and knowledgeable representatives from the media and other sectors of our society.

Normally, papers are commissioned to stimulate discussion of selected policy issues at the meetings, which are attended by small groups led by a chairperson. The purpose is to have policymakers and other experts assess the policy implications of particular security issues and suggest an agenda of initiatives that might assist in better coping with the problems. In most cases, the results of these discussion sessions are published and broadly circulated to selected policymakers and to others interested in national security issues.

The Dinner Seminar Series was one such jointly sponsored effort and stimulated the ideas contained in this book. From November 1980 to April 1981, the Institute hosted six monthly dinner seminar meetings on problems of planning US security. Approximately thirty people involved themselves in the seminar sessions; a list of these distinguished participants is included at the end of this volume.

I can fairly describe myself in the Pentagonese dialect as "dual-hatted" during my association with the 1980-81 Dinner Seminar Series. It was my privilege during that period to serve both as seminar chairman and as editor of this volume; in those two roles I was placed in the debt of a number of thoughtful people whom I wish to acknowledge and thank.

As seminar chairman, first let me thank our host at these sessions, Lieutenant General Robert G. Gard, Jr., former President of the National Defense University, and Ambassador Monteagle Stearns, former Vice President of the National Defense University—our co-host at several sessions—for their hospitality and active participation in the series. Second, I wish to salute the authors and other participants who brought so much to the substance of each session. The quality of their ideas, reflected throughout this volume, and their good humor made my job an easy one. Finally, whatever success the seminar enjoyed is due in no small way to those who handled arrangements and saw to it that we were properly fed and watered but otherwise left alone to conduct our business. The organizing efforts and care provided us by Colonel Gayle Heckel, US Air Force, the Deputy Director of the Institute, and Ms. JoAnne Lewis, its Executive Secretary, deserve our special thanks. Also, the staff of the Officers' Club at Fort Lesley J. McNair in Washington, DC, the site of the sessions, merit our appreciation for their gracious service.

My role as editor and contributing author profited, of course, from the efforts of the other authors, as well as from the rich discussion conducted on a nonattribution basis among the participants that I endeavor to summarize and interpret in chapter 8. I am also beholden to a number of people—including several of our seminar members—who enhanced this book by their candid criticisms of parts of it or their willingness to share with me some of their expertise. Alphabetically, they are: Major General Edward Atkeson, US Army; Dr. Archie Barrett; Lieutenant Colonel Robert Chandler, US Air Force; Dr. David Chu; Lieutenant Colonel Jay Cope, US Army; Major General James Dalton, US Air Force; Captain Nori Endo, US Navy; Colonel Lawrence Farrell, Jr., US Air Force; Lieutenant General Paul Gorman, US Army; Captain William Held, US Navy; Colonel William Jenkins, US Army; Colonel John Landry, US Army; Professor John Lovell; Colonel John Nolan, US Air Force; Colonel Ralph Orey, US Marine Corps; Colonel Stuart Perkins, US Army; Dr. Lewis Sorley; Colonel William Staudenmaier, US Army; Lieutenant Colonel Larry Tucker, US Air Force; and Dr. Victor Utgoff.

The good people at National Defense University Press deserve recognition for their role in the production of this volume. I am very appreciative of the efforts of the staff of the NDU Research Directorate who facilitated the rapid publication of this volume, including Mr. Al Helder who assisted in preparing seminar notes for my final chapter. My special thanks go to Ms. Evelyn Lakes who edited my drafts and administered the publication of the book.

Special credit is due Lieutenant General R. G. Gard, Jr., US Army (Ret.), former President, National Defense University, who retired while this volume was in publication, and his successor, Lieutenant General John S. Pustay, US Air Force, for their interest in the National Security Affairs Institute. That has been central to building the growing reputation of the Institute in the professional community. Recognition is also due the Office of the Under Secretary of Defense for Policy for cosponsorship of Institute programs, and particularly the seminar series that was the basis for this volume. That support has been an important determiner of the success of the Institute.

The congenial *éminence grise* and cruise director of the 1980-81 Dinner Seminar Series was Colonel Franklin Margiotta, US Air Force. Frank developed the original concept for the security planning topic and designed the structure for our Series, including extending invitations to participate to me and the other authors. Great credit is due Frank; I want to thank him for all his help and encouragement with this project. When Frank is not orchestrating conferences or taking seminar notes or contributing to our professional literature, one can find him performing with distinction as Director of Research at the National Defense University, as publisher of the National Defense University Press, and as director of the National Security Affairs Institute.

A final expression of thanks is due Dr. Renee Loeffler for her support throughout this project. Also, I want to compliment her for the fine index she prepared for this book under severe time constraints and for her excellent judgment in the selection of husbands, as of 1973.

PHILIP S. KRONENBERG

Blacksburg, Virginia
July 1981

In war we must always leave room for strokes of fortune, and accidents that cannot be foreseen.

Polybius, c. 125 B.C.

DIMENSIONS OF NATIONAL SECURITY PLANNING

1

PHILIP S. KRONENBERG
Virginia Polytechnic Institute and State University

Of all the institutions in an advanced society, it may be the military which most embodies the essence of planning. Artifacts of its planning nature abound. One sees large-scale military organizations with men and women trained expensively and at length in skills, many of which are born of doctrine, customs, and crafts that have been honed for centuries. There are families of complex weapons, expensively acquired and maintained though not always perfectly matched with the skills and judgment of their human tenders and overseers. Great marvels of technology for acquiring, storing, sorting, and processing information stand as monuments to those who labor to anticipate and deal with unexpected threats. Ambitious programs of research and analysis consume the mental resources and time of many within the defense institutions and then reach out insatiably to draw further intellectual energy from across the society. Finally, monumental effort is applied to coordinate and rationalize this great swirl of people, machines, and ideas and to enforce their application to state purposes—many of which were set in train decades earlier in the heat of international or institutional politics.

To plan well for the common defense is taken to be a necessary thing. Indeed, many see better planning and preparedness as the best hope for the United States to sustain itself in a world of growing insecurity where poor planning can have lethal consequences. As US foreign and national security policy decisionmakers face future planning challenges, important questions— both new and old—need to be raised.

The chapters which follow attempt to identify some of the more significant of these questions and to explore their answers. However, few if any final answers or neat solutions will be found in these pages. Tough problems elude easy solutions. Further-

1

more, thoughtful readers will likely find ideas that both please and displease them. The diversity of our authors and seminar participants assures this result.

PLANNING AND THE ROLE OF STRATEGY

In chapter 2, "On the Need to Reform American Strategy," Edward N. Luttwak offers a provocative critique of strategic thought in the United States and explores its implications for the conduct of military policy. His central thesis is that the formulation and execution of US military policy historically has been bankrupt because of the failure to inform military policy with a strategic perspective. Only a strategic perspective can give a larger context of meaning to the development and use of military force. Strategic thought, in Luttwak's view, requires the connecting of diverse issues into a systematic pattern—a style of thought that is contrary to the deeply rooted American cultural tradition of pragmatism. Earlier in its history, the United States could well afford to indulge this bias toward pragmatism, thanks to its relative detachment from overseas entanglements which might require substantial military commitments.

The emergence of the United States as a superpower ended the luxury if not the practice of pragmatic detachment from matters strategic. The period after World War II saw the emergence of a substantial (relative to prewar commitment) standing military establishment in this country. For Luttwak, this development was not accompanied by an equivalent growth in our national capacity to think and act strategically. No potent grand strategy emerged after World War II other than the passive orientation dubbed "containment."

Whatever limited virtues containment may have had as a strategic perspective, in Luttwak's judgment they were to be overwhelmed by a growing attachment by policymakers and military planners to the cult of systems analysis. His quarrel with systems analysis is that it is based on an economic calculus of civil efficiency that masks the policy rationale for using military force. Furthermore, a primary focus on civil efficiency distracts one from concern with successful military action. The upshot of Luttwak's thesis is that the "how" of using military force cannot be linked with the "why" of using force, because the latter is not framed at a national policy level.

For Luttwak, much of the failure of the United States to achieve a successful result in the use of its armed forces (in the national exhaustion of Vietnam and the abortive rescue attempt in Iran, among others) is due to our reliance on civil efficiency as a methodology to determine effectiveness. In turn, he argues, this produces a bureaucratic orientation with emphases on production modalities (for example, firepower rather than maneuver as an operational method); economics of scale (for example, reliance on large, "cost-effective" systems having high unit costs and force structures built around "heavy" combat units); and upward career mobility (for example, high turnover under rotation policies which enhance one's managerial "portfolio" but are dysfunctional for unit combat effectiveness).

Luttwak places a major share of the blame for these deficiencies in strategic thought—and action—on the American officer corps and the contemporary profession of arms. He argues that the officer corps has abandoned its traditional spheres of tactical and strategic expertise in response to the seductions of a bureaucratic-managerial ethic rooted in the norms of civil efficiency. He sees some potential for constructive change, however, in the shifting national mood around issues of defense spending and Soviet expansionism. Luttwak sees this as a time for shaping a *national strategy* and offers some rules to that end.

THE PLANNING ENVIRONMENT

Chapter 3 by James K. Oliver and James A. Nathan is a probing examination of "The American Environment for Security Planning." Their analysis explores a set of contextual factors that constrain but do not necessarily preclude effective long-range security planning. The first factor they examine is the constitutional framework of government in the United States. This framework reflects two fundamental—and partially contradictory—principles: the centralizing proposals of Alexander Hamilton and the high priority given by James Madison to the restraint of central executive power even if this reduced the efficiency of government. As a result, a fundamental tension exists between the legislative and executive branches of US Government.

A second factor considered by Oliver and Nathan is bureaucracy, which constrains planning not only because of its complex structural and procedural characteristics but also because of the huge staff cadres that tend to accrete in bureaucratic organizations. The authors point out the irony of all this: bureaucracy was initially turned to as a partial solution to the limitations of the constitutional framework.

Democracy itself is the third major constraint on planning cited by the authors. It is their sense that the essence of this "problem" rests with the nature of the electorate to whom policymakers are accountable. Policymakers now have to be somehow responsive to mass and elite opinion, the media, and a complex range of more active and powerful interest groups.

The historical evolution of US foreign and national security policy reflects oscillation between the two poles of congressional limitations and policy intrusion at one end and vigorous, centralized executive initiative at the other. This implies for the defense planner a necessity to work with a structure that is fundamentally ambivalent about the exercise of influence over security policy. Oliver and Nathan conclude that—short of a radical transformation of this structure—all the planner can do is try to develop a clearer understanding of the nature of the planning process; better organize the bureaucratic domain within which planning proceeds; try to identify future security needs, and, ultimately, resign oneself to the debilitating encounters with a political and institutional environment initially contrived and subsequently evolved to frustrate the planner's efforts.

FORECASTING AND PLANNING

Davis B. Bobrow is concerned in chapter 4 with analyzing the elusive relationship between security planning and efforts to illuminate the future with the organized intelligence function. His chapter, "Security Futures: INTELLIGENCE and intelligence," incorporates attention not only to the role of the agencies that are formally part of the intelligence community ("INTELLIGENCE"), but also to the contributions to planning made by other groups, such as internal analysis staffs, think tanks, and university research centers ("intelligence").

Bobrow points up the importance of recognizing that defense plans, INTELLIGENCE, and intelligence have three interdependent purposes: reduce the number, frequency, and intensity of surprises to senior national security officials; reduce their "grasp time" (the time required for them to comprehend the situation they face—thus expanding the time available to them to make decisions); and reduce their "response time" (the time needed to react effectively, thereby increasing their control over security outcomes). The achievement of these three purposes depends significantly on both the plans and the information that support them. The crucial significance for Bobrow of the interdependence among these three purposes is that the national performance of the security function can be no better than the least well achieved of these purposes, a "lowest common denominator" of profound importance.

This chapter argues that the relationship between defense planning and the intelligence function is likely to be troubled and significantly unsatisfactory to all parties concerned. The simple but regrettable explanation for this, offers Bobrow, is that US national security now and for the future poses substantive problems of extraordinary difficulty, yet the institutional resources for dealing with these problems are rather ordinary, large organizations beset with all the pathologies characteristic of the *genre*. Planning and the intelligence function also are seen to be unbalanced in their time perspectives. Investment plans made today determine the means for pursuing national security ends for the next several decades. Although the ends are assumed to be fairly constant, they may in fact change within a single administration. Instrumental strategies, assumed to be constant, may instead be makeshift attempts to reconcile inherited means with partially unanticipated ends. Bobrow concludes that unbalanced planning leads to unbalanced demand and use of INTELLIGENCE and intelligence. This information imbalance, in turn, reinforces the unbalanced planning pattern.

This destabilizing linkage between planning and information produces a number of anomalies which are discussed in this chapter. Among them Bobrow sees a tendency of planners (who should know better!) to embody in their plans a set of important limiting assumptions. These assumptions deny that other global actors have their own agendas and strategies and are affected by what they think to be our plans. Furthermore, planning is largely limited to coping with current enemies and to treating alliances as unitary actors rather than as imperfectly centralized coalitions.

Bobrow proposes a series of measures to improve the planning-information relationship. In so doing, he also questions the importance and desirability of strengthening the role of the Defense Department in the intelligence function and the proposals for giving priority to tactical over other forms of intelligence.

THE PLANNING PROCESS

Chapter 5, "National Security Planning: Images and Issues," was written by me for the purposes of conceptualizing some of the psychological, organizational, and political factors at work in security planning and proposing several general principles to guide the management of the planning process.

The chapter opens with a discussion of factors that undermine our ability to use abstract principles as a substantive planning guide for decisionmakers. I suggest that we should turn from the search for principles to guide substantive planning decisions (for example, resist a Marxist-dominated insurgency in the Middle East or modernize theater nuclear weapons in Europe) because these decisions require political choices that cannot be incorporated usefully into abstract, doctrinal prescriptions. The substance of plans, like policies, cannot be judged as "good" or "bad" in the abstract; they are contingent upon the specific values and interests one wishes to serve. Instead, it is proposed that a more fruitful course of action is to develop principles for *managing* the national security planning process that will produce the plans. The management of planning rather than the selection of substantive plans then becomes the focus of planning principles. The chapter pursues this course by examining planning as both art *and* management.

As an art form it relies on the planner's distinctive personality. Also like the fine artist, the fine planner is limited by the materials, structures, working conditions, and ambiance of the organizational workplace. Finally, like the artist, the planner lives in an interactive relationship with the object of concern. This often subtle interaction provides a series of political and programmatic reference points to give definition to the planner's creativity as constrained by available resources.

When viewing planning as a management rather than as an artistic endeavor, chapter 5 portrays it as the *strategic management* of the national security organizations of government. Thus planning, implementation, and evaluation of policy or program performance become linked together in an integrating concept for managing national security organizations. The intended end result is to control the process whereby these security organizations shape their future missions, jurisdiction, and operating styles so that planning as a function does not become isolated from the operational world.

Planning intends to bring greater rationality—a better fit between ends and means—to national security affairs. Yet planning seldom has the neatly rational quality found in textbooks because the people who plan and use the products of planners are not omniscient calculating machines. The interpretations they bring to events and their decisions and plans are distinctly influenced by psychological, organizational, and political factors.

This chapter examines these factors in some detail in order to prepare a conceptual basis for enunciating six principles to guide management of the national security planning process. These principles are developed in the latter part of chapter 5. They address the composition and purpose of the security planning process, the locus of responsibility for planning, the career incentives for planning assignments, the role of planning as a tool for enhancing decisionmaker sensitivity, and the need for planning to contribute to the policy dialogue.

ORGANIZING FOR PLANNING

"Department of Defense Organization: Planning for Planning," chapter 6, is a sweeping analytical treatment by Archie D. Barrett of the organizational arrangements of the Department of Defense (DOD) and their major implications for planning. Barrett's approach rests on the premise that one cannot *directly* evaluate the impact of organizational patterns on planning capability or performance. Instead, he recognizes that planning and organization are inextricably related and therefore turns to the rich resource of the Defense Organization Study of 1977-80 as a basis for assessing the planning capabilities of the Department.

The Defense Organization Study includes—identifying them with the names of their respective chairmen—the Ignatius Study (DOD headquarters), the Steadman Study (the national military command structure), the Rice Study (resource management: the planning, programming, and budgeting system; acquisition; logistics; personnel career mix; and medical care), the Antonelli Study (defense agencies review), and the Rosenblum Study (combat effective training). Barrett's integrated assessment of these five studies is that they represent a critical indictment of the ability of the Department of Defense to perform its two central functions: maintaining and employing military forces. The *maintaining function* includes recruiting, training, research and development, procurement, administration, logistical support, mainte-

7

nance, and health care. The *employing function* is performed consequent to providing military advice to civilian authorities and involves directing the operations of combat forces in peacetime or wartime—including assessments of enemy threat and friendly warfighting capability, strategic and logistical planning, and command and control arrangements.

Barrett finds a general pattern in the five reports that attributes dominance in departmental functions to the "central management" (the Secretary and the Office of the Secretary of Defense) and the uniformed services; the relationship between central management and the services is the anvil on which the major decisions are formed which affect the maintaining and employing functions. In contrast, the author finds little relative influence among the civilian service secretaries or the joint organizations (the Joint Chiefs of Staff and their supporting joint staffing structures and the commanders in chief of the unified and specified commands).

The indictment of DOD organization in the Defense Organization Study leads Barrett to propose some major changes in the department's organizational design. They involve a streamlined *maintaining* arm, a stronger *employing* arm, explicit delineation of the roles of central management (the Secretary *and* Office of the Secretary of Defense), and increased emphasis on an active higher administrative role by the Secretary of Defense.

These reorganizing thrusts would move in several directions. Barrett envisions that each service secretary would strengthen his oversight of the *maintaining* function by consolidating his relatively small secretariat with the large military headquarters staff and sharing control of this integrated staff with the uniformed service chief. On the *employment* side, Barrett proposes progressive elaboration of a *joint* institution, based upon bringing the unified and specified commands closer to the other joint elements and reducing the dependence of the Joint Staff on service staff influence. He recommends that the Secretary of Defense place increased emphasis on a senior administrative role as chief executive of DOD, in addition to his leadership in the sphere of substantive policy.

IMPROVING THE SYSTEM

The title of chapter 7, "On Making the System Work," captures the thesis of its author, Lawrence J. Korb. His argument is that many of the factors frequently cited as sources of problems in national security planning are an integral part of our system for conducting the business of public policy and will resist most reformist solutions and efforts at reorganization. The more promising approach, in his judgment, is to take the system as a given and work within it.

The diffusion of power in the US Government and the ambiguous delegation of constitutional authority between the Executive and Congress increasingly impede the formulation of consistent national security policy. This basic fragmentation of power goes deeper than the separation of power between the two branches that is fundamental to our governmental structure. Recently, our political system has found that single-issue interest groups are playing a potent role in national affairs. Furthermore, the growth of a large and expert public bureaucracy has had an impact which Korb feels inhibits effective planning. Not only has the size of bureaucracy slowed the decision process but the multiplicity of bureaucratic players requiring coordination and opportunities for participation in decisionmaking has "clogged the system."

Korb agrees with those who find that the Department of Defense is dominated by the "central management" and the military service staffs. In contrast, the service secretariats of each military department (which constitute the staffs of the civilian Secretaries of the Army, Navy, and Air Force), the staff organization of the Joint Chiefs of Staff, and the commanders in chief of the unified and specified commands all have less power than their assigned functions would suggest. The effect of this uneven distribution of power, claims Korb, is that the military services are able to pursue policies which are favorable to their own organizations but are not necessarily beneficial to the Department of Defense; this relative autonomy has resulted in policies which are often inconsistent and short-sighted.

The bureaucratic infighting that accompanies this fragmented system produces, in the author's analysis, a situation where questions of long-term strategic importance are often reduced to short-term victories or losses for the organizations and people involved. It becomes impossible to maintain a future-oriented perspective when policy is increasingly shaped by organizational power struggles and a confusion of priorities. It also becomes difficult, if not impossible, to employ individuals strictly as long-term planners. And Korb feels that those who focus on long-term programs are not rewarded by their organizations.

The author recommends that the best approach is to accept the realities of the system and to work within it, relying on people who understand its characteristics. He calls for action to change obvious flaws in the system but counsels that an incrementalist approach will cause significant benefits to accrue over an extended period of time. Many of our problems are cyclical according to Korb, and even with its flaws, our system compares favorably with allies and adversaries.

A concluding proposal suggests establishment of a Hoover Commission type of inquiry to examine the organization of the national security establishment, perhaps along with other institutions and policy areas. Korb felt that either or both former Presidents Ford and Carter might play useful roles in such a venture.

Chapter 7 ends with the argument that the real issue for debate by those concerned with national security affairs is whether a pluralist democracy with shrinking resources can compete successfully with a determined Soviet oligarchy for influence in a fragmented international system. Korb closes with the charge that if our political leaders and career officials allow the nature of our political and bureaucratic system or our national history to get in the way, "they will have only themselves to blame."

SECURITY PLANNING: RATIONALITY AND POLITICS

The concluding chapter attempts to capture the rich dialogue that characterized the six meetings of the 1980-81 Dinner Seminar Series. This chapter addresses a variety of issues and problems that bear on national security and which were stimulated by the ideas contained in chapters 2 through 7.

The strengths and problems of US security planning were examined in the six sessions, together with recommendations for dealing with the problems. Other than the diversity of views the reader will find expressed in chapter 8, perhaps the most interesting facet of this chapter is the range of nuances explored by the participants. For the most part, the seminar addressed difficult issues which are not amenable to simple, neat solutions. Indeed, many issues are raised where solutions are not at all obvious, due either to political or economic constraints or to the fact that certain issues pose dilemmas with which leaders must cope without the possibility of stable resolution.

Of the many themes examined in the course of the seminar, several stood out because of their importance to the planning enterprise. One was that planning rests on a foundation of fragmented constitutional arrangements, conflictive relations among institutional and bureaucratic fiefs, and a Congress and public that are too often ill-informed and perhaps undermotivated to address tough national security problems. Second, there seems to be no clear consensus among US civilian leaders about the preferred role of this country in the world. We are largely reactive. There is an urgent need to foster a dialogue about these issues in many forums within government and more broadly throughout the society. Third, short of a major crisis, such as a war, to sharpen our sense of national purpose, there seems to be little prospect that our reactive, *ad hoc* style of decisionmaking can be resisted. Thus, it is expected that coping and incrementalism, rather than major policy change or institutional reform, will characterize the conduct of national security policy and planning. More good people with clearer mandates to act rather than structural tinkering seems to be preferred as a strategy for dealing with our problems. A final significant theme in our discussions was that planning is trivialized when it is viewed as the preparation of specific designs for action and actual documents. The essence of planning is the development of an integrative sense of conceptual direction.

These four themes offer little reason for optimism among those who concern themselves with American security in the 1980s. They imply that the political and institutional foundations of our defense posture are deficient in their ability to help us clarify our interests in the world and the price that we should and can pay in their pursuit. Although the chapters in this volume are not filled with dismal prophecy, they do alert us to the sturdy challenges ahead as we attempt to meld rationality and politics in order to provide a better basis for the common defense.

ON THE NEED TO REFORM AMERICAN STRATEGY*

2

EDWARD N. LUTTWAK
Georgetown University

THE ABSENCE OF STRATEGIC TRADITION

The trusty pragmatic approach is to narrow down complicated matters to isolate the key problems and, then, to solve
them one by one with practical solutions. Strategy, however, is
the one practical pursuit requiring a contrary method: to aggre-
gate the diverse issues and then to craft plans (often of long
range) for dealing with the whole. In the experience of the United
States it has not been strategy but, instead, pragmatic problem-
solving that created a most successful society; it is, unsurprising,
therefore, that it is difficult for Americans to accept the fact that
to achieve even moderate success, external policy must now be
guided by the holistic approach of strategy.

It was not always so. Until the beginning of this century, the
United States enjoyed the classic prerogative of a great sea
power: it could take as much or as little of the world's affairs as it
wanted. Neither the US Navy nor the oceans themselves assured
this fortunate state; it was rather Great Britain, then itself exquisitely strategic, that secured for the United States all it most
needed of the outside world. Even in intermittent conflict, there
was a fundamental shared interest: to keep others busy with
large land armies, and, thus, themselves supreme at sea, the
British used both diplomacy and force to maintain that warlike
equilibrium we call the balance of power; hence, the Americans
had the great powers of continental Europe balanced for them,
and kept from their door.

---

*This chapter is based on Dr. Luttwak's previous contributions to *National
Security in the 1980s—From Weakness to Strength* (© 1980 by the Institute for
Contemporary Studies, reprinted by permission); *Commentary* (reprinted from
Commentary, September 1980, by permission; all rights reserved); and PARAM-
ETERS—*Journal of the US Army War College,* December 1980.

Further, to keep trade open for themselves, the British tried to keep trade open for all; thus, the Americans had their markets overseas, and could still protect their own. And to maintain their own moral economy the British also pursued idealism: the suppression of slavery, the reprisals against the Czars for their pogroms, and the teaching of decent practices in international life, sometimes by Mr. Gladstone's sermons, and sometimes by Lord Palmerston's cannonades. Thus, the Americans too could enjoy a world steadily improving in the manners of civilization and in the legalities of international life.

Since the British oligarchy made its greater decisions in discrete privacy, and used a pragmatic language, the fact that British policy was fundamentally guided by a coherent strategy relentlessly pursued was not much in evidence. The upkeep of the balance of power was a harsh business not at all confined to the beating down of bullies: it required favoring the Turk against Christians, and it meant subverting the unification of Europe, no matter how progressive. Hence the need for a certain reticence in explaining British policy.

Until 1945, Americans, thus, merely had to fight in war and then only briefly; it was the British who made strategy, and who chose our enemies. Even after the end of the second World War and the start of the Cold War, Americans had no need of strategy merely to keep the balance of deterrence. The United States possessed an economy so powerful that it could deter by its potential alone; resources so abundant that the world's oil prices were set in Texas, industries so amply productive that any enemy would see in prospect thousands of aircraft and tanks ready to roll off the production lines; and then, above all, the United States possessed the fission and later the thermonuclear bomb. Others could perhaps build them in sample numbers, but only the United States could deliver them on a large scale—and scale still counted in those days when the total number of weapons was quite small.

Thus, that simple strategy "containment," could, nevertheless, be very successful: Europe, Japan, and their appendages duly recovered from the ravages of war safe behind the shield of American power. The task was unknowingly easier than it could have been because during the war we did not know the great secret: behind Stalin's six million men in arms, there was a desert of destruction in all of Russia west of Moscow—cities destroyed and collectives barren and untenanted; even east of Moscow, in those lands that had remained beyond the reach of the Germans, there was an exhausted population and a shortage of men. Stalin and company desperately tried to keep this secret. And, they were successful. By any calculus of power that cold-blooded men have used, Stalin did not have the strength to keep the large part of Europe that Russian arms had won.

With "containment," Americans were able to do what the British had once done for them, until Vietnam. Then it was not so much that the wisdom of policy broke down in the enervation of an elite or that the competent fighting of war collapsed under the weight of a military bureaucracy ignorant of the true phenomena of warfare. It was the very concept of strategy that waned, so shallowly rooted was the idea of strategy, even that passive strategy of containment which required merely that we react.

Even after the final defeat, which brought with it a blow to American prestige and influence unmatched in our history, Americans could, nevertheless, think that the discipline of strategy remained unnecessary. There was still a slim margin in our favor in the "strategic-nuclear" balance (the very term a reminder of the degraded meaning of "strategic" in our discourse); and even if all who desired could very easily project the advent of unambiguous inferiority in the 1980s, more still could imagine that all was well, since few desired to project. And of course by then we had the Strategic Arms Limitation Talks (SALT), whereby as we are even now reminded, the greath strength accumulated by the steady effort of the Russians would be negated, through the drafting of legal documents. In that atmosphere, it was an easy matter for a single tool—arms control—to displace the entire work, for only a national strategy could shape the work, and we had no national strategy. Hence the pursuit of SALT as an end in itself.

And aside from SALT, most of our defense policy was defined by NATO's real or fancied needs. That was not at all a strategic choice, but rather a political compromise: those who were isolationist and those who were still internationalist could find a compromise in an all-for-NATO defense policy. Thus, two acronyms were substituted for the laborious task of creating a national strategy responsive to our needs at home and cognizant of the dangers abroad: SALT and NATO; NATO and SALT. Too bad that a defense policy that made NATO its only real focus under the slogan "no more Vietnams" would mean that we would only be enhancing stability in the one segment of the perimeter of our interests that was the most stable. But NATO and SALT, SALT and NATO had to do duty for the thinking, the planning, and the discipline of a strategy that was absent.

It was perhaps inevitable that sooner or later some official, ignorant of strategy but skilled in public relations, should think of mating the acronyms: therefore, we had the experience of being told insistently that NATO would not survive without SALT. The moment in which Mr. Vance, Secretary of State, chose to pause melodramatically before saying "I don't know" to a Senatorial query (in open hearings) on whether NATO could withstand a rejection of SALT II, shall stand as the nadir of America's unstrategic decade. Such an unawareness of the duties of statecraft demonstrated how far policy could stray without a core of strategic priorities. It is not of course that SALT is incompatible with strategy. It could and indeed should be: in the context of a coherent strategy, SALT could be a most powerful instrument of policy. But the good ingredient unbalanced makes bad medicine, in this case possibly of the fatal variety.

In the absence of strategy, substrategic reflexes govern what we do. The weapons we design, develop, and eventually build reflect the technical ambitions of the engineers as well as the ideal forms of our bureaucrats in uniform; only tactical logic is absent from the process. Our Army, having failed to obtain a new battle tank for a decade, insists on having its new MI tank propelled by a gas turbine—at high cost and greater risk of failure; such propulsion adds little if any to the combat value of the MI, but it satisfies the technological urge, and there is no tactical logic to satisfy anyway. After all, tactics must be derived from the operational method of warfare; and there can be no operational method of warfare unless it is derived from theater strategy; and that in turn cannot be framed except within a national strategy. Without a national strategy it is not unexpected that unguided technical ambition dominates the scene, nor is it surprising that in the military schools our officers study a great deal about management, but scarcely touch upon military history; far better to master those skills so useful in civilian life than to study war—a painful process since the "data-base" is merely the library of military history, and some books are even in languages other than English.

In the absence of strategy, substrategic choices govern the form of the armed forces we deploy. In war, two great phenomena contend: maneuver and fire power. Maneuver is made of circumventing action to by-pass the barrier, to outflank the thrust, and to evade the main strength of the enemy in all instances from weapon design to grand strategy; such maneuver is the product of surprise, deception, and above all agility—in thought, planning, and action. And then there is firepower, which is measured by quantity, by accuracy, and by lethality; firepower is a product of industrial strength, transportation, and efficient logistic distribution. Throughout history, mixtures of maneuver and firepower have contended on a thousand battlefields. Maneuver has generally been the less costly course; but firepower has always been the surer course, and has demanded merely an outright superiority in means. But even in the face of superior firepower and superior resources, maneuver in all its forms—tactical, operational, theater-strategic and developmental, as well as the highest maneuver of grand strategy—has always done better than an outright comparison of forces would reveal and often has prevailed.

THE LOGIC OF EFFICIENCY

But that was before maneuver finally met its match in the figure of the American "systems analyst." When this new apparition came to take its place alongside the Great Captains of history, maneuver was finally undone. Its fatal defect is that no statistical index can be properly attached to surprise, deception, or agility; thus no criterion of effectiveness stated in numbers can be defined for the system analyst's computations. Firepower by contrast is easily quantifiable: volume being tonnage, accuracy being hit probability, and lethality being a known factor. The "simulations" now widely used to define what weapon characteristics are needed, what type and size of forces are to be deployed, and even to evaluate what is called tactics in this system, are all in fact firepower-exchange computations.

All this may seem recondite, but it is the heart of what is wrong. For many years now, the weapons built and the forces deployed have been heavily influenced by mathematical criteria of choice that do not capture the most important dimension of warfare. That is one reason the US Army, half as large in numbers of men as the Soviet Army, has only 16 divisions to their 168—ours being heavy in logistics to sustain firepower, producing it by industrial methods. That is a major reason our aircraft must be so large and costly, since there is apparent efficiency in the economies-of-scale of the large vehicle. One pilot produces more firepower with the larger aircraft—and never mind that one large aircraft can cost the same as several small ones and that numbers give flexibility for action. And that is why our Navy is shaped by the logic of bigness on one side—for on a technical level bigger ships can carry greater firepower and have better sea-keeping qualities—when what is required strategically is a greater number of smaller ships in a greater variety of stations.

And yet, the essence of strategy in such things begins with the rejection of the logic of efficiency. The large thing is often more efficient in producing the unit of firepower, but in war the very aim must be to mingle in the fight, and then the large thing is often almost as vulnerable as the small thing, of which more can be had. In civilian life, one deals with easily predictable phenomena—seldom is there an opponent working his will against yours; but in strategy, there is perpetual contention and the fixed solution of a predictable phenomenon is neatly outmaneuvered.

Thus, a fundamental contradiction exists between (civil) efficiency and (military) effectiveness; until recently this was almost entirely ignored because instead of strategists we have only managers of production and experts of efficiency. And where are our generals and admirals who will rise to protest such methods, who will expose their falsehoods, and who will, if need be, resign? They are busy supervising their own "systems analysts," who make their own suitably rigged calculations, with the same horrifying results. Already themselves far too removed from the true study of war to comprehend its endless unquantifiable complexities, these are not the men who will remind us that the force with the greater firepower has lost more often than not in the record of war; they are not the ones who will insist that maneuver, as well as efficiency, be the criterion of choice.

THE REAL LESSON OF VIETNAM

It has been the bane of the armed services of this nation that since the onset of the Second World War its leaders, its organizers, have been more concerned with managing the military instrument of foreign policy than in being able to win wars. That indeed is the fatal·deformation that has overtaken the armed forces of the United States. To cite the great example: if we stand back from the details of single operations, if we discount those lesser phenomena of error and evil that must attend all armed conflict (and which the critics of course wildly magnified), if we make full allowance for the persistent misdirection of war operations emanating from the White House, American warfare in Indochina still emerges in broad perspective as an essentially bureaucratic phenomenon, scarcely responsive to the realities of that conflict.

Even if the enemy consistently refused to assemble in conveniently targetable mass formations, the artillery fired its ammunition; even if there were no linear defenses to pierce and no flanks to turn, the armor maneuvered; even if there were no targets, the Air Force bombed in close support, in interdiction, and in retaliation against North Vietnamese cities and infrastructures, even if only the last of these missions could find stable and worthwhile targets. Otherwise, much of the air war was simply futile for reasons entirely fundamental: the tactical logic of close air support is to combine air strikes with ground combat against enemy forces that will not or cannot disperse, and this was a condition rarely satisfied in Vietnam. The strategic logic of interdiction is to diminish the flow of supply to an enemy who requires absolutely a certain quantum of supplies to sustain operations which cannot be deferred, and this too was almost entirely absent.

As the war progressed, almost every component of the American armed forces—Coast Guard included—found a satisfactory role for itself in the war; a role, that is, which allowed funds to be claimed for expansion, which allowed careerism to flourish, and which allowed us to lose a conflict whose results have inflicted death and fever on millions of human beings.

The Army, therefore, retained its preferred style of warfare, based much more on the systematic application of firepower than on maneuver; it retained a structure of forces based on extra-large and logistically very heavy divisions; and it retained elaborate headquarters at battalion, brigade, and divisional echelons—even if there were very few targets for the mass application of firepower, little need for the elaborate logistics, and hardly any valid operational functions for all those headquarters in a war of squad and platoon skirmishes. (It is notable that the one clear American victory, the utter defeat of the Vietcong in the

Tet Offensive, was won largely by scattered groups of men fighting with little central direction against an enemy that at last came out in force, thus presenting a stable target.)

The Navy similarly could have taken care of all opposition afloat with a small destroyer flotilla and a few shore-based patrol aircraft, but instead found busy work for its aircraft carriers (and death or captivity for its pilots) in flying attack missions of all kinds by day and by night.

As for the Air Force, every single type of squadron was seemingly needed: fighters; light and heavy bombers; tactical and strategic reconnaissance, both photographic and electronic; and transport squadrons, light, medium, and heavy.

Millions of servicemen worked hard, and a good many lost life or limb, to operate those forces. But, tragically, almost all of this activity had little to do with the true phenomena of the war during most of its stages: the terrorism and propaganda that subverted the authority of the government in each locality to extract recruits, food, and intelligence; the guerrilla who was thus manned, fed, and informed, and whose own opportunistic attacks served to maintain the insecurity in which subversion could progress still further; and then the worldwide propaganda assault on American confidence and morale.

Even when, after Tet 1968, North Vietnamese regular forces largely took over the fighting, the fit between the combat actions performed by the American forces and the nature of the enemy was only very slightly improved. For North Vietnamese regulars still fought as irregulars, that is, elusively. They fought usually when and where they wanted. Only late in the war did the fighting assume the conventional form of large-scale, European-style warfare, complete with sustained artillery barrages and tank assaults by the North Vietnamese. But, by then, almost all the American forces—structured precisely to prevail in that kind of fighting—had been withdrawn (and, of course, the North Vietnamese went over to conventional war operations precisely because the American troops had been withdrawn).

The absurd and tragic ending to the war was dictated by the simple fact that American military organizations, structured, equipped, and trained for warfare on a large scale against regular forces, did not adapt to entirely different circumstances by evolving appropriate small-unit structures. Moreover, they developed neither operational methods related to the context of the war, nor tactics responsive to those of the enemy, which were, of necessity, radically different from traditional structured methods and tactics.

Those in charge at all levels can claim with full justification that Washington continuously interfered in the conduct of the war at the most detailed level, inevitably, much of the interference was ill-informed. They can claim with equal justification that the media were systematically ill-disposed, and indeed functionally structured to denigrate all that the South Vietnamese did and to criticize all that the Americans were trying to do. But responsibility for the utter failure to adapt structures, methods, and tactics to the terrain and to the nature of the enemy must rest squarely and exclusively upon the American officer corps. It was as if there were no body of staff and command officers willing and able to learn the facts of the conflict as it evolved and who could then design forces, methods, and tactics to suit that conflict.

With so many different branches and sub-branches all engaged in war operations in circumstances of luxuriant bureaucratic growth, just the coordination of the different organizational bits and pieces absorbed the work of thousands of officers, especially senior officers. With so much inner-regarding activity, it was all the easier to ignore the war as it was being fought, which was in any case elusive, given the nature of the guerrilla element and the natural silence of subversion.

But for the tactical and operational realities of war to be so largely ignored by tens of thousands of military officers supposedly educated and trained to understand war and fight it, there had to be further and deeper causes of inadvertence, and indeed there were.

First, officers posted to Vietnam tactical commands were rotated in and out of the country at short intervals of a year or less. This meant that officers arrived in the country and then left it again before they were able to come to grips with its complex situation. Characteristically, the first few months of a posting were a period of acclimatization and adjustment. The newly arrived officer could then start to gather in the complexities of his operations, and could begin to rectify the deficiencies he might notice within his unit, only to find his tour at an end, fully aware that his successor would repeat the same pattern.

That fatal lack of continuity not only did great damage in-wardly, since fighting men lost respect for officers who under-stood less of the war than they did themselves, but also denied to the United States all the benefits of a cumulative learning ex-perience in the overall conduct of the war. As the saying went among the cognoscenti, the United States was not in Vietnam for ten years but rather for only one year, ten times over. Of the Romans it has been said that they made all manner of mistakes, but never made the same mistake twice. In Vietnam, by contrast, the same tactical mistakes were repeated over and over again. Since officers were promptly transferred from Vietnam as soon as they began to acquire some experience of war leadership and combat operations, the American forces in Vietnam had no collective memory and the systematic repetition of error was inevitable.

MILITARY BUREAUCRACY AND CIVIL EFFICIENCY

Why was such a devastatingly harmful bureaucratic proce-dure tolerated, let alone perpetuated? This was not one of the malpractices imposed by the interference of civilian officials, but was entirely willed by the military services themselves. The mo-tive, once again, was internal and exquisitely bureaucratic. Since the leadership of combat operations and indeed any service at all in a war zone would confer a great career advantage, it would not have been "fair" to allow some officers to remain in Vietnam year after year, and thus deprive others of useful career-enhancing opportunities.

That people who run bureaucracies are apt to use them in a self-serving fashion to some extent is a thing inevitable, under-standable, even if deplorable. But in the case of officer rotation as practiced in Vietnam, we encounter a gross deviation from efficacy, with enormously damaging consequences.

How could it be that the desiderata of career management were allowed to prevail over the most essential requirements of effective warfare? Although it is true that reserving troop com-mand and staff posts for the few would have caused much re-sentment, it would also have resulted in a much better conduct of the war and the preservation of a fighting army. After all, it is no secret that troops cannot coalesce into cohesive fighting units under leaders constantly changing; and it is only slightly less obvious that the cumulative learning yielded by trial and error can scarcely be achieved by staff officers and commanders coming and going on short tours of duty. Inasmuch as we must assume the good intentions of those involved, it is ignorance of the basics of the military art that we must look for, rather than a conscious, collective selfishness.

But the hypothesis of ignorance encounters an immediate and formidable objection. How is ignorance compatible with the high standards of the contemporary American officer corps? It is after all full of officers with M.A.s and Ph.D.s. The officer corps also contains many highly competent engineers and even scientists, not to speak of very large numbers of skilled managers of all kinds, and in all specialties.

As the list of qualifications lengthens, we begin to glimpse the source of the problem: only one subject of expertise is missing and it is war itself. In the officer corps there are plenty of engineers, economists, and political scientists—but where are the tacticians? There are many skilled personnel managers, logistical managers, and technical managers—but where are the students of the operational level of war? And at the top, there are many competent (and politically sensitive) bureaucrats—but where are the strategists?

And where would these tacticians and strategists come from? Certainly not from the military schools, which teach all manner of subjects—except those essentially military. At West Point, at Annapolis, and at the Air Force Academy, cadets and plebes receive a fairly good all-around education, but they do not study the essentially military subjects. Military history—the only possible "data base" for those who would understand war—is treated in a perfunctory manner as one subject among many.

At the opposite end of the hierarchy of military schools—the war colleges of each branch and the National Defense University, which are meant to prepare mid-career officers for the most senior ranks—there too, management, politics, and foreign policy are taught, but no tactics and little strategy. And in between, at the command and staff colleges, there also, military history is treated as if it were a marginal embellishment rather than recognized as the very basis of military education, the record of trial and error from which today's methods can be developed.

No wonder that the distinguishing characteristic of American officers is their lack of interest in the art of war. No wonder that "military strategy" is a phrase that refers only to budgets and foreign policy in the outpourings of senior officers—men who think that Clausewitz was a German who died a long time ago.

The proximate causes of this extraordinary drift from military professionalism into so many other professions are obvious. The design of the army in 1940-41 and again at the onset of the Korean War, the last of which set the pattern followed ever after, was to process a given amount of raw material (men, ammunition, and so forth) into finished products (soldiers, casualties, and fired rounds). This was realized at the time and apparently approved, for the armed forces set about copying the corporation in its organization and mentality. This was exacerbated by the need to coexist with civilian defense officials who imposed economic criteria of efficiency, and who used mathematical techniques of "systems analysis," creating a demand for officers who understood fancy bookkeeping, and who could beat the mathematical models of civilian budget-cutters with models of their own.

From all the tracks of specialized expertise, officers are promoted stage by stage by way of "ticket punching" assignments to staff or command positions. But since duty tours are short, the experience counts for little. In the present atmosphere of the officer corps, it is the desk jobs in the Pentagon, the assignments to high-prestige outside agencies (the National Security Council is a well-known launching pad to high rank), and high-visibility managerial positions that are most attractive. Staff posts, where war operations are planned, and unit commands, where there is no better company than more junior officers, are seen largely as obligatory stages to better things. And with the up-or-out rules, a soldier pausing too long to master a single field risks dismissal.

If the ambitious officer becomes too interested in the essential military functions of studying the enemy, of inventing suitable tactics, of developing war plans, and of inspiring and commanding men, a glance at the official biographies of the service chiefs will soon show him the error of his ways. It was not by allowing themselves to become bogged down in such things that those men reached the top, but rather by being good managers and smooth bureaucrats.

Some causes of this state of affairs have been mentioned here, but there are others. True students of war are ferreting them out even as I write, and there are many studies available to examine.

In any case, whatever the ultimate causes, the problem is not to be denied. If more general facts and broader assessments are disputed, then a close scrutiny of the details of the Iran rescue debacle certainly reveals the workings of a managerial-bureaucratic approach to the planning and execution of a commando operation, with disastrous consequences.

Commando operations are like all other infantry operations, only more so. They do, however, have their own rules, which the rescue attempt seems to have violated in every respect. The planners involved were, undoubtedly, good managers, economists, engineers, or whatever. But they must also have been quite ignorant of the military history of forty years of British, German, French, and Israeli commando operations. Otherwise, they would not have sent such a small force into action. Here the rule is: "a man's force for a boy's job." Deep in enemy territory, under conditions of gross numerical inferiority, there must be a decisive superiority at the actual point of contact, since any opposition must be crushed before others can intervene to eventually subdue the commando force; there is no time for a fair fight.

If the planners had not been ignorant of the history of all military operations, let alone commando operations, they would not have had three coequal commanders on the spot, and then a "task force" commander back in Egypt, not to speak of the Joint Chiefs, the Secretary of Defense, and the President—all connected by satellite. Here the rule is that there must be unity of command, under one man only, since in high-tempo commando operations there is no time to consult anyway, while any attempt at remote control is bound to be suicidal given the necessary speed and secrecy of such missions.

If not for this ignorance, the planners would not have relied on a few inherently fragile helicopters. Here the rule is that since the combat risks are, by definition, very high, all technical risk must be avoided. If helicopters must be used, let there be twenty or thirty to carry the payload of six.

If the planners had had any knowledge of these affairs, even of the ones in which Americans had performed before, they would not have assembled a raid force drawn from different formations and even different services. Here the rule is that commando operations, being by definition exceptionally demanding of men and morale, must be carried out by cohesive units, and not by ad hoc groups of specialists. That, indeed, is why standing units of commandos were established in the first place. If the suspicion is justified that the fatal accident was caused by a misunderstanding or worse between Marine helicopter pilots and Air Force C-130 pilots—and that procedures, technical jargon, *et cetera,* are different—those involved carry a terrible responsibility. For there is much reason to believe that all four services were involved in the raid precisely because each wanted to insure a share of any eventual glory for its own bureaucracy.

Military force unguided by strategy thus drifts into bureaucratic deformation and the ignorant pursuit of civil efficiency. But of even greater concern is the toll that pragmatism imposes on our national policy. In the absence of strategy, it is substrategic perspectives that govern our comprehension of what confronts us. Thus, over a period of several months in the years 1978-79, Americans debated first the meaning of the supply of Russian submarines to Cuba; then the meaning of the arrival of the high-performance MiG-23s, with Russian pilots; then the discovery in Cuba of modern air-defense weapons for battlefield use; and then finally the revelation that a Soviet brigade was stationed on the island. Each episode was separated from the next by intervals of a few weeks or months, and those intervals proved long enough to ensure that each episode would be viewed in isolation. Of the submarines, it could be said, by those eager for inaction, that they were nonnuclear and thus harmless. Of the MiG-23s, the question was merely asked if they were fitted with pylons for nuclear bombs. Of the air-defense weapons, nothing was said at all, the questions of why and where being too recondite to answer: Cubans in Africa had no need for such weapons; Cubans to be sent to Arabia might well need them, but Arabia is far from Cuba and to connect the two distant places would require a strategic mind. Of the brigade, it was asked only—and ridiculously enough—whether it might threaten the United States of America. The President eventually decided, as the Russians had claimed all along, that the brigade was only in Cuba to train, and not to fight. With that revelation, the matter was then simply dropped, and the question of why the Cubans needed brigade-level training—useless in Black Africa but essential in Arabia—was not asked. Since it is only within the framework of strategic understanding that diverse things may be connected to form a view of the whole, the genuine profile of the danger, that is to say not the submarines as such, not the MiG-23s on their own, not just the air defense, not merely the brigade, but rather the transformation of Cuba into a higher class military power, never emerged at all. That indeed was the one issue not debated, even while hawks and doves spoke and wrote millions of words on each fragment of a whole that was never even recognized as such.

Until the later years of the 1970s there was still a residual of power, or at least residual delusions that the United States could prosper even in weakness. Only now, as of this writing, is the long holiday finally over, at long last and so very late. The agencies of our education were several: the display of the most intricate details of our "strategic-nuclear" weakness in the Senate hearings on the SALT II accords; the growing realization that a NATO-only defense policy meant a fatal lassitude before a Soviet strategy that created alienation between us and some of our most vital interests; and then, finally, at the hands of the mobs of Iran, a belated education in the necessary, hard value of the intangible of prestige. Of course, deep emotional resistance is not so easily overcome, but at least the mood of the nation has changed, and the need to upgrade the nation's armed power has been widely accepted.

A TIME FOR STRATEGY

The time may have finally come when the acknowledgement of weakness and the understanding of its unacceptable price have taught us all the necessity of strength and a national strategy that can use it. The contours of such a strategy must of course be dictated in many lesser decisions made over time by the Executive and the Congress, but the broad rules are the same for all nations, and we too must frame our desires within them:

—Never deal with the single issue, or the single affair of any kind, in isolation. When, for example, Soviet power intervenes to decide the outcome of war in Ethiopia—do not look at Ethiopia alone but at the consequences of action or inaction for the whole of East Africa, for the Middle East, and for the world.

—Do not seek partial, practical solutions without considering their effect on the general equilibrium of power. If SALT offers an "equivalence" of strategic-nuclear weapons, ask if there is also "equivalence" in theater-nuclear weapons, in nonnuclear weapons and forces, and in other means: in clandestine military and covert political action and the constructive instruments of aid and trade. Otherwise, a guaranteed parity in one class of weapons alone may result in overall inferiority. Of course, the partial solution may still be desirable, and practical solutions will almost always be less than total solutions, but they cannot be framed in a less than total view: if there is a national strategy, there may well be need of SALT negotiations also, but let not those talks usurp strategy.

—Do not battle strength head on, but maneuver around it; do not allow the enemy to exploit every area of weakness without acting similarly, for otherwise there is no hope of success. If it is Soviet policy to separate the Alliance, active measures of Alliance solidarity are essential, but they must be complemented by a relentless campaign to undermine the Soviet Union in Eastern Europe: it is neither useful nor moral to incite Hungarian children to confront Russian tanks, but it is merely abasement to have our officials speak of "socialist" countries when we should speak only of Russia and of captive nations. More substantially, if it is Soviet policy to conspire against us in Iran, let us reciprocate in Afghanistan or other places where Soviet interests are engaged.

—Do not confuse ethics and aesthetics. Ethics must reflect the moral calculus of least human suffering. Aesthetics merely reflects the superficial appearance of things. If OPEC uses the market strength of a cartel to inflict inconvenience upon us, we may merely suffer inconvenience, but poverty increases in such countries as Turkey and Brazil; when the marginal countries suffer impoverishment, less fortunate peasants actually starve for want of crops, that is to say for want of water for their crops, that is to say for want of diesel oil for their tube wells. And so let armed power be brought in to balance market power, for our own good—and for that of many others.

—Do not pretend that others are not as they are. The Soviet Union is the vehicle for the aggrandizement of the Russians. The Russians have a strategy, and it is an imperial strategy of traditional build: to protect Muscovy, the Ukraine and Byelorussia must be held; to protect those, a further cordon of non-Russian lands from Estonia to Moldavia must be annexed to the Soviet Union; to protect the latter, the states of Eastern Europe too must come under Russian power, lest their freedom inspire revolt in the non-Russian fringe. But, Eastern Europe will remain restless so long as the nations of Western Europe parade their liberties and prosperity before the peoples of Eastern Europe; thus, Western Europe must be responsive if Eastern Europe is to become permanently obedient, so that the non-Russian fringe lands will be obedient also, so that the cordon will be safe, so that Moscow will remain powerful over all. But, Western Europe will never be responsible so long as American protection exists to allow its elected leaders to defy Moscow's demands for "reasonableness." And so the Soviet Union's imperial strategy relentlessly pursues the struggle to diminish American power, and to separate Europeans and Americans. Now, the new prospect of achieving that objective by acting against another, the Persian Gulf, has opened vast new possibilities for Moscow. We must defend the perimeters directly under threat, but that cannot suffice: hence, the need to maneuver and articulate power where opportunity offers scope and in East Asia in particular. The best defense for Europe is most probably located somewhere between Outer Mongolia and the banks of the Ussuri. Thus, the folly of a "Eurocentric" strategy, precisely because Europe is justifiably held to be most important for us.

And then finally, and above all, we need tenacity. That is not a quality as easily admired as creativity or compassion. But it is the one quality that strategy unalterably requires.

THE AMERICAN ENVIRONMENT FOR SECURITY PLANNING*

3

JAMES K. OLIVER AND JAMES A. NATHAN
University of Delaware

DOMESTIC CONTEXT OF NATIONAL SECURITY POLICY

Analyses and assessments of the inherent capabilities and limits of the domestic environment and institutions that shape the American approach toward long-range national security policy and planning frequently echo de Tocqueville's conclusion that, "As for myself, I do not hesitate to say that it is especially in the conduct of their foreign relations that democracies appear to me decidedly inferior to other governments." De Tocqueville continued:

> Foreign politics demand scarcely any of those qualities which are peculiar to a democracy; they require, on the contrary, the perfect use of almost all those in which it is deficient. . . . [A] democracy can only with great difficulty regulate the details of an important undertaking, persevere in a fixed design, and work out its execution in spite of serious obstacles. It cannot combine its measures with secrecy or await their consequences with patience.[1]

Underlying de Tocqueville's lament and contemporary concerns about the adequacy of the American system to face the task of long-range national security planning is the fear that American culture, political institutions, and bureaucratic politics might be inadequate. Americans have always harbored fears that their domestic institutions and politics at a minimum constrain and at worst may preclude efficient and effective planning and conduct of national security policy.

---

*This chapter is derived from arguments developed more extensively in the authors' *Foreign Policy Making in the American Political System* (Boston: Little, Brown & Co., 1981).

There is ample evidence that policymakers responsible for the formulation and conduct of foreign and national security have been troubled as much as or more with these environmental and institutional "limits" than with the foreign objects and international conditions that are presumably the essence of foreign and national security policies. For example, at the onset of the Cold War, Truman and his administration seemed nearly as concerned about mobilizing public and congressional opinion behind the Truman Doctrine, Marshall Plan, and containment as about the Soviet threat to the Western world. Indeed, there seemed to be less doubt about American capability to deal with the external threat than about the will of the American people to respond and stay the course. There were similar worries about the adequacy of the governmental structure itself. Thus, there was a perceived need to reorganize and coordinate disparate foreign and defense agencies and departments into a coherent national security policy establishment. During the Truman years, there was Acheson's admitted oversimplification and overstatement of deteriorating and threatening global conditions in order that, as he put it, the "mass mind of government" could be "bludgeoned" into accepting the world view and prescription of that quintessential long-range national security plan, NSC-68. And, of course, the Truman Presidency was closed by twin events with dramatic domestic consequences. The first was Truman's only partially successful confrontation with General Douglas MacArthur and American public opinion concerning civil-military relations. The second was the issue of the conduct of "limited war" in a domestic environment wrought up by earlier, strident calls to contain the Communist threat at home and abroad.

During the 1950s, Eisenhower and Dulles were preoccupied with the McCarthy wing of their own party. The presumption of the 1950s was that there existed in America a large, inchoate, but atavistic segment of public opinion always susceptible to mobilization at the slightest hint of "appeasement." Kennedy, Johnson, and Nixon were no less concerned that the "essential domino" of public opinion not fall during their respective administrations' prosecution of the Vietnam War. The Johnson and Nixon administrations, especially the latter, became nearly obsessed with mastery of what came to be an adversarial relationship with an increasingly aggressive media during the late 1960s and 1970s. Simultaneously, Nixon and Kissinger engaged in studied attempts to preempt and circumvent the national security bureaucracy as they sought the latitude to conceive and pursue their conceptions of national security policy. The Nixon-Kissinger vision was immensely complicated and in some measure frustrated by yet another major domestic constraint of the late 1960s and the 1970s, the virtual collapse of executive-legislative bipartisanship and congressional submission to executive initiative and leadership. Finally, as the United States entered the 1980s we had yet another example of the constraining effect of the American political context: the unedifying spectacle and questionable efficacy of "planning" American strategic policy and forces under the press of the Presidential election campaign.

These examples suggest that one could very nearly write a history of American foreign and national security policy after World War II solely from the perspective of policymakers straining against the limits imposed by the American cultural, constitutional, institutional, and political milieu. Such an account is, however, clearly beyond the scope and beside the point of this chapter.[2] Instead, we will first survey those elements of the American domestic context that constrain and impede long-range policy planning and execution. We will then examine some of the approaches advanced over the last few decades to deal with and overcome these factors.

CONSTRAINTS AND LIMITS

Whether during the late 1940s, throughout the 1950s, or the early 1960s, when the apparent combination of international anarchy and strong ideologically antagonistic enemies armed with nuclear weapons dominated the American world view, or whether during the late 1960s and throughout the 1970s, when political economics and economic power perplexed the policy establishment, a set of images and concerns about the American policymaking and domestic political milieu were in evidence. The fragmented policymaking and decisional processes and the generally uninformed and unpredictable character of a democratic society were liabilities in the planning and conduct of foreign and national security policy. The implication of this for many observers of the national security machinery is that such a system is inefficient, even dangerous, within the contemporary international system. For a policymaking system of fragmented and diffused power would seem to frustrate the needs of a state that would operate in, or impose order upon, the international system. Accordingly, the policymaking institutions and processes had to be somehow "protected" from the "excesses of democracy"; and the institutions and processes themselves had to be centralized and "rationalized" so as to permit flexibility and responsiveness in dealing with a dangerous and complex international environment.

CONSTITUTIONAL CONSTRAINTS

Advocates of centralized control of foreign policy have been confounded by a number of difficulties. Not the least of these is the basic constitutional framework of the United States. The Constitution militates against coherence and efficiency. From the very onset, an unresolved tension has lain at the nexus of constitutionally prescribed foreign and national security policy-making authority. On the one hand there is Alexander Hamilton's assertion that:

> The authorities essential to the common defense are these: to raise armies; to build and equip fleets; to prescribe rules for the government of both; to direct their operations; to provide for their support. These powers ought to exist without limitation, *because it is impossible to foresee or to define the extent and variety of national exigencies, and the correspondent extent and variety of the means which may be necessary to satisfy them.* The circumstances that endanger the safety of nations are infinite, and for this reason no constitutional shackles can wisely be imposed on the power to which the care of it is committed. The power ought to be coextensive with all the possible combinations of such circumstances; and ought to be under the direction of the same councils which are appointed to preside over the common defense.[3]

In contrast, however, there was the conviction of James Madison that:

> In time of *actual* war, great discretionary powers are constantly given to the Executive Magistrate. Constant apprehension of war, has the same tendency to render the head too large for the body. A standing military force, with an overgrown Executive will not long be safe companions to liberty. The means of defence against foreign danger, have been always the instruments of tyranny at home.[4]

Although Hamilton felt that his position "is one of those truths which to a correct and unprejudiced mind carries its own evidence along with it, and may be obscured, but cannot be made plainer by argument or reasoning,"[5] Madison's fear of tyranny proved the stronger force in the construction of the constitutional design. While accepting Hamilton's concern that the exigencies of the common defense demanded centralization of decisional authority in the national government, that authority was itself subject to the now familiar Madisonian approach of "so contriving the interior structure of the government as that its several constituent parts may, by their mutual relations, be the means of keeping each other in their proper places."[6] Thus, decisional power was fragmented and processes were established that would, it was hoped, at least minimize the possibility of preponderant decisional authority and responsibility accruing to any single individual or institution. "In republican government," Madison asserted, "the legislative authority necessarily predominates,"[7] but Hamilton's arguments were not without force. Accordingly, a unitary "commander in chief" was established to whom was given treaty-making and other diplomatic functions, but the war-declaring powers, the authority to raise and maintain armies and navies, and the treaty-ratification powers were vested in the Congress. It was not an especially neat structure, but the pattern of overlapping, shared, and even conflicting powers present in the system was deemed a necessary price to pay to protect the transcendent value of nontyrannical government. This position was reaffirmed by the twentieth-century jurist, Mr. Justice Brandeis:

> The doctrine of separation of powers was adopted by the Convention of 1787, not to promote efficiency but to preclude the exercise of arbitrary power. The purpose was, not to avoid friction, but, by means of the inevitable friction incident to the distribution of the governmental powers among three departments, to save the people from autocracy.[8]

Viewed from this perspective, these policymaking inefficiencies are by no means "irrational."

But if the problems presented by the original constitutional design could be rationalized in terms of transcendent principles of political liberty, subsequent developments seemed to demand structural modifications. Once committed to the course of global activism in an international context of ambiguous Cold War, the mobilization and deployment of resources, as well as the permanent possibility of nuclear war, led inexorably to the modification of constitutional interpretation. By the 1960s, the executive-legislative relationship had undergone a near transformation.

Hans Morgenthau, perhaps the foremost scholar of international relations of this century, frequently quoted to those audiences who desired and applauded decisive and swift remedy to the ills of American policy, the Roman saying, *Senatores bone veri, Senatus aulem mala bestia* (The Senators are good men, but the Senate is an evil beast).[9] The Congress, in this view, is the epitome of the weakness of the American system. It is a large body of autonomous policymakers whose political survival is a function of 585 different constituencies to whom all of the House of Representatives and one-third of the Senate are accountable every two years. Notwithstanding whatever larger and more long-term vision individual members might develop concerning international affairs and American participation in them, as a practical matter the next election (usually two and no more than six years away) is the most important fact of life for the legislator. Nonetheless, under the constitutional design substantial foreign policy power was given to the Congress, presumably with the expectation that the institution would exercise that power with responsibility to a larger vision of interest than the individual member's political survival. Unfortunately, the critics asserted, the reality was too frequently contrary to the constitutional theory, and nowhere was de Tocqueville's critique of democracy more appropriate than with respect to Congress.

The exigencies of mid-century recalled the Hamiltonian argument and his "axioms as simple as they are universal; the *means* ought to be proportioned to the *end;* the persons from whose agency the attainment of any *end* is expected ought to possess the *means* by which it is attained."[10] The end of global management required, it seemed, an energetic Executive, and thus throughout the 1950s and 1960s authority and instrumentalities were extended to and assumed by a succession of Presidents. As Senator J. William Fulbright noted:

> The circumstance has been crisis, an entire era of crisis in which urgent decisions have been required again and again, decisions of a kind that the Congress is ill-equipped to make with what had been thought to be the requisite speed. The President has the means at his disposal for prompt action; the Congress does not. When the security of the country is endangered, or thought to be endangered, there is a powerful premium on prompt action, and that means executive action.[11]

With the onset of the crisis-ridden 1960s, the notion of congressional acquiescence in its relationship with the President was firmly established. Thus, in 1959 a new Chairman of the Senate Foreign Relations Committee summarized the congressional mind:

> So it is the President that must take the lead, and we would help him. We would accede to his requests. If he puts it the other way around, it is going to fail, and I think he makes a mistake in not taking a stronger stand in this field. . . .
>
> I'm talking about political management . . . of the Congress. Our strong Presidents always have, if they are successful in this field, to counteract the parochial interests of our Congress.[12]

But if events and circumstances had seemed to resolve the constitutional tension in favor of the Presidency by the 1960s, the fate of the policy response to those circumstances once again called forth the constitutional constraints. As America's Vietnam involvement accrued more and more costs, popular and congressional reaction turned negative. (The congressional response was led by the same Senator Fulbright who had earlier called for congressional accession to Presidential requests.) Presidents Johnson and Nixon resorted to increasingly blatant assertions of Presidential prerogative, thereby forcing the issue of the fundamental imbalance that had developed between the Presidency on the one hand and the Congress on the other. Thus, by the 1970s it had become commonplace to speak of an "imperial Presidency"[13] with powers, as Harry Truman had once put it, that "would have made Caesar, Genghis Khan or Napoleon bite his nails with envy."[14]

As the excesses of the Nixon Presidency became more manifest and culminated in the Watergate scandal, attention concentrated on the swollen institution and powers of the office. By the middle and late 1970s, some scholars had begun openly asking whether the kind of Presidency seemingly demanded by American foreign policy was compatible with traditional American freedoms. The resort to secrecy, control and manipulation of information, deceit, and spying on and interference with the legitimate exercise of the political rights of American citizens was deemed by some to have become an inherent and ongoing necessity of a national security bureaucracy increasingly out of, and perhaps beyond, control.[15] The Madisonian fears now seemed more compelling.

Paralleling these concerns about the dangers and even pathologies of the Cold War Presidency was a renewed interest in what was taken to be a renascence of the Congress. The Congress had emerged as a focal point of organized and effective political opposition to the Vietnam War and the claims of Presidential power advanced by the Johnson and especially the Nixon administrations. Accordingly, many concerned themselves with the capacity of the institution for "congressional government." It was clear that the congressional reaction to the war and the Nixon administration had contributed to significant internal reforms within Congress and the assertion of new powers, such as the legislative or congressional veto. However, it was not self-evident that the Congress had succeeded by the end of the 1970s in establishing a means whereby the legislature could become a full and responsible partner in the policy planning and formulation phase of American foreign policymaking. Rather, Congress remained an essentially reactive participant in the process; policy initiative could be exercised by Congress only spasmodically. Indeed, to the extent that Congress had become more effective as a check on Presidential power and initiative, concern began to mount by the end of the decade that the American system was becoming bogged down in institutional deadlock and political stalemate and, therefore, incapable of exercising world leadership.[16]

Thus, on the threshold of the 1980s, the constitutional constraints of two hundred years ago retain their force. For the small, isolated nation that constructed the Constitution, institutional deadlock and political stalemate were desirable outcomes. World leadership was explicitly abjured by Washington, in part out of a fear of what such a role would do to the constitutional design and the values it was to protect. For the framers of the constitutional constraints, structural tension and policymaking complexity were necessary, even elegant, accoutrements of a republican form of government. For late twentieth-century American foreign and national security policymakers, the constraints have also taken on the attributes of intractable impediments to planning and implementing policy.

BUREAUCRATIC CONSTRAINTS

Constitutional constraints are "givens" in the planning and policymaking environment. They have come to be viewed as constraints in no small measure because the institutional framework has been called upon to serve a perceived national interest far beyond anything imagined in the eighteenth century. Yet, other institutional constraints are present in the American system that have resulted precisely from the effort to augment the constitutional structure to deal with the demands of a foreign policy predicated on the construction and maintenance of world order. Specifically, to implement a foreign and national security policy as multifaceted as containment had become by the early 1950s required thousands and eventually tens of thousands of people organized around planning and administering the programs designed to mobilize the money, people, information, and technology necessary for the establishment and maintenance of world order. In a word, a large and growing bureaucracy, a foreign and national security policy establishment has developed. And though conceived and established as a means to plan and implement national security and foreign policy, the establishment's very size, diversity, and resultant policymaking processes have come to be viewed as constraints as important as the constitutional structure itself.

A growing literature, conferences, courses, and entire programs at prestigious universities all emphasize the necessity of looking to the bureaucratic structure and milieu that undergird the modern nation-state as the most important level of analysis of the formulation and substance of foreign and defense policy.[17] As Stephen D. Krasner notes in an important critique of the approach, "the bureaucratic interpretation of foreign policy has become the conventional wisdom."[18] In recent years Graham Allison and Morton Halperin have climbed atop decades of research into organizational theory, bureaucratic dynamics, and Presidential power to advance their now widely accepted paradigm of bureaucratic politics and its effects on policy planning and formulation.

"Decision" and "actions" are viewed as the outcomes of a complex process of "compromise, conflict, and confusion" best summarized as a fluid and very dynamic intragovernmental bargaining process. The process is, in fact, a "game." "Players" are seen as "men in career jobs." Their "position" vis-a-vis a "central arena" of Presidential decision "defines what players both may and must do." What becomes an issue, how stakes are defined, what face of an issue is perceived, and what stand is taken is determined by a player's position within an organization, his conception of "organizational interests."

The bureaucratic players' organizational interests are derived from the desire to achieve or maintain for their organizations autonomy, organizational morale, organizational "essence," roles and missions, and budgets.[19] This compulsion to protect and maximize these "organizational interests" is, therefore, the crux of the foreign policy process and affects in turn foreign and national security policy outcomes because the bureaucratic players assume that "what is in the nation's security interests are the interests of the organization to which they belong. [They] come naturally to believe that the health of their organization is vital to the nation's security."[20]

Entering into and constraining the perception of issues, stakes, and stands are personal objectives, domestic interests, and widely accepted but essentially nonoperational conceptions of the national interest. The game is not seen as a free-form exercise proceeding in a structural vacuum, for there are a number of "action channels," for example, the budgetary process, which, along with the formal and informal "rules of game," structures the bureaucratic struggle—the dynamic essence of the foreign policymaking process. Moreover, the resultant "outcomes," that is, decisions, do not "end" the game, for the "pulling and hauling" of bureaucratic politics will continue as decisions are implemented and become "actions."[21]

The proponents of this bureaucratic politics model of the policymaking process have proved somewhat unclear whether they applaud or deplore these processes. The process has a pluralistic and adversarial air that undoubtedly appeals to men and women socialized in the pragmatic traditions of American history. However, other observers have emphasized the negative implications of this "bureaucratic-pragmatic leadership" style.

Henry Kissinger in a concise and highly critical commentary on the bureaucratic-pragmatic style emphasizes its undermining effect on foreign and national security policy planning.[22] Inasmuch as pragmatism carries with it a "problem-solving" emphasis, there is a tendency to reduce foreign and national security policy to a series of discrete technical puzzles that must be resolved because they are forced onto the bureaucratic milieu by events. Indeed, pragmatism within a bureaucratic context is predisposed to await events or "developments" because relevant technical and bureaucratic expertise can be mobilized only within a particular "real" context. Within such a leadership style and under highly bureaucratized conditions "planning and policy formulation" tends toward the often intensely conflictual "game" of bureaucratic politics as actors struggle for access to and control of the "action." In such an environment, the adversarial skills of lawyers and the managerial talents of business entrepreneurs are at a premium. At the same time, however:

> This procedure neglects the long range because the future has no administrative constituency and is, therefore, without representation in the adversary proceedings. Problems tend to be slighted until some agency or department is made responsible for them. When this occurs—usually when a difficulty has already grown acute—the relevant department becomes an all-out spokesman for its particular area of responsibility. The outcome usually depends more on the pressures or the persuasiveness of the contending advocates than on a concept of overall purpose.[23]

The historical, hypothetical approach—with its sensitivity to complex interrelationships, which are all essential to planning—is discounted; for "pragmatism, at least in its generally accepted form, is more concerned with method than with judgment; or rather it seeks to reduce judgment to methodology and value to knowledge."[24] But as recent analysis of the Vietnam War suggests, the bureaucratic-pragmatic dynamic can lead by discrete, technically well-informed, and bureaucratically "sweet" steps to catastrophes.[25]

The fragmentation of a now enormous foreign policy establishment is, therefore, a legitimate source of concern. For it pushes the inherent and constitutionally mandated fragmentation of the American Government and policymaking processes to a point where it is fair to ask whether the difficulties of forming and administering policy in such a complex bureaucratic milieu may not undermine the very national interests and security the bureaucracies are purportedly serving. Might not the ponderous process of "coordinating" these many departments, agencies, and bureaus move too slowly and produce an ultimately inadequate compromise of many departments' interests rather than a foreign policy that serves the interests of the American people? Or, failing such compromise and coordination, might not so many actors promoting so many and often conflicting perceptions of the national interest contribute to a chaotic congeries of foreign policies that work at cross-purposes?

The National Security Act of 1947 anticipated this problem of a growing national security policy bureaucracy to a certain extent. The National Security Council (NSC) was to serve as a means for coordinating the activities of the various departments and agencies. But, by the late 1960s, the NSC and especially the Security Adviser had become a powerful locus of national security advice and formulation. Indeed, many critics contended that the Special Assistant and the NSC staff had become the center of an inordinate and dangerous concentration of policymaking power within the White House. Thus, critics of American foreign policy and policymaking could contend that even as the growth of the foreign policy bureaucracy constituted an excessive and dangerous caricature of the Madisonian separation of power, the attempt to counter organizational and administrative disarray had resulted in an excessive and dangerous centralization of power.

DEMOCRACY AS A CONSTRAINT

But the dilemmas of foreign policy formulation, planning, and management in the American political system are more complex yet, for the American system has during the two centuries of its existence developed into a far more democratic system than perhaps the original constitutional designers foresaw. Thus, with expansion of voting to a larger enfranchised electorate and with the number, range, and access of organized interest groups also expanding, the problems of contemporary policymakers have become even more complicated. The nature of the electorate to whom policymakers are accountable is frequently cited as the essence of the "problem." Hence, one student of the American political system, having evaluated research findings on public opinion and attitudes, concludes:

> The masses are incompetent in the tasks of government. They have neither the time, intelligence, information, skills, nor knowledge to direct the course of a nation. . . . Governing a nation is a task which is too vital, too complex, and too difficult to be left to the masses.[26]

Furthermore, some claim that in no area of public policy are most Americans so ill-informed and unconcerned as in foreign policy:

> The "ordinary citizen" does not seem to have enough information at his command to play even his limited public part with full efficiency. Public opinion polls reveal a startling lack of knowledge about such important matters as the United Na-

tions, NATO, the nature of Communism, and so on. Without basic data, it is a near-impossibility for individuals to make intelligent decisions—or even any decisions at all.[27]

In much of the conventional wisdom, therefore, the image of the American public is not unlike that described by George Kennan, who once characterized the American public as a kind of pea-brained monster:

> But I sometimes wonder whether in this respect a democracy is not uncomfortably similar to one of those prehistoric monsters with a body as long as this room and the brain the size of a pin: he lies there in his comfortable primeval mud and pays little attention to his environment: he is slow to wrath—in fact you practically have to whack his tail off to make him aware that his interests are being disturbed; but, once he grasps this, he lays about him with such blind determination that he not only destroys his adversary but largely wrecks his native habitat. You wonder whether it would not have been wiser for him to have taken a little more interest in what was going on at an earlier date and to have seen whether he could not have prevented some of these situations from arising instead of proceeding from an undiscriminating indifference to a holy wrath equally undiscriminating.[28]

The combination of an uneven public awareness of foreign affairs and the frequently "disruptive" nature of the American electoral process has contributed to a certain uneasiness on the part of some concerning the relationship of democratic processes and foreign policymaking. Kennan reflected this ambivalence when he lamented that "it is sometimes easier for a strong and authoritative government to shape its external conduct in an enlightened manner, when the spirit so moves it, than it is for a democratic government locked in the throes of domestic political conflict."[29]

Of course, the problem is more demanding than this oversimplified view of the American public would suggest. In fact, poll data for the late 1960s and throughout the 1970s suggest that the public is in most respects as pragmatic as its leadership. Moreover, insofar as the public displays swings of mood, one cannot always be sure whether this is caused by some deep, inherent inadequacy of the people or is not reflective of no less significant shifts in mood of political elites or, even more implicative, deep division and disorientation among those who claim foreign policy leadership.[30] Furthermore, the frequent and media-dominated character of the contemporary American electoral process can only compound the disruptive effects on policy planning and formulation. American electoral campaigns seem less and less issue-oriented; or if issues are apparent, they are quickly drained of substance and converted into symbols to be manipulated in pursuit of the affections of an increasingly benumbed, even cynical, public. When political leaders arrive in Washington as the result of their survival skills in, and are then preoccupied by their next encounter with, such domestic political conflict, it is little wonder that policy formulation has about it a certain disjointed character. "Planning" in such an environment is of value only if it can produce politically marketable payoffs within an electorally defined timeframe. Thus, the political context serves to exacerbate and reinforce the fragmenting pragmatism of the bureaucratic dynamic.

Finally, taking note of the collapse during the 1970s of whatever foreign policy consensus might have existed during the Cold War years, another group of observers has emphasized yet another difficulty posed by democracy. Inasmuch as American constitutional theory always presupposed limited government so as to protect and allow for the development and exercise of substantial private initiative and freedom, especially with respect to economic activity, concentrations of private nongovernmental power have always been an important part of the American system. Such power has never been evenly distributed. Thus, throughout most of American history—and in contrast with the largest business and corporate interests—women, blacks, ethnic minorities, labor, and other groups were not organized and, therefore, were relatively weak within this "private sector." By the middle of the twentieth century, however, this situation had begun to change and by the late 1950s and 1960s, the American system underwent a veritable explosion of political and economic organization as various groups sought to emulate the success of the labor and civil rights movements during the 1930s and 1960s respectively. Moreover, articulated demands became increasingly direct and intensely focused on the Congress and the Presidency. The traditional intermediary role played by the political parties was in some measure short-circuited as political, economic, social, and environmental activists exploited the immediate and pervasive presence of modern media, such as television, to bring their demands and political pressures to bear on the governmental system.

The pervasiveness of contemporary electronic and print media has had additional effects beyond serving as a ready means for more highly mobilized activists to gain a hearing. More subtle but no less important consequences flow from the pervasiveness of media in that the public is now exposed to numerous alternative "views" of international reality other than those traditionally provided by policymaking elites. In addition, the aggressiveness of the media—given legitimacy by the Pentagon Papers case and the Freedom of Information Act—now makes it more difficult for the government to maintain a public posture of consistency. "Leaking" becomes virtually endemic and the government quickly loses its monopoly on information and hence the command of the loyalties of the public. Under such circumstances the legitimacy of governmental policy is easily challenged, and with the challenge goes an undermining of authority and the erosion of policy coherence.

Perhaps nowhere were the consequences of this combination of higher public mobilization and media influence more apparent than during the late 1960s and throughout the 1970s. First with respect to Vietnam, but then concerning a volatile mix of "single issue" campaigns, the governmental structure yielded wherever the pressure became most intense. But as Samuel Huntington has argued in one of the seminal analyses of the phenomenon, such a response was ultimately inadequate:

> Polarization over issues generated distrust about government, as those who had strong positions on issues became dissatisfied with the ambivalent, compromising policies of government. Political leaders, in effect, alienated more and more people by attempting to please them through time-honored traditional politics of compromise.[31]

By the 1970s, therefore, some observers felt that the ultimate and dangerous democratic character of the American system was manifest. The result, they asserted, was democratic excess whereby the American political system had degenerated to little more than an arena in which intensely felt but conflicting demands contended, but out of which the common purpose necessary to successful foreign policy had not, indeed, could not emerge. The failure of Vietnam, the sordid spectacle of Watergate, and the seeming inability of government to protect and cushion people against the shocks of economic interdependence in the form of high energy prices and foreign competition combined to undermine the legitimacy of political institutions and the authority of the formal and informal policy establishment. The upshot was a "zero-sum society" in which no one was willing to pay the social and economic price of adjustment required by the international position of the United States. Furthermore, the scale of political, economic, and social organization combined with the fragmented character of the American governmental system made it extraordinarily difficult to apportion the costs and shift the burdens of adjustment with the decisiveness and speed that international circumstances seemed to demand.[32] There was, in short, a "democratic distemper"—the fulfillment of de Tocqueville's gloomy prognosis.[33]

MADISONIAN FRAGMENTATION, PRESIDENTIAL POWER, AND THE LIMITS OF PLANNING

The governmental fragmentation and democratic character of the American political system, therefore, combine to confront American foreign and national security policy planning, formulation, and administration with complex dilemmas. For well over 150 years, observers have questioned whether the complex and clanking machinery of American democracy was equal to the demands of world politics. But especially during the decades after World War II when the United States assumed a position of activist leadership in world affairs, one or more of the elements of that machinery were always found to be out of adjustment. And whenever governmental cogs slipped or democratic wheels squeaked, foreign policy analysts were usually present with their tool kits filled with "conceptual frameworks," "models," and "levels of analysis" designed to realign the machinery, as well as prescriptive reorganizations to lubricate points of friction.

The great fear, at the height of the Cold War, was that America would lose in the cockpit of international society unless it found a mechanism for overcoming the centrifugal forces inherent in American constitutional principles, design, and democratic ideals. At the apogee of the Cold War, textbooks reflected a common despair for democracy's chances of survival in bitter and sustained international conflict.[34] It was feared, in the words of one text, that

the more civilized and non-violent a democratic nation becomes in its internal institutions and behavior, the more peaceful and frank the outlook and conduct of its people, the more it may find it difficult, as a nation, to survive and prosper in the semi-anarchy of international affairs, in which secrecy, suspicion and violence always lurk in the background.[35]

Essentially, what these textbooks and scholars agonized over was the deliberate division of responsibility for foreign affairs. These divisions are both enumerated by the Constitution and established by practice. Scholars and diplomats commonly bemoaned, in print, the "grave dangers" to the successful conduct of diplomacy imposed by the constitutional parceling of responsibility for foreign affairs.[36] The logical response it seemed was to increase the powers of the Presidency by means of an expanded bureaucracy to handle the many new demands imposed on American foreign policy, and to design a new set of institutions to facilitate the coordination of the burgeoning national security policymaking institutions and processes.

After slightly more than a decade of operation, the national security policymaking system was the subject of intense analysis both in and out of government. Much of the public discussion and debate about the most appropriate structures for the 1960s, which were perceived by the new Kennedy administration as a time of maximum testing and peril, came to focus in an extended set of hearings held by Senator Henry Jackson's Senate Subcommittee on National Policy Machinery. From 1959 through 1965, the various hearings and studies undertaken by the Jackson Subcommittee provided a forum for discussing the problems of the Presidency and especially the foreign policy bureaucracy. There was much discussion and lamenting of the plight of the Department of State and the need to reinvigorate the role of the Secretary of State. Nonetheless, the thrust of the analysis followed that of Richard Neustadt's scholarly and influential paean to a strong Presidency, *Presidential Power:* the "needs of the President" came first and in a nuclear age beset by Soviet-American hostility this meant a strong, Presidentially-dominated national security process.[37] In sum, Hamiltonian centralization was the necessary and presumably sufficient organizational antidote to an excess of Madisonian fragmentation.

Such centralization has not proven beyond the capacity of recent Presidents. Thus, throughout the 1960s, the now familiar accretion of policymaking and bureaucratic power was developing in the office of the Special Assistant for National Security Affairs. More often than not, this trend has been at the expense of the Secretary of State and his department. The personalities of the President's Security Advisers and Secretaries of State have undoubtedly played a part in this development. But one cannot escape the conclusion that the institutional position of the Security Adviser offers fundamental advantages over that of the Secretary of State for a President bent upon an activist foreign policy. The Security Adviser is above all accountable only to the President. The Secretary of State, however, is encumbered by a department, a diplomatic tradition no longer regarded as central to American policy, and a more public role than the Security Adviser. The Security Adviser can, of course, assume high public visibility and engage in diplomacy—in the past he has also commanded significant staff resources. But, above all, the Security Adviser has been for five Presidents over the last twenty years, the "Presidential alter ego for foreign affairs"; he has thereby assumed the role that one of the most thoughtful and comprehensive analyses of needed organizational reform would have given to the Secretary of State:

—To be responsive to the President's need for options, for tough-minded advice that challenges pet bureaucratic doctrines, and thereby to make it in the President's interest to maintain [the Security Adviser's] primacy;

—To achieve maximum influence on the day-to-day actions of the foreign affairs government, aiming not only at prompt and faithful implementation of explicit Presidential decisions but also at a more general line of action consistent with top-level objectives and priorities.[38]

Yet, such centralization has not always meant policy coherence. Apart from the question whether any single individual, no matter how unencumbered by bureaucratic constraints or close to the President, can, alone, manage the entirety of American foreign and national security policy,[39] there remain other sources of incoherence: the executive-legislative relationship and democratic dynamics. For a time in the early and mid-1970s there seemed some prospect that a form of "congressional government" might emerge from the travail occasioned by an expiring Vietnam War and Watergate. But, as noted previously, this approach to resolving the institutional crisis of American policy-making has led back to a closer approximation of the executive-legislative and institutional deadlock prescribed by Madison. Moreover, the intensification of democratic or, as Maynes and Ullman have put it recently, "populist" dynamics[40] has sharpened the dilemmas of a centralized but ultimately stymied Presidency. The juxtaposition of a Presidency stridently asserting its prerogatives in the face of a "populist" foreign policy, that is, one "less confined to elitist prescriptions, but more subject to popular whims; less conscious of past mistakes, but more open to new errors; less understanding of foreign cultures and more strident about America's own,"[41] gives rise to a spectacle that evokes wonder and ultimately contempt abroad.

The concern that American democracy has become paralyzed by an excess of institutional checks, balances, and democratic expression of demands and mobilization of previously marginal social and economic groups, such as racial minorities and women, had been originally advanced by Samuel Huntington in the Trilateral Commission's report, *The Governability of Democracies,* in 1975. But by the end of the decade the analysis had been extended to the increasingly narcissistic character of the American people and the extension of these trends to the nation's troubled economic prospects.[42] This recent emphasis on the paralysis of democracy has been for the most part descriptive. By 1980, however, the combination of deepening national and international economic stagnation and renewed concern about Soviet intentions in the wake of the Afghanistan invasion, had led some who viewed American foreign policymaking from this perspective to echo Huntington's earlier call for yet another reassertion of Presidential energy and leadership.[43] But while some saw the "central challenge" as "not to reduce the president's power to lead, to govern or to persuade, but while checking the president's power to mislead and corrupt to ensure that a president has the means to lead, govern and persuade,"[44] the question remained as to how this was to be done. The preceding thirty-five years of American foreign policy have confirmed the extraordinary difficulty of achieving and then maintaining precisely such a balance in the face of the demands of an activist foreign policy.

Alternatively, one might pursue a more "democratic foreign policy" in which national leadership "practice[d] seriously the democratic arts of governance and consultation."[45] But unless one pins one's hopes to the emergence of a succession of extraordinarily self-contained Presidents, such an approach presupposes creating some approximation of a responsible party model of American government. And that entails, in turn, reconsidering the entire federal structure (yet another Madisonian obstacle) or, at a minimum, reforming campaign finance laws regulating congressional elections far beyond those acceptable to Congress thus far.[46]

One should, therefore, have no illusions about the task of changing either the institutional or the environmental constraints on foreign and national security policy. One seeks to change a structure originally conceived to inhibit, if not preclude, the very systemic efficiency one would presumably seek to arrange through the effort at reform. Indeed, the very concept of strategic planning for an activist global role would undoubtedly have struck many of the men who framed the institutional structure of the American political system as simply beyond the capacity of the system they devised. In fact, one suspects they would regard such planning and the international behavior that must flow from it as a threat to the values they sought to protect. The bureaucratization of policymaking, the democratization of the system, and the salience of concentrations of private power all compound the systemic and contextual constraints.

In sum, attacking the environmental or institutional constraints on foreign and national security policy planning, formulation, and execution is an immense *political* and *social* task; no mere "adjustment" of institutional relationships, but an act of truly radical proportions. Barring such a political transformation or the time necessary for social change to work, the planner can try to be clear as to the nature of the planning process, can try to better organize the bureaucratic domain within which planning must proceed, and can try to identify future security needs. At the same time, however, the planner must be resigned to debilitating encounters with a political and institutional environment initially contrived and subsequently evolved in a manner to frustrate the planner's efforts.

NOTES

1.   Alexis de Tocqueville, *Democracy in America,* vol. 1 (New York: Vintage Books, 1945), p. 243.

2.   For a review of American policy after World War II that emphasizes (though in balance with other factors) the role of domestic forces and constraints, see James A. Nathan and James K. Oliver, *United States Foreign Policy and World Order*, 2d ed. (Boston: Little, Brown and Co., 1981), and idem, *A Decidedly Inferior Form? Foreign Policymaking in the American Political System* (Boston: Little, Brown and Co., 1981).

3.   Alexander Hamilton, "Federalist Paper No. 24," in *The Federalist Papers* (New York: New American Library, 1961), p. 153 (emphasis in the original).

4.   James Madison, *Notes of Debates in the Federal Convention of 1787* (New York: W.W. Norton & Company, Inc., 1969), p. 214 (emphasis added).

5.   Hamilton, "Federalist Paper No. 24."

6.   Madison, "Federalist Paper No. 51," *The Federalist Papers,* p. 320.

7.   Ibid., p. 322.

8.   *Meyers vs. United States,* 272 US 293 (1926), Mr. Justice Brandeis dissenting.

9.   Hans J. Morgenthau, *Truth and Power: Essays of a Decade, 1960-1970* (New York: Praeger Publishers, 1970), p. 159.

10. Hamilton, "Federalist Paper No. 24," p. 153.

11. Statement of Senator J. William Fulbright before US Congress, Senate Subcommittee on Separation of Powers of the Judiciary Committee, *Separation of Powers,* 90th Cong., lst sess., 1967, p. 42.

12. Fulbright, "Meet the Press," 7 June 1959.

13. Arthur M. Schlesinger, Jr., *The Imperial Presidency* (Boston: Houghton-Mifflin Co., 1973).

14. Cited in Clinton Rossitor, *The American Presidency,* 2d ed. (New York: Harcourt, Brace, Jovanovich, 1960), p. 30.

15. For an expression and elaboration of the latter view, see Morton Halperin et al., *The Lawless State: The Crimes of the Intelligence Agencies* (New York: Penguin Books, 1976), and Halperin and Daniel Hoffman, *Freedom vs. National Security: Secrecy and Surveillance* (New York: Chelsea House Publishers, 1977). See also Frank J. Donner, *The Age of Surveillance: The Aims and Methods of America's Political Intelligence System* (New York: Alfred A. Knopf, 1980). For a discussion of the development of the Presidency during the late 1960s and early 1970s, in addition to that presented by Schlesinger, see Thomas Cronin, *The State of the Presidency,* 2d ed. (Boston: Little, Brown & Co., 1980), and Cronin, *The Presidency Reappraised* (New York: Praeger, 1977).

16. Perhaps the most comprehensive reviews of Congress and foreign policy during the 1970s are Alton Frye, *A Responsible Congress* (New York: McGraw Hill, 1975), and Thomas M. Frank and Edward Weisband,

Foreign Policy by Congress (New York: Oxford University Press, 1979); see also, Cecil V. Crabb, Jr. and Pat M. Holt, *Invitation to Struggle: Congress, the President and Foreign Policy* (Washington, DC: Congressional Quarterly Press, 1980).

17. The literature on bureaucratic politics has grown enormously in the last few years. Perhaps the most important of these works are Graham T. Allison, *Essence of Decision: Explaining the Cuban Missile Crisis* (Boston: Little, Brown & Co., 1971); Morton H. Halperin, *Bureaucratic Politics and Foreign Policy* (Washington, DC: The Brookings Institution, 1974); Allison and Halperin, "Bureaucratic Politics: A Paradigm and Some Policy Implications," *World Politics* 24 (Supplement, Spring 1972): 40-79; Halperin and Arnold Kanter, eds., *Readings in American Foreign Policy: A Bureaucratic Perspective* (Boston: Little, Brown & Co., 1973), especially the "Introduction," pp. 1-42; Richard Neustadt, *Alliance Politics* (New York: Columbia University Press, 1970); and the critiques of the perspective by Robert Art, "Bureaucratic Politics and American Foreign Policy: A Critique," *Policy Sciences* 40 (1973), and James A. Nathan and James K. Oliver, "Bureaucratic Politics: Academic Windfalls and Intellectual Pitfalls," *Journal of Political and Military Sociology* 6 (Spring 1978): 81-91.

18. Stephen D. Krasner, "Are Bureaucracies Important? (or Allison Wonderland)," *Foreign Policy,* no. 7 (Summer 1972), p. 159.

19. Halperin, *Bureaucratic Politics and Foreign Policy.*

20. Ibid.

21. Allison, *The Essence of Decision.*

22. Henry Kissinger, "Domestic Structure and Foreign Policy," in Kissinger, *American Foreign Policy,* 3d ed. (New York: W.W. Norton & Company, Inc., 1977), especially pp. 29-34.

23. Ibid., p. 31.

24. Ibid., p. 30.

25. See Leslie H. Gelb with Richard K. Betts, *The Irony of Vietnam: The System Worked* (Washington, DC: The Brookings Institution, 1979).

26. Thomas R. Dye, "What to Do About the Establishment: Prescription for Elites," in Thomas R. Dye and L. Harmon Zeigler, *The Irony of Democracy: An Uncommon Introduction to American Politics,* 2d ed. (Belmont, Calif.: Duxbury Press, 1972), p. 365.

27. Charles O. Lerche, Jr., *Foreign Policy of the American People,* 3d ed. (Englewood Cliffs, NJ: Prentice-Hall, Inc., 1967), p. 120.

28. George F. Kennan, *American Diplomacy, 1900-1950* (New York: New American World Library, 1959), p. 59.

29. Idem, *The Realities of American Foreign Policy* (Princeton, NJ: Princeton University Press, 1954), p. 44.

30. See the findings of Ole R. Holsti and James N. Roseman in "Cold War Axioms in the Post-Vietnam World," to appear in Holsti, Randolph M. Sinerson and Alexander L. George, *Change in the International System* (Boulder, Colo.: Westview Press, 1980), and Holsti and Rosnan, "Vietnam, Consensus, and the Belief Systems of American Leaders," *World Politics* 32 (October 1979): 1-56.

31. Samuel P. Huntington in his contribution to the Trilateral Commission's report, *The Governability of Democracies,* Rapporteurs: Michel Crozier, Samuel P. Huntington, and Joji Watanuki (Trilateral Commission, May 1975), p. 21. Huntington's argument is also published as "The Democratic Distemper," in *The American Commonwealth,* eds., Nathan Glazer and Irving Kristol (New York: Basic Books, 1976).

32. See Lester Thurow's analysis of the economic implications of this situation in *The Zero-Sum Society* (New York: Basic Books, 1980).

33. Huntington, *The Governability of Democracies,* passim.

34. See for example, Robert Dahl, *Congress and Foreign Policy* (New York: Harcourt, Brace, Jovanovich, 1950).

35. W. Ebenstein et al., *American Democracy in World Perspective* (New York: Harper and Row, 1967), pp. 645-46.

36. Charles Thayer, *Diplomat* (New York: Harper and Row, 1959), p. 80.

37. See US Senate, Committee on Government Operations, Hearings before the Subcommittee on National Policy Machinery, *Organizing for National Security,* 86th Cong., 2d sess., 1960; idem, Hearings before the Subcommittee on National Security Staffing and Operations, *Administration of National Security,* 88th Cong., 1962-63; and idem, Hearings before the Subcommittee on National Security and International Operations, *Conduct of National Security,* 89th Cong., 1st sess., 1965. See also Richard Neustadt, *Presidential Power* (New York: John Wiley & Sons, 1960). There have been subsequent revisions of Neustadt's book, but the 1960 edition remains the clearest statement of his thesis. On the reinvigoration of the Department of State, see I.M. Destler, *Presidents, Bureaucrats, and Foreign Policy: The Politics of Organizational Reform* (Princeton, NJ: Princeton University Press, 1974).

38. Destler, *Presidents, Bureaucrats, and Foreign Policy,* p. 261.

39. Destler, "Can One Man Do?" *Foreign Policy,* no. 5 (Winter 1971-72).

40. Charles William Maynes and Richard Ullman, "Ten Years of Foreign Policy," *Foreign Policy,* no. 40 (Fall 1980), p. 17.

41. Ibid.

42. On the narcissistic character of contemporary America, see Christopher Lasch, *The Culture of Narcissism* (New York: W.W. Norton, 1978); on the economy, see Thurow, *The Zero-Sum Society.*

43. For Huntington's position, see *The Governability of Democracies: USA,* pp. 37-38; see also Cronin, "Presidential Power Revised and Reappraised," *The Western Political Quarterly* 32 (December 1979): 381-95.

44. Cronin, "Presidential Power Revised and Reappraised," p. 394.

45. Maynes and Ullman, "Ten Years of Foreign Policy."

46. For a proposal along these lines, see James K. Oliver and Jerrold E. Schneider, "Congressional Government and a Scenario of Change," *Short Essays in Political Science,* proceedings of the 1975 Annual Meeting of the National Capital Area Political Science Association, Georgetown University, Washington, DC, 19 April 1975.

SECURITY FUTURES: INTELLIGENCE AND intelligence

4

DAVIS B. BOBROW
University of Maryland

DEFENSE PLANNING AND FORESIGHT

The defense sector differs from other areas of US public policy and public institutions in many ways. The most pertinent here are in the trappings of explicit planning (some would say the obsession with it), the priority claim on and, indeed, command over most of the resources of "big i" US Intelligence agencies (financial, technological, and human), and the extensive funding for "small i" intelligence (produced by internal analysis staffs, think tanks, and university research centers). One might, then, expect the relationship between planning and organized illumination of the future to be particularly good and widely accepted as relatively satisfactory. In fact, there is widespread doubt about the quality of defense planning and of the Intelligence and intelligence contributions to it. Indeed, external criticism and internal acrimony and bitterness have led to intense conflict among high officials responsible for defense planning and Intelligence, and noticeably declining real investment in and optimism about the contribution from intelligence.

The following observations and suggestions deal with several of the various types of defense planning (requirements, capabilities, and operations) agencies that are officially part of the intelligence community (referred to as providers of "big i" intelligence), and other recipients of government funds to provide foresight about the external world (referred to as providers of "small i" intelligence).

Some blame shortcomings in national security foresight and preparations on individuals and others on particular institutions. Such devil theories may have short-term parochial benefits. They do little to advance the national welfare because they skirt the far more fundamental and pervasive problems posed by the content of defense policy and the large organizations in which that policy must be made and carried out. The following pages single out a few of the fundamental problems and put forward some modest suggestions to ameliorate—not eliminate—ongoing difficulties.

This paper is not about techniques or methods. These matter, but in themselves improved methods will do little to improve defense planning, and the contributions of Intelligence and intelligence to it, unless underlying problems are dealt with more adequately than they have been. Neither does this paper attempt to be judicious and balanced. It is hoped that some blunt and oversimplified judgments will stimulate discussion and action sufficiently to compensate for their perhaps irritating lack of recognition of efforts to improve the situation. Finally, I will not repeat analyses available elsewhere of the sorts of forecasts and forecasting approaches that can improve the quality of planning decisions, if not the ease of generating plans.[1]

It is important to recognize that defense plans, Intelligence, and intelligence have three interdependent purposes. These are to:

—Reduce the number, frequency, and intensity of surprises to senior national security officials;

—Extend the decisionmaking period by reducing the time required for those officials to comprehend or grasp the situation they face, that is, to reduce "grasp time";

—Increase their control over international security affairs outcomes by reducing the time required for those officials to respond effectively to shape external situations, that is, to reduce "response time" and increase response effectiveness.

How the United States performs on these three counts depends significantly on both plans and information to arrive at and support them. The national benefits from plans and information can be no greater than whichever is weaker. National security performance is limited by the one of the three purposes least well achieved.

One of the critical dependencies of defense planning, and one not addressed by Intelligence or intelligence about the external world, involves domestic US futures. Changes in economic performance, willingness to favor defense programs over social programs, influence on the part of organized groups in the United States affecting security relations with other countries, all can and do make an enormous difference with regard to security futures. Organized foresight on these matters properly lies outside of the mission of the Defense Department or Intelligence agencies. That does not spare defense planning from the adverse consequences of operating rather blindly in these respects. In particular, there is a persistent tendency to plan on the basis of capabilities assumed to be available at a particular time in the future. The presumption of availability often rests on grossly unrealistic budgetary assumptions.

EXTRAORDINARY PROBLEMS AND ORDINARY BUREAUCRACIES

The relationships between, and the substance of, defense planning, Intelligence, and intelligence are inherently likely to be troubled and significantly unsatisfactory to all parties involved.[2] The national security of the United States now and for the future poses substantive problems of extraordinary difficulty. Yet, the organizations involved are ordinary in the sense of embodying standard pathologies found in large organizations.[3] Volumes have been and will be written on these difficulties and pathologies. I have selected a few that seem especially important in the present US national security context.

MEANS NOW, ENDS LATER, INSTRUMENTAL STRATEGIES LAST

The US defense planning process and the support from Intelligence and intelligence show a particular pattern of emphases with regard to time horizon. First, investment plans are being made now that set the limits on the means (advanced weapons, transportation, and communication systems) in service a good thirty years from now. These planning decisions are driven by perceptions of technical feasibility (ours), technical possibility (theirs), and current political appeal. Second, the national security ends those means will be called on to achieve are assumed to be constant, or, at most, extrapolations of those now in fashion. Yet, there is abundant evidence that national security ends, that is, aims and commitments specific enough to have practical military implications, often change within the life-span of an administration, let alone between administrations. Finally, instrumental strategies are either assumed to be constant or not thought of as plans at all, that is, as judgments shaping current resource allocations for future uses. Instead, beneath the slogan level, instrumental strategies are rather makeshift attempts to reconcile inherited means with at least partially unexpected ends. If relevant to prevailing national aims and commitments, they are usually suboptimal with respect to the available means and *vice versa.*

This unbalanced pattern of planning leads to unbalanced contemporary demands for Intelligence and intelligence. Unbalanced demand leads to similar unbalanced production and consumption of "big i" and "small i" analyses. This information imbalance, in turn, reinforces the planning pattern just described. The distant futures of hardware requirements planners involve information about science and technology. In contrast, those responsible for the instrumental application of force (warfighting, deterrence, and crisis management) seek information about the present or immediate future, that is, "current intelligence." They are rather uninterested in distant futures. Moreover, they often prefer to trade-off analytic depth for rapidly available observations (collection, processing, and reporting). Of course, instrumental applications of force succeed or fail, are appropriate or inappropriate, in large measure because of the capabilities, intentions, and reactions of other participants in international security affairs. Thus, the information needed to support such judgments is military, political, and economic rather than scientific and technological.

Accordingly, there is little demand for and consumption of information that illuminates the political, economic, and non-hardware military dimensions of the future. To the extent that demand and consumption determine supply, there will be little production of or investment in such forecasts either. Priorities are not expressed or followed for these kinds of information that bear directly on future national security aims and challenges. Accordingly, there will be little attention to information to support timely development of strategies to reconcile means with changing ends and changing foreign intentions. A reactive posture is almost assured as political, economic, and military realities impose themselves.

Parenthetically, similar patterns occur within the intelligence community itself. Investments in means that involve advanced technology have a far longer planning horizon than investments in human capital to analyze areas and subjects of interest that may well have more importance in the future than the present. Strategies to integrate the two are usually arrived at in an analogously ad hoc and catch-up manner. The planning pattern in Intelligence works then to reinforce rather than compensate for that in the Department of Defense. Information from "small i" intelligence usually results from particular task requests, and these, in turn, are driven by needs to justify technology or achieve expressed national aims. Therefore, at least so far as that deliberately produced under Defense auspices, it fits rather than counterbalances the patterns presented.

AH, SWEET CERTAINTY

Defense planners have an enormous appetite for the reduction of uncertainty. It would be surprising if they did not given the awesome costs of error in defense matters, the gap between available resources and conceivable threats, and the persistence of institutional habits. Intelligence and intelligence are welcome, as they make the consequences of policy alternatives very clear, establish that some events will definitely happen and others definitely will not, or contend that some institutions of other governments are fixed. At an extreme, the sweetness of certainty takes the form of a preference for "bad news" that reduces uncertainty over "good news" (opportunities) that increases it.

Unfortunately, the world is not so deterministic. Outcomes are rarely the consequence of a single policy or even a single nation. Governments rarely make irrevocable decisions to produce particular events.[4] Intentions are usually extraordinarily vague with respect to timing and, indeed, to the priority of any one intention compared to others. International security affairs present defense planners and analysts with an extraordinarily "open" system with numerous paths between intention and action, cause and consequence. Diverse outcomes can follow from the same set of purposes and capabilities. Diverse sets of purposes and capabilities can produce the same outcome. Nevertheless, in the cafeteria of information about defense futures, few planners rush for the items that increase uncertainty in any way, let alone proliferate relevant futures.

The understandable aversion to uncertainty creates preferences for Intelligence and intelligence more helpful for generating defense plans than for effective defense preparations. First, forecasts that stress possible discontinuities from previous behavior receive less serious attention than those that stress continuity. That is true whether the forecasts are about current allies, neutrals, or enemies. Second, reports about physical capabilities, especially ones in being, are treated as somehow more definitive and reliable as bases for defense planning than reports about less tangible factors such as morale, command performance, economic sacrifice, or politics. This preference confuses what is measurable with what has importance, what is tangible with what has clear security implications, and what is quantitative with what can be treated systematically. Third, since it is obviously easier to be certain about what it will be possible for a government to do as contrasted with what it will believe it should do or what it will do, preferences for long time horizon forecasts emphasize military hardware.

These information preferences are compatible with defense plans that bet strongly on a narrow range of possible futures, feature special rather than general purpose assets, and dedicate rather than pool military resources. They yield a defense posture vulnerable to being out of touch with reality and unadaptable to a great many situations. Because such plans make it very important to have made the right bet, officials locked into such a planning mode will never believe that they have sufficient information. Instead, they have an almost insatiable appetite for additional information and information resources in the areas of apparent certainty that provided the foundation for the prior pattern of defense planning bets. Absent shocks to the defense system, a smaller and smaller fraction of the universe of defense futures comes to consume a greater and greater fraction of resources for and attention to Intelligence and intelligence. Departures in response to fleeting shocks or short-lived crises erode quickly. Shifts in information demand and production that come after shocks hardly aid in planning to avert or cope with them.

THE ONLY GAME IN THE WORLD

Most defense plans are drawn with reference to some foreign government, coalition of governments, or political movement that are assigned one or several of the roles of threat sources, targets, or associates in receiving and generating threats. Thus, in the United States, defense planning is highly self-centered. For example, it organizes the world around US concerns and assumes that others are primarily addressing their relations with the United States and its enemies within the rules of conflict that the United States envisions. In that sense, the US security agenda is treated as the only game in the world. Others either play in it or are somewhat irrelevant. Reality is, of course, much more complex and much less controllable. Other governments and movements, and their component institutions and factions, engage in numerous games other than those that the United States sees as central. Even without such diversity of defense interests, most governments bring their own rules, experiences, and values to these potential security conflicts emphasized by US planners. The international security environment contains many simultaneous games with different sets of players often using different rules.[5] Further, a rather mechanical and deterministic view of how others reach and implement decisions makes for little alertness to the problem of self-fulfilling prophecies. One need not accept extreme action-reaction conceptions to admit that prudent hostile governments will take into account signs of the future challenges the United States will pose to their objectives.[6]

Of course, most defense planners do know that others have their own agendas and strategies and are affected by what they think to be our plans. The problem is that much of the time the plans *per se* embody a set of limiting assumptions that denies such diversity.

This chauvinistic oversimplification, combined with the two difficulties discussed previously, yields some expectations about defense planning and the role of Intelligence and intelligence. Most planning focuses on currently active sources of threats or targets for coercion. In a climate of defense of the status quo, planning is largely limited to coping with current enemies. Allies and neutrals are treated in a rather mechanical fashion, as if they were devoid of free will. Accordingly, alliances are often held for planning purposes to be unitary actors rather than imperfectly centralized coalitions. In effect, the world is "red," "blue," or vacant rather than, in many respects, gray or chameleon-like. Relatively little planning attention is given to conflicts between two or more enemies, or between two or more associates. Other than current enemies, few, if any, nations or movements are thought of as acting in ways that will change US national security aims or undercut instrumental strategies. Even enemies are treated as playing by our preferred rules in at least some respects. In particular, enemies are not viewed as adapting to long-lead time choices of means by the United States in ways that may deprive those choices of the merits they originally had. One sign of this tendency involves comparisons of future US forces with current enemy forces to show the value of the former. Another is planning that treats enemy attacks for which we have prepared most extensively as the most likely.

If these expectations do characterize defense planning, much information about the world will have little or no effect. Most information about most governments simply is beside the point. There is little reason to be informed about nations that are neither allies nor enemies in terms of their own internal and regional dynamics. Associated countries are expected to share the US focus on some enemy. Accordingly, information about them can be limited to the assets they can bring to cooperation (economic, military, and demographic). As for enemies, information has interest as it deals with their relations with the United States in fairly direct fashion, their threats to us and vulnerabilities to responses by us.

Information appetites would be far broader if one were to emphasize instead the diversity of the agendas of different governments (and their bureaus) and their adaptability. One would still not plan for all eventualities, but one would want information to keep updating sets of planning contingencies and considerations. More fundamentally, one would want information to help comprehend and respond to surprises and situations that occur without the effective guidance of the United States or its current major adversary. That is, one would at least want information available about pertinent participants in international security situations as purposeful decision systems. Foreign officials and institutions need to be viewed as engaging in many endeavors and trying to succeed as best they can within the limits of their resources, information, and political processes. These endeavors —be they on the part of allies, neutrals, or enemies—largely involve domestic problems, aspirations, and struggles. Intelligence and intelligence would then be asked to provide a foundation level of understanding of how other parties to international security affairs function and of the agendas they have set for themselves. With improved information about the political economy shaping the policies and practices of others, US defense planning could be more realistic and more sensitive to unwarranted premises. Defense plans would themselves become the source of a multitude of information requirements whenever they assumed some particular action (including inaction) by any foreign party.

DEFENDING PAST CHOICES

Neither defense planners nor information suppliers operate from a clean slate. Therefore, all have a stake in demonstrating the correctness of their previous choices. Recognition of current and likely future realities becomes constrained by previous positions, whether these involve force structure, investments in Intelligence collection assets, or estimates about the intentions of a foreign government. Among long-lived bureaucracies and staffs, this situation often results in tacit treaties to minimize conflict. The treaties lessen displays of fallibility that would comfort political enemies within the US decision process. When such treaties are operative, the involved bureaucracies cooperate to play down needs for drastic changes. When the treaties are fragile, the bureaus become more interested in laying a record for offense and defense against each other in the future than in relatively selfless cooperation to face uncomfortable developments. All parties become tempted to engage in protective behavior that will lessen future vulnerabilities. Information providers shun falsifiable predictions and seek protection in a welter of caveats and conditional statements. Defense planners make sure that there is some Intelligence and intelligence that can be cited to justify their choices.

MY BUDGET'S ENEMY IS MY ENEMY

Institutions responsible for defense planning and for Intelligence are developers and custodians of budgets and of expensive, "big-ticket" systems. Both seek justifications for their budgets and resent demurs to their claims on resources. Just as the previous pathology makes treaties to preserve images of competence, this pathology makes treaties to rationalize budget requests. From the side of defense planners, this creates a special appetite for Intelligence and intelligence supporting the need for and efficacy of major new weapons systems and procurements that one or several of the military services desire. From the side of high Intelligence officials, the treaty creates or ratifies special appetites for plans which justify expensive collection systems.

MY MONOPOLY IS MY POWER

Defense planners and information providers are subject to the judgments of third parties, in the US case even the more senior military and civilian Defense officials, the President, and the Congress. In a world of finite resources, they are in some sense competitors although the relationship between them is not zero-sum. The last two pathologies note tendencies toward collusion. This pathology suggests tendencies to strengthen their respective hands by monopolizing expertise. In its simple form, this tendency leads to defense planners monopolizing information about US plans and forces and to information providers monopolizing information about what is known and can be known about the exterior world.

Bureaucratic incentives for "green doors," "black boxes," and restrictive classification compartments are extremely strong. Defense planners' positions will be stronger if these planners or their masters in the defense establishment monopolize information about both ourselves and others. Should that not be possible, the second best is to break the information monopoly of Intelligence and intelligence institutions by having some subordinate to defense planners. Those subordinates would be expected to be more "appropriately sensitive" to the need for making past defense planning choices and current defense budget desires look good. In a weakly centralized system of defense planning, such as the Office of the Joint Chiefs of Staff provides, one would expect subordinate Intelligence and intelligence activities in each of the military services and some defense agencies if only for justification in budget battles. Defense planners also will be reluctant to supply Intelligence and intelligence analysts with information about US forces or plans. The pressures of bureaucratic life work, then, to stimulate the desire for and defense of a monopoly of expertise and the quest for "hired guns" to break the monopoly of other institutions.

LET'S GET ON WITH IT

The large organizations with diverse competing interests involved in defense planning and in Intelligence make any binding decision difficult to achieve, and even more arduous to implement coherently. There is, then, an understandable resistance to reopening past decisions and a great desire to get on with the job. Major alterations in defense plans, or in characterization of important foreign participants in security matters, imply the need to at least review and possibly alter decisions thought to be settled once and for all. Such alterations make bureaucratic life miserable for those obligated to respond. The first response is usually to do little and hope the change will go away, and to attempt quietly to discredit it. The second is to change, but use the occasion to pursue reassignments of missions and assets to avoid another disruption. Recognizing the unexpected is, then, a risky course of action. At most, it produces a higher level of critical scrutiny and, at worst, it occasions attacks on institutional prerogatives. Facing up to change calls into question the treaties with respect to competence and resources referred to above.

PRIORITIES AS RESOURCE SHIELDS

In a bureaucratic context, resources are insufficient to meet all demands for them. Agencies are more likely to protect the resources they have, and get more, when they can credibly portray all their current resources as allocated to high-priority, widely recognized problems. Allocations to high-priority accounts are relatively shielded. Allocations to low-priority accounts are vulnerable. Experienced defense planners, Intelligence executives, and intelligence funders, all are repeatedly reminded of these laws of resource competition. Those who allocate resources as insurance against changes in national security ends or challenges take risks in resource terms. Of course, they will look "golden" if low-priority problems become salient. In the interim, they can easily be portrayed as irrelevant, willful, and "fat."

In national security policy as in personal life, the main motives for insurance are to discharge obligations to future generations and to reduce anxiety about unforeseen disasters. Insurance expenditures seem to be luxuries when one is already extraordinarily anxious about current, manifest dangers and the survival of one's own generation. As the world seems more threatening to the United States, the disincentives mount against allocating resources to distant or low-priority problems.

The distortions and limitations these tendencies place on defense planning, Intelligence, and intelligence are serious. They operate regardless of the ideology or security viewpoints of the individuals involved. They foster a situation where there is no powerful institutional voice for reality before it poses crisis conditions, unless reality is ultra-stable. By ultra-stable, I mean that the world only changes in line with fixed preconceptions. When other changes occur, there will be little in the way of planning and information to minimize grasp and response times and maximize response effectiveness.

SOME MODEST SUGGESTIONS

The tendencies just discussed seem rather inevitable. Accordingly, an important national security management problem is how to build some partial correction into defense planning, Intelligence, and intelligence. The viability of these suggestions does not lie in the hands of defense planners, Intelligence executives, or intelligence funders acting singly. Only mutual, shared recognition of their desirability and of the need for their active support will give the following recommendations much of a chance.

Before turning to positive recommendations, it seems important to question the importance, and even the desirability, of two suggestions currently in wide circulation. The first calls for a greatly strengthened Department of Defense role in monitoring and forecasting the external world; the second, for giving priority to tactical over other forms of Intelligence. Even greater Defense Department dominance of Intelligence than now exists would foster many of the pathologies noted above. The present overwhelming emphasis on military matters, including military science and technology, to the disadvantage of political and economic information would become even worse. The inattention to nations other than the Soviets and their allies would become even more pronounced. There are even grounds to argue that the major shortcomings of Intelligence for defense planning are largely within the domain already assigned to Defense. Expanding that domain may well divert attention from seriously needed internal reforms. As for tactical versus other claims, framing the issue in those terms is bureaucratically natural but substantively misleading. Intelligence means, intelligence perspectives, and the information both can provide simply are not neatly divided into single-purpose bins. The need for tactical information is genuine and important; it is best met by better mechanisms to set priorities for specific situations and improved information sharing and integration. Otherwise, we risk an even greater lack of attention to developments and situations marginal to the current responsibilities of major theater commanders. Yet, those currently marginal developments and situations need to be addressed before they become flashpoints of crises and theaters of war.

The suggestions that follow are addressed more to the "grasp" and response areas of performance than to avoiding surprises. This largely reflects my pessimism and that of many others about the feasibility of improved predictions or warnings sufficiently precise about timing to provide positive guidance for defense planning.[7]

FORECASTS AND THE INFORMED NATIVE STANDARD

The Holy Grail of perfect warning sufficiently ahead of events to help response planning creates unrealistic expectations and a bottomless sink for resources. That standard should be replaced with a more modest one—comprehending the future with as much clarity as well-informed, thoughtful native observers of the foreign institutions in question. Picking the observers whose expectations provide the standard is by no means easy. It will be important to refrain from automatically assuming that high officials in the foreign government are necessarily very perceptive about the future. Under this standard, one will often conclude that foreign governments and movements have yet to decide conclusively what they will do and when and how they will do it. Acceptance of this standard will argue for defense planning based on uncertainty rather than clarity about the future.

PLANNING AND INFORMATION PRIORITIES BASED ON RISK

Salient priorities in national security policy at any point in time only partially reflect risks, that is, developments which may pose critical difficulties to national decisionmakers. Instead, such priorities reflect the fraction of such developments made salient by recent US experience, and bureaucratic missions and resource investments. A sounder approach proceeds to planning and information priorities from a broad view of developments that would be upsetting, that is, would pose risks, and preparation to comprehend and respond to them.[8] This list will unavoidably exceed available resources, a problem that calls for the means to "surge" planning and information capacity as risks clarify.

SURGE CAPACITY—INFORMATION

The ability to rapidly surge information about foreign participants in international security affairs and theaters of operation can usefully be broken down into collection, processing, and analysis. For collection, there is a need for reserving a fraction of observation means for low-priority areas and actors. Otherwise, there will not be the baseline of observation required to notice changes or the capability to engage in expanded, quickly useful observations. For processing, there is a need for more flexible information management systems which allow for rapid retrospective search of observations, messages, and actions hitherto stored but ignored, or never addressed in a newly pertinent fashion. For analysis, and some forms of processing, especially of statements and messages, there is no substitute for people with appropriate language, area, and topic skills.

It is unrealistic, given the complexity and diversity of the international environment, to expect the full-time staffs of the US Government for Intelligence and intelligence to have staffing depth across the board. What should be feasible is to emulate the model of the active military reserve. An analogous *International Affairs Reserve* would enroll and be able to quickly mobilize persons with language, foreign area, and international-topic expertise. Like the members of the active military reserve, these individuals would have a regular part-time obligation to use their expertise and would spend several weeks a year on pertinent "active duty." They would, therefore, be ready to contribute quickly and not require extensive retraining. By focusing membership to complement full-time, regular executive branch personnel, the modest expense would produce a high rate of information return should circumstances warrant.

SURGE CAPACITY—PLANNING

The ability to rapidly surge the provision of defense plans argues for, first, modular planning, and second, practice at quickly assembling and patching the relationships between existing modules. My suggestion, here, rests on the view that defense plans for different specific contingencies in large measure involve drawing from a set of more generic primitive mini-plans. These are the modules which, when assembled and properly linked for compatibility, make up a full-fledged plan. It should be recognized that many of these modules, to move and support a fighter wing, for example, will have to contain "blanks" to be filled in for the particular situation at hand. Nevertheless, they can still lessen response time and provide guidance to Intelligence and intelligence efforts by identifying, in advance, specific types of information that will be needed. The modular planning suggestion could be implemented through a well-documented, computer-based library of planning modules and through exercises in which planning staffs use the library. It would at least narrow the considerations that would require planning from scratch.

LONG LEAD-TIME INVESTMENT UPDATES

Although the long lead times for high technology systems development and procurement surely can be shortened, they will still be long. What seems desirable are far greater efforts to review periodically, and seriously, the merits of such systems in terms of changing international security circumstances and US national security priorities. Intensive procedural steps are necessary to give those considerations clout in the acquisition process (in Defense and Intelligence) and to lessen the autonomy of those who arrange technology futures from those responsible for policy futures.

REDRESSING THE NON-MILITARY VERSUS MILITARY IMBALANCE

Intelligence, intelligence, and defense plans now give primary attention to military matters. One does not gainsay their importance by observing that many national security problems and the desirability and feasibility of many military responses are crucially affected by nonmilitary factors. Gaps in military information are outweighed by a paucity of economic, political, and sociological information. Steps to increase effective demand for and supply of these other forms of information should be a major national priority. That will probably not be the case until the institutions for which these factors are culturally salient come to exercise a far stronger claim on Intelligence and intelligence resources than is now the case. This implies far more information access and resource control by the Departments of State and Treasury. The major purpose of this suggestion is not to downgrade the influence of the Department of Defense on how the United States relates to security futures, although it may have that consequence. Rather, my major concern is that information be available to place military possibilities in a politically and economically realistic context. It may well be that there also is a need for more competitive analysis on military matters, but there are, for most purposes, no competing centers of analysis on political and economic matters.

COMPARATIVE APPRAISALS AND PLANNING QUALITY CONTROL

Defense plans rest on more or less implicit judgments that compare how the United States and its adversaries will perform. Yet, very few of those comparative appraisals are subject to rigorous scrutiny by independent experts well informed about both the United States and its possible allies and our enemy and its possible allies. The mistakes that can then enter into plans multiply erroneous expectations as the plans themselves come to drive subsequent preparations for contingencies. Since plans can well outlive realities, independent comparative appraisals of their premises need to be done periodically and in depth. Stress should be laid on the independence and comparative knowledge of those who do these appraisals. It is asking too much to assign this task primarily to individuals who were personally involved in the initial appraisals, or whose careers are captive to the institutions that provided the initial information and estimates on one or the other side to a conflict.

ASSUMPTIONS IN COMPETITION

The realities of international security affairs make it quite easy to find examples to support the merits of almost any view. One responsibility of elected officials and their appointees is to make judgments when the burden of expert judgment is inconclusive. These are some of the more fundamental reasons for competition between well-informed experts in a pluralist manner, and for competition in which institutional incentives are at least varied. The quest for a right set of assumptions about foreign governments may have its satisfactions, but it overlooks the quite frequent situation in which several sets of assumptions are partially valid. The United States will be served far better by procedures and a climate that encourage vigorous, reasoned tracing through of competing sets of assumptions supporting different defense plans. At present, support for the set of assumptions that "lose" in the ultimate policy judgment entails great risk to those involved. To avoid misunderstanding, let me add that the well-known "Team A, Team B" episode was a travesty of this suggestion, whatever its intent.[9] Among other things, it raised the perceived risks incurred by some of the experts to a high level and did not include a well-distributed representation of the available competing assumptions about Soviet intentions and behavior.

To conclude, the suggestions put forward are not freshly minted. There has been progress with some of them.[10] My plea is that the steps involved need to be made routine rather than exceptional.

NOTES

1. A useful review can be found in Nazli Choucri and Thomas W. Robinson, eds., *Forecasting in International Relations* (San Francisco: W. H. Freeman, 1978).

2. Harold L. Wilensky, *Organizational Intelligence* (New York: Basic Books, 1967).

3. For example, see Anthony Downs, *Inside Bureaucracy* (Boston: Little, Brown, 1967); Graham T. Allison, *Essence of Decision* (Boston: Little, Brown, 1971); Morton H. Halperin, *Bureaucratic Politics and Foreign Policy* (Washington, DC: The Brookings Institution, 1974).

4. Thomas G. Belden, "Indications, Warning and Crisis Operations," *International Studies Quarterly* 21 (March 1977): 181-98.

5. For examples, see Davis B. Bobrow, Steve Chan, and John Kringen, *Understanding Foreign Policy Decisions* (New York: The Free Press, 1979), and my "Ecology of International Games," *Peace Research Society (International) Papers* 11 (1969): 67-88.

6. Albert Wohlstetter, "Theory and Opposed-Systems Design," in Morton A. Kaplan, ed., *New Approaches to International Relations* (New York: St. Martin's 1968), pp. 19-53.

7. For examples, see Richard K. Betts, "Analysis, War and Decision," *World Politics* 31 (October 1978): 61-89; Steve Chan, "The Intelligence of Stupidity," *American Political Science Review* 73 (March 1979): 171-80; Michael Handel, "The Yom Kippur War," *International Studies Quarterly* 21 (September 1977): 461-502; *Planning for Problems in Crisis Management* (Washington: CACI, Inc., 1976).

8. For examples, see several papers by Ralph E. Strauch, *The Operational Assessment of Risk* (Santa Monica: RAND, R-691-PR, March 1971; *Risk Assessment as a Subjective Process* (Santa Monica: RAND, P-6460, March 1980).

9. "The National Intelligence Estimates A-B Team Episode Concerning Soviet Strategic Capability and Objectives," Report of the US Senate Select Committee on Intelligence, 95th Cong., 2d sess., 16 February 1978.

10. A notable example is the work on net assessment under the direction of Andrew Marshall in the Office of the Secretary of Defense.

NATIONAL SECURITY PLANNING: IMAGES AND ISSUES

5

PHILIP S. KRONENBERG
Virginia Polytechnic Institute and State University

What general principles should guide national security planning by the United States? There is widespread concern about the state of US military preparedness; dissatisfaction with America's ability to coordinate the political, economic, and military dimensions of its foreign policy; and a sense of being eclipsed by the vigorous expansion of Soviet military power. Given the firm commitment of the Reagan administration to enhance the vitality of US defenses, one would expect that national security planning needs to be made more effective. What guiding principles can best serve to improve security planning?

The answer to this question seems rather straightforward. If one were to ask this question of an experienced planner in any national security agency, the answer would likely include the following:

—Clarify national objectives defined in terms of US values and interests and the international conditions the United States prefers.

—Develop a foreign policy consensus at home around an integrated national strategy toward the world and the US role in the world. This consensus should fully support our national objectives and be clearly articulated by US political leadership.

—Derive active policies, strategies, programs, and capabilities or force structures in the military, economic, and politico-diplomatic spheres which are consistent with our national strategy and which serve US national objectives in the world. In so doing, the United States should deemphasize reactive approaches to the initiatives of other international actors.

—Provide the political support for the policies, the institutional and doctrinal support for the strategies, and the resource support and operational plans for the programs, that are appropriate to the successful accomplishment of US national objectives.

—Adjust policies, strategies, programs, capabilities or forces, operational plans, and actions in response to shifts in current or expected global and regional opportunities, competition, and threats—but always in a manner consistent with US national objectives.

Advocacy of principles such as these appears to be a continuing source of despair for many experienced planners. Simultaneous with articulating these principles, they frequently acknowledge some fundamental problems in making them work. First, is the absence of a well-defined political consensus among national leaders—and the general population—about US national objectives, values, and interests. Where agreement is found it tends to be pitched at an extraordinarily general level of definition, providing uncertain guidance to planners. Also acknowledged is the lack of clarity among leaders and the populace about acceptable strategies or modes of behavior in the conduct of foreign policy (the sharply defined current *exceptions* to this point being the use of covert operations or programs of security assistance which might encourage "another Vietnam" and actions which could precipitate a confrontation with the Soviets and resort to nuclear weapons). Additionally, planners see persistent conflict in the country over the allocation of resources across the full range of national policy spheres, with some contentious debate periodically evoked over the relationship between defense and social expenditures.

A second deficiency that some planners concede is the fragility of resource commitments to national security programs, even during periods of relative popular sentiment on behalf of defense spending. The erosion by inflation of the value of monies directed into defense programs and the deterioration of the industrial base and the human resource accessions characteristic of unfavorable demographics undermine the doctrinal and means-ends logic of several planning principles.

A third problem with these principles is the limited capacity of planners to forecast the future. Coupled with this is the great variation one finds in the acceptance of planners' forecasts by decisionmakers who would use their product. These traits produce real problems for the fifth principle above, which calls for the adjustment of policies and plans in response to shifting events.

Finally, some planners will acknowledge the difficult problem of interaction effect. The world is not simply "out there" like some great, complex physical object that can be acted upon successfully once competent forecasts have been provided our policy diagnosticians. The international system is not so deterministic. As the United States chooses to initiate, omit, or maintain programs or policies based on expectations of the near or distant future, the effect of these choices alters certain conditions in the world and the "reality" we thought we were dealing with has been changed, often in ways that are obscure to even the most astute planner.

The solutions some planners offer to deal with these shortcomings in the planning principles summarized above seem to be *more of the same.* For example, one is told that the lack of a sufficient political consensus can only be solved by "clarifying our objectives" and "reaching broader agreement among America's political leaders" about the appropriate direction of US policy. This circular approach to principles and the problems it raises may be due to an underlying epistemological issue: What can we understand about planning and the objects of planning?

It would appear that planning principles of the type listed above keep running into problems for which ineffective circular solutions are offered because such principles try to direct our attention toward making national security policy and program *choices* based on substantive, doctrinal consistency. (For example, should the United States resist a Marxist-dominated insurgency in the Middle East? Should we modernize theater nuclear weapons in Europe?) Perhaps this is one of the implications of the conclusion reached by Gelb and Betts that "the need for pragmatism more than doctrines, formulas, and ideologies is the basic lesson of the Vietnam War. . . . Doctrine demands a dangerous consistency; a workable policy requires discrimination and choice."[1] The substance of plans, like policies, cannot be judged as "good" or "bad" in the abstract. They are contingent on the specific values and interests one wishes to serve. Instead of principles intended to help us *make* the substantive planning *decisions* themselves, perhaps what we need—and can more feasibly articulate as abstract, general principles—are principles for *managing* the national security planning *process.* Thus, the management of planning rather than the selection of substantive plans becomes the focus of planning principles.

The purpose of this chapter is to contribute to the discussion of how to improve the management of the national security planning process by (1) examining how the circumstances of the people who are engaged in planning and the organizational context in which they work bear on the planning process and (2) proposing several principles which may enhance the management of that process.

PLANNING AS MANAGEMENT AND ART

Put simply, a plan is a design, a way of doing something. The focus of this chapter, however, is not on the design of *all* the "somethings" associated with agencies such as the Defense Department, National Security Council, Central Intelligence Agency, or Department of State. That would cover too much. Instead, the focus is on thinking of planning as being the *strategic management*[2] of the national security organizations of the US Government. Strategic management consists of a process of planning *and* implementing plans for the future involvement or "positioning" of each national security organization with respect to:

— The domestic environment of other agencies, organizations, and key individuals
— The international environment of national and supranational players on the world scene, and relevant international organizations
— Its distinctive operating doctrines and styles
— The goods and services each provides
— Operational capabilities of military combat organizations
— Evaluation of the performance appropriate to these
— Values sought by those who shape organizational action
— Criteria used to evaluate organizational action
— Geographic spheres of operations

The purpose of viewing national security planning in this way—as the control over planning and executing of attempts by organizations to be *strategic* by shaping their future missions, jurisdictions, and styles of action—is to minimize the notion that planning is an exercise somewhat isolated from the operational world. Plans that, in prospect, have no impact on the world are like a tree falling unobserved in a forest. They are irrelevant, at least at that moment. This strategic management view of planning suggests that one should reject any notion that plans can be evaluated separately from their pragmatic implications for action. A "good" plan that is implausible in resource or political terms, therefore, cannot pass muster without a sturdy defense of its exceptional premises. The idea here is not intended to be an endorsement of mindless incrementalism or unimaginative art-of-the-possible thinking. It is instead the simple point that a plan should involve a concept or set of action directions that seasoned people in the operational world would wish to use under selected conditions.

Newcomers to the Washington bureaucracy who advocate reforms are soon put a question intended to bring them quickly to their senses: "If it's not broken, why fix it?" Whether broken or not, there are clear reasons to want improvement in defense planning.

First, defense efforts consume enormous quantities of scarce resources. A more efficient use of resources for defense will allow alternative uses of resources in domestic programs of government or in the private sector. Second, better planning improves the quality of advice to policymakers and sensitizes them to the nuances of alternative courses of action and their consequences. Third, to the extent that representative elements of a high-quality planning debate enter the public domain, there should emerge an enhanced political dialogue on these issues and a more thoughtful political basis of popular support for defense policies and institutions. We need to move beyond the polarization and frustration that grew from the Vietnam conflict. Fourth, high-quality planning with the longer term commitments that are possible may improve the defense resource picture. Stable expectations based on more careful commitments can produce a solid base to attract human resources and expenditure patterns which can minimize the bidding-up of program costs with crash procurement efforts. Fifth, careful planning and investment programs can help limit and perhaps reverse the decay of the industrial base. Sixth, planning in the sense of strategic management (the linking of planning-implementation-evaluation) can help convey our commitment to a steady course to our allies and uncommitted states, together with an expression of greater national will to our adversaries.

Although planning for the security of a postindustrial society uses complex organizational arrangements and the tools of high technology, it is basically an art form. National security planning is art not only in the sense of requiring technical craft but also in the political sense of statecraft.

As in the domain of the artist, good planning relies on the planner's distinctive personality, requiring at times great imagination, strategic sensitivity, insight into the issues and problems of economy and society as well as military affairs, reliable skill, tenacity, great energy, and occasional daring. Also like the fine artist, the fine planner is limited by the materials, structures, working conditions, and ambiance of his organizational workplace. Finally, and again like the artist, the planner lives in an interactive relationship with the object of concern. As in the relationship between artist and model, this often subtle interaction provides a series of external reference points to give *definition* to the planner's creativity as constrained by available resources. These are political and programmatic definitions which shape the character of allies and adversaries—and those in between—in the mind's eye of the planner.

Thus, principles of planning must deal with (1) the people who plan and interact with the planners, (2) the orientation of the planners toward the objects of planning, and (3) the organizational context in which they plan.

PLANNING AND PEOPLE

RATIONALITY AND UNCERTAINTY

Planning is labor intensive and involves people in creative roles. These creative roles clearly have a rational dimension. Planners seek to interpret objectives and to design approaches to action which will serve these objectives. Although planning is rational in the instrumental sense of trying to relate means and ends, this rationality does not necessarily achieve on a routine basis the formal characteristics of rigorous analytic logic dictated by textbook planning. Competing values are not always integrated into single dimensions of utility. Alternatives are not always arrayed in coherent preference rankings with probabilistic outcomes. Choices are not always made on the basis of current information. Instead, the choices made and plans developed are often better explained by what John Steinbruner calls a "cybernetic paradigm" supplemented with cognitive theory.[3] Decision-makers do not confront a complex problem in its full variety. Rather, they subjectively impose meaning on complex events as a means to reduce their uncertainty and act on alternatives assumed to have single outcomes, using a narrow, perhaps out-dated, information base. For example, Washington decision-makers tended to rely on out-of-date information about the relative strength of the South Korean and North Korean armies in their deliberations during the first week of the Korean conflict in 1950. These estimates understated the greater strength of the North Korean forces in spite of the opportunities to update these impressions with objectively available data.[4]

Although crisis decisionmaking and more routine defense planning may not be identical phenomena, one may argue that those who plan and those who use the products of planners are not utterly rational, omniscient calculators. Planners, as people, pursue their self-interest within a kind of bounded rationality in which they have neither the wit nor the will—much less the time or data—to continually maximize a single value or integrated concept of utility. Most of the time planners seek satisfactory ("good enough") solutions to problems rather than maximum ("best possible") solutions.[5] Finally, their interpretations of their own purposes and the *meaning* of events or "realities" are largely determined by the efforts of others to control the social and political processes in which they are embedded. The point being argued here is that the meaning of reality in a climate of uncertainty is actively structured by human intellect.[6] And, at least at the margin of interpretation, there is never an objective standard which can give meaning to events. When does the half-full glass become half-empty? When does the vigorous thrust toward parity in strategic weapons by an adversary country become a first-strike capability? The *construction of meaning* by human mental processes is the product of social relationships, especially power relationships, in which individuals and groups seek to control events.[7]

MEANING, UNCERTAINTY, AND ACTION

What are the psychological factors that shape how people give meaning to very uncertain situations? What are the mental linkages between social or political relationships and the way an individual interprets uncertainty and acts on that interpretation? These psychological mechanisms associated with high uncertainty are not well understood but several that bear mentioning have some currency in the organization theory literature. What follows by no means exhausts the list.

First, values are not necessarily selected before plans are formed or actions initiated.[8] Values play an important symbolic role to justify the action plans undertaken. Often, individuals will defer making their values explicit to others (or themselves) to retain room for maneuver. Certainly there are cases when values or considerations of ends are the point of departure in designing action. But more frequently, the function of values in means-ends relations is problematic, especially as one moves closer to policy levels. When values are expressed with much specificity, they may become a major source of contention; thus, they are seldom addressed directly. Their ultimate avowal is often a *post factum* rationalization of actions influenced by intuition, emotion, organizational habits, ideological and political considerations, or the weight of accumulated policy, program, or budgetary commitments. The last of these is especially influential. Earlier choices become heavily value-laden over time. Given this normative baggage, few policy or planning questions can be approached *de novo*.

Second, the selection of the information requirements for action and the interpretation of information are biased by sociopolitical factors. As with values, the selection of information, judgments about the veracity or reliability of information sources, and its interpretation are influenced by ideological and political constraints and by the work habits and subculture of organizations. An example of this is the exaggerated expectations and results claimed for strategic bombing in World War II by its proponents.[9]

A third mechanism has been called "problemistic search."[10] This means that people follow familiar procedures and decision rules and rely on familiar information sources—based upon social reinforcement in their work situation—until they encounter a problem for which established routines do not work. Thus, the problem "motivates" them to search for a solution. There may be a kind of Law of Social Inertia compelling people to keep doing what they are used to doing—and what is rewarded—until a major problem surfaces. Most organizations sustain stable routines for "coding" or imposing a structure of meaning on events which can then serve as a basis for calling forth programmed action (or inaction) in response to these events. Events that do not fit these structuring codes tend to be ignored. For example, emphasis on offensive strategic weapons—especially ballistic missiles—with their supporting doctrine and the assumption of their superiority over plausible defensive systems may block proper attention to the development of ballistic missile defense technologies and concepts, especially at the level of fiscally constrained long-term planning.

A fourth, and related, psychological mechanism is "opportunistic surveillance"[11] consisting of monitoring behavior that scans the environment for opportunities. This scanning does not wait to be activated by the emergence of a problem nor does it necessarily stop when a solution has been found. Opportunistic surveillance represents a kind of *curiosity* because it involves monitoring events for opportunities. This seems to be stimulated by three impulses: (1) a preference for novelty, (2) ambition which seeks to differentiate one's individual or organizational product from that of coalitional or interorganizational competitors, and (3) a strategic sense which compels efforts to control uncertain but plausible futures. Some elements of opportunistic surveillance may be seen in the evolution of Army and Air Force initiatives related to the "Assault Breaker" concept of the Defense Advanced Research Projects Agency (DARPA) in the Department of Defense.[12] The concept concerns a ground- or air-launched standoff weapon to attack moving, rear echelon armor massed deep behind enemy lines. The Army proposes a ground-launched missile, perhaps using Air Force PAVE MOVER targeting radar while the Air Force wants an air-launched Assault Breaker, perhaps using an Army-developed missile. The General Accounting Office believes that each of the services "would be more inclined toward a system over which they have total direct control." Several years before DARPA initiated the Assault Breaker program, both the Army and Air Force had programs to develop a weapon to attack rear echelon armor.

Opportunistic surveillance would seem to become more vigorous under conditions of growing uncertainty. The codes which help structure meaning and are associated with problemistic search may be adapted or even abandoned under circumstances of perceived turbulence or high stress. Individuals in these situations begin to reinterpret in a uniquely personal way those events that have salient but uncertain meaning and are perceived to involve high stakes. This starts a process of "discovery" of meaning and mental imposition of structure in reaction to these uncertain events, influenced in part by resource, ideological, and political constraints—and by what has worked in the past.[13]

A fifth item could be added to this partial list of factors that give meaning to uncertain events and help link sociopolitical relationships to actions or planning. This factor is more a result of the working of the other four factors than a psychological mechanism in its own right. Under circumstances of increasing uncertainty, these other factors seem to combine to produce a situation where consensus on the definition of the problem or the values to be served does not necessarily predict which action plan will be designed for its solution. Situations of substantial certainty are characterized by "familiar" problems which tend to produce plans or actions that are widely expected by knowledge-able insiders. In these situations the person who can set the agenda of debate or can define the nature of the problem or set key assumptions will likely have a major influence over resulting actions. But less familiar problems carry with them an increasing burden of uncertainty that people are motivated to dispel. Here, increasingly, the linkage between the definition of the problem (and the perceived occasion to act) and the action alternatives selected grows less predictable. Here, actions—like values or ends—are subject to one's external social influences, like ideo-logical, political, and resource factors. But action is also subject increasingly under growing uncertainty to uniquely personal in-terpretations of meaning associated with the "curiosity" and "discovery" processes of opportunistic surveillance. The notion of "discovery" implies a dynamic kind of interaction over time between each individual and the puzzling setting in which he or she is operating. The *post factum* rationalization of a series of actions taken during several cycles of interaction and reinterpre-tation of what things "really" mean may look erratic and unpre-dictable to the observer but can be justified as value-consistent by the actor involved. An example of this process is seen in a description of one facet of a pattern referred to as "uncommitted thinking":

> The high-level policymaker, beset with uncertainty and sitting at the intersection of a number of information chan-nels, will tend at different times to adopt *different* belief pat-terns for the same decision problem. Since his own experience does not commit him to a particular belief pattern, he will adopt several competing patterns, not at once, but in se-quence.[14]

One implication of this fifth factor may extend our under-standing of the practice of using staff representatives rather than their principals to "test the waters" as policies or plans develop. The usual interpretation is that principals use this device to avoid having to advocate a preferred position "prematurely," before they can determine its political basis of support. The fifth factor points to an additional reason for the practice: the principal may not yet know what he or she wants. Interaction with one's staff representatives and the sequences of internal and external discussions and actions may *produce* the meaning that flows from discovery.

All of this is not to suggest that national security threats are somehow "unreal." Instead, the point is that the interpretation of that reality is a human and political act in which, at the margin between *no threat* and *threat,* the interpretation is debatable and tends to be made as a product of the efforts of some actors to control events by controlling the interpretation of uncertainty. The process described here is not *necessarily* bad or devious. It is simply descriptive of the conditions of planning in an uncertain, dangerous world.

THE MIND-SET OF THE PLANNER

One ingredient that contributes meaning to planning is the mind-set of the planner. Planners and other decisionmakers rely on habits of thought—which constrain action—that are rooted in earlier conceptual learning, work experiences, and intense personal events. Principal decisionmakers at the beginning of the Korean War exhibited a tendency to supplement information they were getting concerning the *objective* state of affairs at the outbreak of hostilities with information drawn from their own past experiences with acts of aggression by Germany, Japan, and Italy prior to World War II.[15]

One might expect that the mind-set of each planner is unique to that individual. However, there is likely to be some patterning to mind-sets because they are a joint product of life experiences, the institutional context in which planning occurs, the technical or design assumptions associated with the objects of planning, and the events that elicit a need to plan. The human distinctiveness or variability of each planner's mind-set will be somewhat countered by the tendency of highly differentiated, complex organizations, such as found within the Department of Defense, to cluster together those who plan based on variables such as experience, rank, age, work specialty, technical background, and self-selection. Of the several consequences of these likely patterned variations in planner mind-sets, one of the more interesting may be the *orientation of the planner toward political influence* or the making of policy or strategic choices for one's organization. Although there seem to be no relevant research findings which might shed light on the specific orientation of defense planners toward politics, one can uncover some insights by turning to the literature about one of the most highly organized communities of professional planners—the urban and regional planners. Three different patterns can be seen in their mind-sets toward politics in the planning function.[16]

First, some planners assert they should be *apolitical technicians or professionals.* One position associated with this mind-set argues that planners should emphasize objective research on the functional aspects of the city and ignore the value implications of planning decisions because values are so difficult to measure and are so poorly understood. This emphasis on means to the exclusion of ends and values suggests that the techniques of the planner are rooted in an ethically and politically neutral science. According to this mind-set, such a science can set immediate objectives and make important instrumental decisions that are valid on their face and do not acquire any of the attributes of politics. This mind-set would be viewed within the national security community as naive, sterile, and perhaps simplistic by those located at or above the level of general staff agencies in the military services or civilian counterpart agencies. However, this mind-set can be found in field agencies among operations planners and logistics planners who are immersed in the instrumental milieu of unit exercises and operations, acquisition schedules, capability refinements, cost and delivery problems, and the like.

A second mind-set is that planners should be *above interest-group politics.* This means that both goals and means are the province of the planner, but the planner must remain true to commitments to the higher good of the *community* and not become ensnared in partisanship or the polemics of vested interests. In a defense context, this mind-set might reflect some of the style of the joint planner or National Security Council staffer who is sensitive to the need for consensus-building and skillful negotiation on behalf of broader security values. It may also reflect the mind-set of the programmer. The successful practitioner of this mind-set would seem to require a strong grasp of the political elements needed to develop consensus within resource and policy constraints.

A third mind-set is offered by those who could be called the *advocates.* This view starts with the premise that there is no "one best way" to plan in any complex policy arena, and, therefore, no single component of the system should dominate the planning effort. Plural plans should be advanced based on the vigorous advocacy of several interest groups which compete for approval of their priorities, methods, and claims on resources. Component planners in the unified commands, service staff planners, representatives of consulting firms or contract research institutes, as well as congressional advocates and systems groups in prime contractors within the private sector may all be imbued with this mind-set.

CAREER CONSTRAINTS

Like any job, the job of planner has more than short-term implications for the incumbent. It is a unit in his or her career. As such it is heavily molded by the incentive system of that career, as constrained by certain organizational or institutional traditions.[17] Where does this leave national security planners, especially force planners who are engaged in more contemplative planning tasks oriented toward intermediate or long-term futures?

Career incentives tend to be shaped by factors that cause stress to an organization. Typically, those who tend to help an organization deal in the short-term with contingencies and stress are rewarded more generously than others.[18] Within the national security establishment, as in all large-scale bureaucracies, a two-culture problem exists not unlike that identified by C.P. Snow. In this case the dichotomy is between responsive action in the short-term (focusing *reactions* on local crisis symptoms) and contemplation-based action over the longer term (emphasizing *initiation* of more comprehensive exploration of options, risks, and opportunities). One major consequence of this reaction-contemplation dichotomy has been described by Nobel laureate Herbert Simon and James March as a kind of "Gresham's Law of Planning" where highly structured tasks tend to drive out attention to less structured tasks, such as planning.[19] Structured tasks which produce problems are generally more amenable to solutions or "fixes" in the short-term. Also, it is more difficult to *evaluate* (and thus reward) the contributions of given individuals to helping their organization identify and deal with problems which have less immediate and structured solutions.

This bureaucratic reaction-contemplation dichotomy is evident in the armed forces, with some variations among the services. No doubt this is due in large part to the premium placed on decisive action within the military, especially on the part of combat leaders. Indeed, the reaction-contemplation dichotomy may be better explained by a leader-staffer distinction than an implicit military-civilian distinction. Consistent with this interpretation is the fact that a number of organizations within the Defense Department and other national security agencies encourage long-range thinking, with military and civilian personnel in primarily staff roles. Among these are the headquarters staffs of the several services, the National Security Council staff, the Joint Staff, the senior service schools, and various plans and analysis units within the Office of the Secretary of Defense. Also consistent with this interpretation is the impression that careers within the closed cadres of the uniformed services or Foreign Service Officer corps give preference to action-oriented roles related to current operational problems with short time perspectives, such as command roles in the military services and political officer roles in the diplomatic service. Long tours in staff or managerial roles may disadvantage one's senior promotion prospects. Similarly, planning mind-sets more attuned to shorter term issues—such as operations, budget, or program planning issues—may be *advantaged* in careers relative to those concerned with, say, long-term force development or strategy planning issues. Research by Lewis Sorley provides evidence from recent history that a preoccupation with short time perspectives and the associated career advantages led some Army general officers to adopt career development strategies based on rapid movement through a series of brief assignments.[20]

Having said all this, what accounts for the career success of a Dwight Eisenhower or a George Marshall—both of whom demonstrated substantial planning genius? The answer seems to be that they rose to prominence in the military institution under unique circumstances that may not be duplicated today in institutional and professional incentives to pursue longer range concerns. The time before World War II was one of lean years for the American military. The prewar climate was captured in Forrest Pogue's description of the innovative "Spirit of Fort Benning" which produced some 200 of the future general officers of that war from its students and instructors.[21] The US armed forces under those circumstances experienced a period of revitalization which placed a premium on the vision, role, and skills of the strategist and planner. This appears to have happened in much the same way as the twenty years of neglect of the armed services after our Civil War produced a great flowering of professional military study and conceptual development.[22] But these were temporary phenomena.

After World War II the locus of many planning roles and skills seems to have shifted increasingly from military to civilian agencies, especially with the major growth of the Office of the Secretary of Defense in the sixties and seventies. It may be that this shift of influence over the planning function from the uniformed services toward the civilian establishment has undermined the desirability of planning assignments for career officers, but that is not obvious. What is clear, however, is that the structure of incentives and decisionmaking patterns embedded in organizational arrangements are an important ingredient in determining the character of national security planning. Although good people are crucial to planning, they must be organized properly within a context of tasks, incentives, and information if they are to have a useful influence on long-range decisionmaking. The United States may not be able to build and operate a competently planned military establishment based on people of below-average ability. But even the "best and the brightest" cannot do the job if they lack the proper tools, work structure, information, and policy guidance. This suggests we must look beyond the obvious need for good people and examine the organizational context of planning.

ORGANIZATIONAL CONSTRAINTS

MULTIPLE INSTITUTIONS SHAPE PLANNING

Human beings tend to be ethnocentric at several levels. The species *Homo bureaucraticus* is especially prone to: view the world as revolving around one's outer office; take seriously only those plans originating within or bearing directly on one's own program, budget, and career; and sustain mere clinical interest in plans initiated ("invented") elsewhere—unless, of course, these proposals come down from "on high," in the person of a ranking official or policy officer who can affect one's future. Despite the elaborate formal structure of planning embedded in that elegant confederation, the Department of Defense, it is the case that significant planning actions occur in multiple organizations of national government (not the least of which include the White House, National Security Council, Central Intelligence Agency, the Congress, Office of Management and Budget, Departments of State and Treasury, and Arms Control and Disarmament Agency). Furthermore, important actions are constantly being taken by quasi-public and private sector institutions across this society which constrain the purposes, content, and style of national security planning. Beyond these, there is little need to comment on the obvious role of foreign governments and the political economy of their societies which condition US defense planning in elusive ways.

I am not here trying to make the point of a vulgar general systems theorist who sees the connectedness of the cosmos. Instead, I am directing attention to the matter that national security planning involves multiple institutions beyond a single lead agency or the boxes in a formal planning flow diagram—and certainly beyond the simplistic journalistic formulations of "interservice rivalry" or a "military-industrial complex." The planning process is not described properly as a neatly bounded, machine-like network of correlated organizational actors. It is more like what has been characterized as a "semilattice"[23] of overlapping, often loosely connected multiple actors,[24] some of whom are unevenly dependent on certain others, but *no one of whom* totally controls all planning premises or needed resources. Put simply, there are many planners (including those who do not formally call themselves planners or who are not fully aware of their impact on security planning) and no one of them is or can be "in charge."

PLANNING AS INTERORGANIZATIONAL PROCESS

The preceding comments about the locus of planning and the multiple organizations which give it tone and texture suggest their interaction. However, the planning process involves more than an elephantine dance of great departments around issues of turf, policy, program, and resources. One's conceptual vision should break apart the totality of each great institution into its intricately nested organizations and suborganizations. For example, one cannot properly understand the United States Navy as an organization unless its essence is seen as defined by three navies—submariners, surface sailors, and aviators—and possibly a fourth: the nuclear navy. Each of these nested and often loosely coupled organizational subsystems contains multiple coalitions of human actors, and each coalition may pursue different purposes with variable intensity of effort.

One finds much more autonomy within these interorganizational settings than might be expected. There are complex interactions around resource and information exchanges and turf questions, internal *and* external to each parent organization. Within each organization, one also finds planning *and* decision-making strongly influenced by coalitional politics which are variably sensitive to these interorganizational processes.

COALITIONAL POLITICS

The internal coalitional processes of organizations and the way they relate to interorganizational processes are largely influenced by *dependencies* on *uncertain* resources, information, and political support. Another important source of dependence in these relationships is unpredictable technology, typified by heavy commitments to programs and doctrine which rely on weapons systems that have not yet been refined and developed to their promised operational capability. Dependencies are a source of power or influence: Smith's legitimate dependence (for whatever reason) on Jones gives Jones some power over Smith. The quest to use power to manage these dependencies in a context of uncertainty evokes patterns of conflict and cooperation within and among organizations engaged in the planning process.[25]

The coalitional politics within organizations and the interorganizational processes among them permit individual organizations to operate with internally inconsistent goals; they often engage in "quasi-resolution" of conflict[26] by not trying to rationalize all goals simultaneously. As a result, organizations frequently react to one "fire" at a time and make only half-hearted commitments to reconcile a range of inconsistent priorities all at once. This phenomenon is due both to coalitional resistance to turf accommodation around goals and individually held value or perceptual constraints. The effect of quasi-resolution of conflict is variable. It may be beneficial in some situations: although it may not fit some planners' ideal of comprehensive rationality, it may provide a realistic response to complexity by allowing a decisionmaker to defer choice in the hope of finding a more acceptable, consistent solution in the near future. However, the consequences may be negative. Of course, these may be of minor import and represent an acceptable trade-off. The program manager of the Army's new M-1 Abrams tank judged that major revisions to correct deficiencies of the caliber .50 machine gun at the tank commander's station were not worth the cost when compared to the vehicle's combat effectiveness derived from its main gun, "the tank's reason for being."[27] On the other hand, the consequences of quasi-resolution of conflict may be of great significance. For example, failure to resolve major jurisdictional conflicts may frustrate effective planning and readiness efforts. Army General Volney Warner, while commanding the US Readiness Command, was reported as deciding to retire prematurely from military service in part because of conflict within the Joint Chiefs of Staff over which unified command should direct the Rapid Deployment Force.[28]

GOAL CONFLICT AND INTERORGANIZATIONAL PROCESSES

It is the nature of interorganizational processes that there will be conflict *among* organizations which may well add to the problems flowing from the quasi-resolution of conflict *within* organizations. In the private economic sector, the myth and reality of interorganizational competition and conflict is generally thought to be desirable. The public sector is viewed differently. Generally, a dim view is taken of conflict among organizations that operate in the same policy arena of the public sector. Except for an occasional genuflection to "healthy competition" among the four armed services, there seems to be broad disapproval of conflict among national security organizations. There has been some historical advocacy of total unification of the services in order to deal with this problem. There seems to be little current political support for total unification.

The problems of conflict among the services was raised again after the failure of the 1980 attempt to release US hostages in Iran using a combined operation with participation by the four services. Subsequent to that abortive rescue attempt the US national security leadership was criticized—as they are in the Luttwak chapter elsewhere in this book—for self-serving parochialism. The charge of parochialism is important to examine as a planning issue because it goes to the heart of the effort to *manage* the national security planning process. The heart lies in the allocation and evaluation of resources and the assignment responsibilities.

The basic thesis of the parochialism argument is that the narrow career goals and organizational interests of senior leaders in each service—and those who aspire to senior leadership roles—produce their efforts to: protect their turf from other services and civilian establishments ("Don't give anything away!"), insure that their service gets a fair share of "the action" (budgets, missions, and new systems), and deny other services disproportionate growth in resources, mission, or strategic role. General Maxwell Taylor's critique of the Eisenhower administration's "New Look" could be interpreted as a parochial, pro-Army critique of strategies and policies that advantaged the US Air Force at the expense of the Army.[29] One cannot easily penetrate the mind and soul of a Maxwell Taylor or anyone else to ascertain the true scope of their motives. No doubt one's interpretation of reality will be shaped by a lifetime of service in a branch of the military concerned with land warfare and by being an important spokesman and leader of Army interests. But the parochialism argument seems too limited and bald an attempt to account for complex behavior in terms of narrow self-interest alone.

The parochialism thesis is intended to undermine the *legitimacy* of conflict among the services or, say, between the Departments of Defense and State. The view that conflict among national security organizations is illegitimate may be based on the myth that there should be no policymaking activity in the executive branch of government once the Congress—the "political" organ of government—has spoken. Whatever the basis for this myth, it serves to deny legitimacy to the natural goal conflict which is characteristic of *all* interorganizational processes.

Conflict is a natural part of interorganizational behavior, not necessarily due to venal self-interest. Even if we would wish otherwise, organizations have vigorous impulses to conflict with each other because certain of their goals reflect the differing priorities or interests of different classes of participants in the life of each organization. These different classes of internal and external participants in each organization produce different categories of goals which may be in conflict and which may be pursued simultaneously or in some sequence. Thus, it is possible to have two specific organizations interacting cooperatively in an exchange relationship serving certain goals while at the same time conflicting with each other over other goals. Certainly goals can be in conflict within an organization, as well.

Perrow has identified five levels or categories of goals found in every organization and defined by *whose* preferences are being served.[30] *Societal goals* are the diffuse, often indirect, moods and systemic needs or preferences of the larger society. Oil imports from the Persian Gulf to support our petroleum-based economy reflect such a goal. *Output goals* suggest the type of intended consumer. The development by the Air Force of capability to provide theater airdrop of Army airborne units would be an output goal. *System goals* reflect the priorities of policy officers or executives quite apart from the product produced or the client served. Goals such as organizational personnel growth or maintaining budgetary position are goals of this type. *Product characteristic goals* embody attributes of the goods or services produced. The establishment of a lightly armored, high technology, easily transported Army division would express product characteristic goals. Emphasis on quality, quantity, uniqueness, or innovativeness are goals of this type. Finally, one can think of the uses to which an organization puts the influence or power it generates in pursuit of other goals as *derived goals.* The ability of political leadership to use the armed forces to change minority housing or employment practices in communities adjacent to defense installations illustrates the pursuit of derived goals.

The intractable nature of goal conflict among organizations can be seen in the controversy over the M-16 rifle as it was developed from the AR-15. James Fallows' analysis[31] of the M-16 program levels a devastating charge at the Army ordnance establishment: "The M-16 was a brilliant technical success in its early (that is, AR-15) models, but was perverted by bureaucratic pressures into a weapon that betrayed its users in Vietnam."[32] Fallows seems to attribute a malevolent quality to the M-16 program when he cites the House Armed Services Committee hearings on the M-16 as a "pure portrayal of the banality of evil."[33] Although Fallows could find no "actual corruption" in the relationship between the M-16 manufacturer, Colt, and representatives of Army ordnance, one could infer from Fallows that corruption was one plausible explanation of events. But from Fallows' viewpoint, the *better* explanation is that the interorganizational process surrounding military supply

> is always full of power plays and bureaucratic games which distract attention from the goals that in a rational world would always be pursued. Only occasionally does chance make the effects of these games catastrophic.[34]

Without assessing its factual accuracy or depriving Fallows' analysis of its unique insights, one can note a significant problem of his study. It diverts us from coming to grips with the underlying reality of coalitional politics and interorganizational processes: No legitimacy—no resources or power. Legitimacy comes from serving distinct organizational interests supported by important internal and external participants in the life of each organization. Pursuit of support may produce conflict. My point here is that one need not search for an evil plot in order to account for behavior of the kind described in Fallows' M-16 study. Conflict—and attempts to enforce one's organizational priorities—are natural and virtuous in a relativistic world. They serve the quest for legitimacy by unique organizations. One problem faced by planners is to reduce unnecessary conflict without undermining the *uniqueness* of essential organizations from which they derive their legitimacy—and hence the resources and power they need to operate.

The "power plays and bureaucratic games" mentioned by Fallows may well have been a normal part of the reality of the Army ordnance department—as it is in most other large bureaucracies. However, if one examines Fallows' description of Army ordnance through the lenses of Perrow's goal levels—mentioned above—some cross-cutting organizational motives within the Army ordnance department are revealed which temper the interpretation that a chief culprit in the M-16 case was bureaucratic power plays.

The *societal goal* of Army ordnance was to contribute to national security by providing all Army troops with reliable and effective weapons conforming to practical, time-tested concepts used throughout the history of US ground forces. The *output goal* was to provide a rifle for regular infantry troops who would fight according to tactical doctrine calling for slow, aimed fire at distant targets. A major *system goal* of the department was to support the arsenal system of the Army, a system which had produced the M-14 rifle—the then standard infantry weapon of the US Army—and which had encouraged its eventual replacement with another heavy "marksmen's rifle" in the tradition of the M-14. Furthermore, the Frankford arsenal, part of the arsenal system, discredited the gunpowder known as IMR 4475 which worked very well in the ammunition of the early AR-15 and which satisfied US Air Force and US Marine Corps specifications. But the Army ordnance department specified a higher muzzle velocity that could not be satisfied by the original AR-15 powder, IMR 4475. Instead, the Army switched to "ball powder" which achieved the mandated muzzle velocity but which contributed to far higher rates of malfunctioning of the AR-15 turned M-16. The *product characteristic goals* were to provide a rifle that was optimumly suited for slow, deliberate fire—consuming less ammunition and thereby placing less strain on the Army's distribution network (predominant Army use of ball powder also eased logistical problems)—and to rely on a large, heavy bullet fired through a barrel with sufficient twist in its rifling to assure the bullet would remain steady in flight and be less sensitive to wind effects over long distance. Also, the rifle was to be equally effective in all environments in which Army troops might fight, from the Arctic to the jungle (Army tests concluded that AR-15 rounds wobbled in flight during Arctic tests at 65 degrees below zero). The *derived goals* of Army ordnance are more difficult to pin down in Fallows' study. Surely one of them was to use the department's procurement process to insure that certain types of reliable industrial capacity be maintained in the civilian economy for military applications. Evidently, this reliable capacity goal was served by Colt (manufacturer of the M-16, using the AR-15 design owned by Armalite Corporation); Remington Arms (which produced the M-16 ammunition); and Olin Mathieson Company (which was the sole American manufacturer of ball powder).

A light, small caliber rifle with full-automatic capability and plastic stocks like the AR-15 did not fit the conflicting goal premises of the Army ordnance department. The fact that the US Air Force and the Army Special Forces adopted the original AR-15 was largely irrelevant from the viewpoint of the Army ordnance people; the Air Force and Green Berets were outside of the mainstream of Army tradition and global operational planning concepts.

The ultimate irony in this case seems to have occurred when Secretary of Defense McNamara centralized military procurement as an efficiency measure and assigned the Army the task to procure the small-arms for all the armed services. At that point, all AR-15 procurement was brought under the jurisdiction of Army ordnance; the AR-15 rifle was then "militarized" into the M-16 and became subject to the Army ordnance standards which appear to have gravely reduced its reliability as a weapon for use in the Vietnam conflict. If this was an "evil" result, it was a product of the natural inclination of decisionmakers to respond to their own organization's mandate and to minimize dependence upon and the influence of others who were serving different goals. The decision by Secretary McNamara to centralize procurement served to spread the consequences of any Army ordnance department errors more broadly throughout the armed services.

The lessons about goals and interorganizational planning to be learned from the M-16 experience are not primarily lessons about corruption and evil plots—although there may have been some of these. Rather, it serves to warn us of the inexorably predictable efforts of organizations to maintain their legitimacy around traditional norms, concepts, and styles they judge to have served them well and to pursue sensible goals in terms of their responsibilities within a bureaucratic division of labor. Furthermore, the M-16 case illustrates the interorganizational processes at work that lead organizations to encourage cooperation with other organizations which support their legitimate missions and doctrine (for example, the Colt and Olin Mathieson companies) and to treat as irrelevant or actually to engage in conflict with other organizations that do not, such as Armalite Corporation—or DuPont, which produced a gunpowder for the original AR-15 cartridges which did not conform to Army ordnance specifications (but which did perform well in the AR-15 according to Fallows' research). These lessons should inform efforts to manage the planning process and should be used to help decisionmakers gain perspective on issues of goal conflict that may be masked by simple charges of parochialism.

TOWARD MANAGING THE PLANNING PROCESS

The basic thesis of this chapter is that national security planning does not obviously accommodate itself to efforts to frame general substantive principles that can then be used to guide planning choices. The reasons for this, developed above, are the persistent tendencies of human nature, organizational dynamics, and political realities to undermine the usefulness of hierarchically stratified networks for rational choice. Instead, it seems more useful to explore several tentative principles to guide the *management* of the national security planning process.

1. *National security planning should involve the strategic management by the national government of the society's interorganizational networks which provide for the common defense.*

Strategic management concerns itself with the full spectrum of choices by the national government that have consequences in the long term for national security. The values, priorities, and resources of the entire society are germane here. Planning viewed as strategic management extends the concern of the planner to how each national security-related organization—and the entire national security network—are positioned for the future with respect to security responsibilities. This expands the scope of planning as a design function. It includes not only the design of policy, rules, and concepts, but also the design of action capabilities, modes of execution of action, and evaluation of performance.

The purpose of viewing planning in this way—as strategic management—is to try to close the loop that historically has been characterized by a failure to sustain reliable linkages among those who formulate plans; those who identify, acquire, and transform resources; those who direct and support action structures, forces, and programs; and those who evaluate the performance of all major players in the network. Planning as a form of strategic management attempts to integrate formulation, implementation, and evaluation within that network. A more vigorous application of this first principle might have retarded the serious deterioration over the past decade of the US defense industrial base. Congressional hearings in 1980 revealed continuing inaction by the Department of Defense to enhance military industrial base preparedness, including a general insensitivity in defense planning efforts to the realities of the industrial base, especially in its capacity to satisfy surge requirements.[35]

2. *The purpose of national security planning should be the design and control of action, including its evaluation.*

National security planning has no substance if it fails to be a preparation for action. It is especially empty if it fails to take into account resource constraints, coalitional politics within the same agency, and politics involving the major interorganizational players. For example, if plans come out of the Joint Staff which have minor impact on program and budget decisions because of vetoes from the military services, such plans are substantively irrelevant. Plans need consumers who are in a position to exercise effective demand over resources to evoke actions that are relevant to the plans. Lack of consumers today may be changed tomorrow by a gifted marketing strategy or, more likely, a dramatic shift or expansion in the appropriate interorganizational constituency. The latter was exemplified by the growth of support for increased defense spending in the late Carter and early Reagan administrations. The essence of planning is to manage the priority setting and future behavior of environmental actors important to the national security network and the society. The environmental actors may be other organizations or other states.

Our enduring preoccupation with the failure of plans to be fully implemented—or implemented at all—perhaps distracts us from the need to incorporate the evaluation of performance *and* the goals of action into the planning responsibility. The point of putting evaluation into the planning logic is not so much to "check up and take names" as it is to stimulate redesign of planning premises. Effective evaluation cannot only aid in determining whether planned goals are being met but can also reassess their validity as goals. The image of the compliance audit is clearly contrary to the spirit of this proposal. An image of *research-on-action* is more to the point.[36] This latter viewpoint would try to interpret the discovery of problems and the development and application of solutions as if they were tests of tentative hypotheses in order to feed better information into a broadly participatory planning and policy cycle. The working assumption of research-on-action that elites would have to foster is that people and programs are seldom *fundamentally* deficient. Instead, they would encourage the premise that actions taken in a complex and changing environment—characterized by many interactions among the players—are always flawed choices which solve some problems but create others.

Another feature of this view of planning is that it must contain the means for its own evaluation. This does not necessarily mean self-evaluation by "planners"—although that could well be a part of the larger picture. Rather, it suggests that strategic management of the planning process would include a basis for deciding when "more" planning may not be better and how to best allocate expensive planning resources so that they will have a higher quality impact on the level of national security.[37]

3. *Principal policy officers and executive actors should have the central responsibility for planning.*

Commanders have traditionally been responsible for the health and moral well-being of their troops. They and their policymaking and executive kin should likewise be held accountable for making planning work in the sense of strategic management. Those who would use the resources must plan and control their effective use. If the "strategy man" or the "long-range planner" or the "concepts and doctrine woman" are irrelevant, that is the doing of the people who profess to lead these great organizations. These elites should be held accountable for their lack of practical judgment and their dereliction of duty. At its core, planning is *not* a staff function. It is the central obligation of strategic management to get the most talented people to address the key problems and produce appropriate action.

4. *Incentive systems should be modified to attract to planning assignments and make effective use of the most talented people in national security careers.*

Personnel systems and informal cues from elites should encourage the best people to compete for planning assignments. This will require some changes. Given the uneven incentives for planners at present, one is tempted to paraphrase E.J.M.D. Plunkett, the 18th Baron Dunsany, in saying: "Planning assignments, like whiskey, lose their beneficial effect when taken in too large quantities."

One approach which might offer some pro-planning incentives would take the form of a military general staff. The general staff concept, however, has tended to be resisted on several grounds: antidemocratic elitism, "group-think" of a conservative bent, fostering of intellectualism in the combat-oriented military subculture, and a hint of militarism associated with the German General Staff. An interesting recent proposal by William Hauser for an American General Staff System without formally establishing a General Staff *Corps* may curb these deficiencies in the general staff concept and offer fertile ground for enhancing professional opportunities in planning roles.[38] In the next chapter Archie Barrett examines some related issues in the context of DOD reorganization. However, even these innovative proposals would not completely eliminate concern that such a system would facilitate a monolithic staff mind-set in an essentially pluralistic military establishment. The problem remaining is how to ensure creative interaction between a culture of action and a culture of contemplation. Perhaps an experimental effort to build a reserve component general staff system from a pool of civilian policy analysts and academic specialists might have merit. Ultimately, however, the subculture of the active service staff system would have to nurture the proper work climate if the thing is to be more than window dressing. But adjustments in staffing patterns may not be the proper focus. The mandating of primary planning (as strategic management) responsibilities for senior commanders, policy officers, and executives may be far more effective in recasting the incentives for younger career personnel.

A related issue is the effectiveness with which good people may be used in planning assignments, especially the upwardly mobile people at mid-career. A facet of this issue is turnover policy. Those who shape personnel policy should examine the implications for the quality of planning throughout the national security system of practices affecting the length of assignments and differential turnover rates among the services and several nonmilitary agencies. The Sorley study cited above did not focus specifically on defense planners. However, it did suggest the likelihood that rapid turnover of senior officials inhibits the professional development of those officials and produces decay in the effectiveness of their organizations. The turnover patterns described in this study offer important career cues for young professionals.[39]

The planning network should offer structural incentives to resist *pro forma* plan reviews across agencies or among levels within the same organization. Factional advocacy and rivalry can play a constructive role, but they may be insufficient or even counterproductive if not well managed by key elites. The planning staff system should be structured so that advanced substantive skills exist at all levels. Formal mechanisms for *advocacy planning* at each level might be salutary—but the process is expensive in terms of staffing requirements. Under advocacy planning several staff planning groups are given the task of preparing positions on a given planning decision. Each group becomes an advocate for a given position and operates in an adversarial style. The ambiance surrounding advocacy planning would have to be developed with great care—and supported by interested elites—to prevent undermining of the research-on-action evaluation approach associated with the second planning principle. A senior interagency planning audit staff (similar to some of the broad-scope program evaluation staffs at the Central Intelligence Agency and the General Accounting Office) might be explored with this in mind.

Such an audit staff might also engage in a serious review of the qualifications of all personnel assigned to planning roles in the national security system. Substantial conceptual ability and operational experience should be demonstrated. It may be that low regard for "paper pushing" tasks leads some commanders or staff leaders—especially in field organizations—to assign planning jobs to inexperienced people. Without a very tough review mechanism at all points in the planning system, inept or distorted premises may get built into planning products as they move from the periphery of the system to the center.[40] Also, personnel policymakers might reduce the "experience problem" in planning billets by making tours longer. However, this might drive some ambitious, talented people away from these longer tours unless (1) the general assignment practices provided for longer tours and (2) planning assignments were clearly rewarded as one key to upward professional mobility. One other contributor to the "experience problem" is the retirement system. Although "double-dipping" has been curtailed, the seductions of a second career and the disincentives of pay caps appear to contribute to a migration from public service of some excellent people who are in their prime as contributors to an effective planning system.

5. *Planning should enhance the sensitivity of senior decision-makers to the larger implications of action and choice.*

This principle has several dimensions. One is the need to enrich decisionmakers' comparative analytical sophistication. Experienced people understand that the conceptual basis of operational or contingency planning is military strategy while force planning is rooted in issues of resource planning. The former is concerned with current or near-term conditions while force planning is more future oriented. Planning should encourage exploration of significant nuances beyond such distinctions.[41] For example, one possible difference between resource planning and other types of planning is based on fungibility. Resource fungibility refers to the extent that resources can easily be exchanged or reallocated. Money is a very fungible resource. Main battle tanks are less fungible. The resources being allocated by different government agencies are not equally fungible. The issue of fungibility becomes interesting when one speculates about the implications of different levels of fungibility for another comparative dimension of interest to senior decisionmakers: the time perspective. Do the planners who allocate budgetary resources have shorter time perspectives than planners who allocate tank assets? If this is so, does fungibility represent a partial explanation? Decisionmakers may need to understand this in order to grasp more clearly the effects on them of the organization of the planning system. The planning process should provide that understanding and clarify its implications for the decisionmaker.

Environmental sensitivity is another element of this principle. Planners need to "map" the principal environmental actors and how they are linked together. It is not enough to evaluate the internal structure and leadership of complex organizations; much of their behavior is conditioned by interactions with their external environments. In doing this, planners should distinguish among the several subenvironments of each organization with respect to human, physical and financial resources, political support, and goals. The internal and environmental structures and dynamics of a strategic missile wing have a different style and pattern—and set of implications for the planner and the policy officer—than those of an infantry brigade.

Planners should also alert their principals to other implications of environmental structure. They may wish to challenge the tendency to rely heavily on organizational designs involving large-scale systems. These are often too tightly linked and fragile because of their interdependence and complexity. Perhaps more loosely coupled, semiautonomous organizations are appropriate. Although highly complex, interdependent organizations can be maintained—given our superior communications technologies—they break down or do not survive resource or information "trauma" very easily. Planners may need to recommend the building of more self-reliant support units, command structures, and operating forces. We may have tried too hard to be "efficient."

Another aspect of environmental sensitivity arises with the design of planning units and how it is proposed they be linked to the clientele, markets, and allies toward which their planning efforts will be oriented. They need a political base to have an impact. Personnel recruitment, public relations efforts on behalf of certain planning options, and other key decisions will be affected by the kind of political base they acquire and how this base links them with their principals.

A final element of sensitivity concerns organizational life cycles. Organizations seem to have three interrelated problem cycles that require constant adjustment if they are to survive:

(1) technical problems concerning production, (2) allocation of power and resources, and (3) the mixture of internal ideological values and cultural norms. Since cycles are dynamic and move in different patterns, the problem of their adjustment is never fully solved.[42] The planning process should facilitate an understanding of these cycles in relevant organizations and their implications for national security objectives.

6. *Planning should contribute directly to the policy dialogue and induce senior decisionmakers to address key issues.*

This final principle is derived from the other five. It builds particularly on the earlier principles that the ultimate responsibility for planning must rest with policy principals and must revolve around the strategic management of action among and within national security networks. Thus, planning should focus on influencing the policy dialogue among and within these networks in setting priorities, refining and focusing the discussion of issues, and resolving conflict. Planning should not be reduced to paper shuffling; a good planning system should not be trivialized by merely producing reports and planning documents which can acquire a life of their own. Its more important function is to encourage key decisionmakers to clarify their assumptions and preferences and their expectations of the future. This should be done in order to *resist* the erosion of their long-range choices caused by the individual, organizational, and political factors discussed earlier in this chapter. In effect, the planning system must play a *compensatory* role in helping to inhibit the working of factors which undermine high-quality decisionmaking.

This role puts a heavy responsibility on planning staffs to engage in strategic analysis to assess the effectiveness of various means to serve preferred ends and to clarify these ends. *Strategic analysis* can be differentiated from *systems analysis* which tends to compare the costs of technical performance among seemingly comparable means, without necessarily relating means to missions or longer term objectives.[43]

The management of the planning process and the preparation and reviews of planning documents should serve to keep goals and assumptions visible so that principals are aware of the substantive *and* political-organizational premises of choice. Furthermore, these assumptions should be given critical scrutiny from competing perspectives. It is often difficult for planning staffs to get their principals to commit themselves on priorities or assumptions. It is even tougher to get principals to evaluate premises and assumptions in the light of emergent conditions in order to (1) test their continuing validity, (2) refine them, and (3) enforce their *evaluated* implications and resist decay in commitment to them by conscious choice or by selective or strategic *neglect*.

Several potential hazards for the quality of planning and action may flow from failure to engage principals in the explicit evaluation of key assumptions. First, one can discern a "Chicken Little Syndrome" associated with risk assessment. Plans tend to be developed around alternative scenarios which posit "worst case," "best case," or "most likely case" assumptions with respect to the relationship between one's own security capability and the estimated threat. While "most likely" conditions tend initially to be accepted due to the implausibly extreme assumptions of "worst-case" and "best case" scenarios, the actual content of the assumptions guiding planners and their principals may well move inexorably in the direction of worst-case conditions as uncertainties and the price of error increase. Problems of faulty intelligence estimates or technological breakthrough related to strategic nuclear weapons compel one toward the adoption of worst-case assumptions as a prudent "insurance policy." But insurance policies are seductive and tend to move planning toward worst-case assumptions as a matter of orthodoxy rather than as a selectively used norm.

The Chicken Little Syndrome involves too broad an application of an approved mind-set toward risk which numbs the analytical sensitivity of planning and risk assessment. It may be important, for example, to *stratify* the planning assumptions of worst-case, "total surprise" conditions; worst-case expectations may be highly implausible at a global or even theater level. The expectation may not be persuasive that the Soviets can mount a serious theater-wide assault in Europe from a standing start without warning. However, local and subtheater commands may need to be very sensitive to worst-case assumptions and to develop critically realistic assessments of their local situations. If worst-case assumptions become too broadly used, "Chicken Little" will be ignored and the capacity to discriminate among threats will erode. Few, other than some conscientious planners and exercise officers, will long take worst-case assumptions seriously. We need to invest in mind-sets that are more sensitive to local perceptions of what is plausible and real in order to involve more vigorous participation of planning staffs in the conceptual development and operation of preparedness efforts. Pearl Harbor might have been limited to a tactical tragedy if local planning were not afflicted with the creeping ennui of a tired, worst-case mind-set that could concentrate major fleet elements in the harbor and have aircraft lined neatly wing-to-wing on the apron—and allow scarce Navy aircraft to be committed to training for attack on Japanese mandated islands rather than used for long-range reconnaissance (which could have provided alert on 7 December).[44]

A variation of this particular problem of failure to examine assumptions in a critical, explicit manner is the "Cry-Wolf Syndrome" identified by Betts.

> *Unambigious* threat is not an intelligence problem; rather, the challenge lies in the response to fragmentary, contradictory, and dubious indicators. Most such indicators turn out to be false alarms. Analysts who reflexively warn of disaster are soon derided as hysterical.[45]

Betts points to evidence from General William Westmoreland that for several years before the 1968 Tet Offensive the US Saigon headquarters had predicted a winter-spring offensive by the Viet Cong and North Vietnamese forces. Every year the season came and went without dire results; therefore, the warning of the "new offensive" in 1968 was thought to be just another overly cautious prediction. As Betts concludes, "Seeking to cover all contingencies, worst-case analysis loses focus and salience; by providing a theoretical guide for everything, it provides a practical guide for very little."[46]

A second hazard of failure to evaluate key assumptions is *doctrinal eccentricity,* a haphazard quality surrounding the ideas influencing the way decisionmaking processes are organized. For example, Wilensky observes about doctrines of organizational information processing that decisionmakers "often evince anti-intellectualism, narrow empiricism, and a demand for secrecy in odd combination with a demand for scientific prediction and quantitative estimates." The combination leads to foolish ideas "about the way to organize and use information in decisionmaking."[47] When accompanied by overwhelming uncertainty, doctrinal shifts may allow indifference to expert advice and its replacement with trial-and-error.[48] In some instances, doctrinal eccentricity can produce a near-equivalent to *doctrinal surprise* for one's own people as well as one's adversary: "doctrinal innovation may be a surprise when it unfolds on the battlefield because it is almost a surprise to the attacker who uses it."[49]

One of the factors other than uncertainty that may contribute to doctrinal eccentricity is the symbolic universe in which planners and their principals operate. The use of manufacturing and production terms like "assets" and "inventory" when referring to people may distract or remove decisionmakers somewhat from the reality of their operational milieu and its doctrinal basis. The symbolic system of national security planning should help decisionmakers to understand the ideological, normative, and interpretive bases of their actions. Other than a step such as the periodic evaluation of the symbolic bases of action, planning systems might usefully encourage the research function to direct attention to an area like problem identification, given the strongly reactive character of much planning. What symbolic gates and filters mask or elicit a sense of uneasiness or alert one to define a situation as a "problem"? How are these built into the routines or structures of national security agencies? Also, research on hazard mitigation should be encouraged so that the doctrinal repertoire may include explicit concern for planning based on opportunistic surveillance to limit damage from events that cannot be stopped, controlled, or even clearly identified.

A fourth problem that may flow from inadequate evaluation of assumptions is technologically derived instability in the quality of national security. The unfolding development of military weapon and nonweapon technologies—especially but not exclusively associated with strategic nuclear conflict—and their likely proliferation outside of the current group of existing nuclear weapon countries, present some disturbing images. The acceleration of cumulative and interactive military technological innovations seems to be producing greater strategic flexibility and more warfighting options for an increasing number of states while adding to their "uncertainty and insecurity."[50] The genie may indeed be out of the bottle as growing technological capability combines with increasingly rapid obsolescence and its attendant vulnerability to produce a decreasing sense of calculability in international relations and defense. There is no obvious way to deflect this dynamic. It adds a new spirit of increasing uncertainty about the likely decisiveness of military operations to the long-standing uncertainty about the politico-military intentions of adversaries. Greater evaluation of assumptions associated with the development and deployment of new military capabilities is warranted not as a "solution" but as a prudent effort to retard thoughtless growth of this dynamic. Brooks' illustration of the dynamic is instructive:

> MIRV, adopted posthaste to counter an apparently mythical Soviet ABM, has left us with a situation in which the MIRVing of heavy Russian missiles casts doubt on the survivability of our land-based ICBM forces. Would the Russians also have moved more slowly on MIRV if we had been more restrained in its testing and deployment? Would moderate progress have slowed the Russian buildup and permitted a less pressured SALT II negotiation?[51]

PLANNING AND THE NATIONAL POLICY DIALOGUE

Long-range planning is the function or level of planning where the greatest potential lies for addressing policy and power. This potential is rarely realized, however, possibly because of the prominence of programming and budgeting in the national security policy process. Long-range planning is not obviously cost-effective, especially when large staff is laid on. Nonetheless, long-range planning can help sensitize policymakers to the opportunities and threats of the future.

A unique responsibility falls to those engaged in planning, especially those whose labors shape long-term choices. They may be in a position to sharpen the concepts and clarify the issues that characterize policy deliberations, both in official and more popular forums. Senior planners may well assume a role in helping to inform the dialogue on security matters that parallels that of the research scholar in other fields. The planner is in the position of "speaking truth to power"[52] at the nexus of ideas and action.

There is a great need today to communicate to others with clarity and specificity the character of US strategic interests. There is a related obligation to *act* periodically, with equal clarity, to reinforce the resolve of US commitments to these strategic interests. The United States should leave no doubt about (1) the geopolitical locus of primary commitments, and (2) the firm determination of the US national leadership to preserve these interests with swift action using the mixture of national sanctions that will be effective. These means must include a component that is visibly coercive in its potential, not because physical force is effective over time (its protracted application is counter-productive in the long term because it brutalizes and evokes counterforces among all parties), but because it establishes a sociological baseline. This baseline helps create a local deterrent dynamic and a premise of legitimate authority *within which* more effective legal, economic, political, and cultural instruments can be accommodated. Without this baseline the other instruments are likely to offer little more than atmospherics.

There is not much in our short history as a major power to encourage us in the expectation that our political leaders will have the political courage and wisdom, in Maxwell Taylor's words, to "tell the military exactly what you want."[53] The political qualities desired in such leaders are unlikely in the best of times in any society. Nonetheless, a clearer consensus on objectives is needed. Apart from the problem of building a consensus around leaders and their goals, there is the further problem that the logic of capabilities (central to the military's sense of its responsibilities) and the logic of intentions (central to many policy planners and their principals as well as the normal analytical biases of people who operate in benign—rather than hostile—environments) may ultimately be irreconcilable. But the effort to narrow the gap is compelling, given the risks involved.

The destabilizing potential of military technology in a context of superpower parity and weapons proliferation produces an inherent and perhaps chronic ambiguity in the logic of capabilities. For this reason, the efforts of planners to promote closer evaluation of technological choices which shape the emergent logic of capabilities must be coupled to their possibly greater contribution in the form of help to build clarifying perspectives within the shifting logic of intentions. The machinery of planning cannot tell us what are the "right" things to do. But its evaluative mind-set, its concern with issue-forcing and dialogue, its role as a source of institutional memory, its aspiration to bring policy formulation, implementation, and evaluation into the same loop, its expanded time horizon—these offer a methodology that might make a difference.

NOTES

1.   Leslie H. Gelb with Richard K. Betts, *The Irony of Vietnam: The System Worked* (Washington, DC: The Brookings Institution, 1979), p. 368-69.

2.   Several representative studies of strategic management are: Robert C. Shirley, Michael H. Peters, and Adel I. El-Ansary, *Strategy and Policy Formation* (New York: Wiley, 1976); H. Igor Ansoff, *Strategic Management* (New York: Wiley, 1979); Russel L. Ackoff, *A Concept of Corporate Planning* (New York: Wiley, 1970); Peter Lorange and Richard F. Vancil, eds., *Strategic Planning Systems* (Englewood Cliffs, NJ: Prentice-Hall, 1977); Richard M. Hodgetts and Max S. Wortman, Jr., *Administrative Policy* (New York: Wiley, 1980); Dan E. Schendel and Charles W. Hofer, eds., *Strategic Management: A New View of Business Policy and Planning* (Boston: Little, Brown, 1979).

3.   John D. Steinbruner, *The Cybernetic Theory of Decision: New Dimensions of Political Analysis* (Princeton: Princeton University Press, 1974).

4.   Glenn D. Paige, *The Korean Decision* (New York: Free Press, 1968), pp. 294-95.

5.   Herbert A. Simon, *Models of Man, Social and Rational* (New York: Wiley, 1957).

6.   Karl E. Weick, *The Social Psychology of Organizing* (Menlo Park, Calif.: Addison-Wesley, 1969).

7.   Jeffrey Pfeffer, *Organizational Design* (Arlington Heights, Ill.: AHM Publishing Corp., 1978).

8.   Cf. Charles Lindblom, "The Science of Muddling Through," *Public Administration Review*, Spring 1959, pp. 79-88, and Weick, *The Social Psychology of Organizing*.

9.   Harold L. Wilensky, *Organizational Intelligence* (New York: Basic Books, 1967), p. 24.

10. Richard M. Cyert and James G. March, *A Behavioral Theory of the Firm* (Englewood Cliffs, NJ: Prentice-Hall, 1963).

11. James D. Thompson, *Organizations in Action* (New York: McGraw-Hill, 1967), p. 151.

12. US, General Accounting Office, "Decisions to be Made in Charting Future of DOD's Assault Breaker," Report by the Comptroller General of the United States, MASAD-81-9, 28 February 1981.

13. Steinbruner, *The Cybernetic Theory of Decision;* Weick, *The Social Psychology of Organizing*.

14. Steinbruner, *The Cybernetic Theory of Decision*, p. 129.

15. Paige, *The Korean Decision*, p. 295.

16. These three patterns in the urban and regional planning literature are analyzed in detail in Philip S. Kronenberg, "Micropolitics and Public Planning: A Comparative Study of the Interorganizational Politics of Planning," Ph.D. dissertation, University of Pittsburgh, April 1969, chap. 2.

17. Thompson, *Organizations in Action,* chap. 8.

18. Charles Perrow, "Goals and Power Structures," in Elliott Freidson, ed., *The Hospital in Modern Society* (New York: Free Press, 1963), pp. 112-46.

19. James G. March and Herbert A. Simon, *Organizations* (New York: Wiley, 1958), p. 185.

20. Lewis Sorley, "Turbulence at the Top: Our Peripatetic Generals," *Army,* March 1981, pp. 14-24.

21. Forrest C. Pogue, *George C. Marshall: Education of a General, 1880-1939* (London: MacGibbon & Kee, 1964), chap. 15.

22. Russell F. Weigley, *The American Way of War* (Bloomington, Ind.: Indiana University Press, 1977), p. 171.

23. Todd R. LaPorte, ed., *Organized Social Complexity: Challenge to Politics and Policy* (Princeton: Princeton University Press, 1975), chap. 1.

24. Karl Weick, "Educational Organizations as Loosely Coupled Systems," *Administrative Science Quarterly,* March 1976, pp. 1-19.

25. Thompson, *Organizations in Action,* chap. 2.

26. Cyert and March, *A Behavioral Theory of the Firm.*

27. Letter to the editor from Major General Duard D. Ball, USA, *Wall Street Journal,* 21 May 1981, p. 27.

28. Reported in the *Washington Post,* 21 May 1981, p. A3.

29. Maxwell D. Taylor, *The Uncertain Trumpet* (New York: Harper, 1959).

30. Charles Perrow, *Organizational Analysis: A Sociological View* (Belmont, Calif.: Brooks/Cole, 1970), chap. 5.

31. My treatment of the M-16 case is based entirely on Fallows' research. See James Fallows, "M-16: A Bureaucratic Horror Story," *The Atlantic,* June 1981, pp. 56-65.

32. Ibid., p. 56.

33. Ibid.

34. Ibid., p. 65.

35. US, Congress, House, Committee on Armed Services, "The Ailing Defense Industrial Base: Unready for Crisis," Report of the Defense Industrial Base Panel, 96th Cong., 2d sess., No. 29, 31 December 1980.

36. For one approach to organizational research applications of this kind, see Jack Rothman, Using Research in Organizations (Beverly Hills, Calif.: SAGE Publications, 1980).

37. Aaron Wildavsky, "If Planning is Everything, Maybe It's Nothing," *Policy Sciences* 4 (1973): 127-53.

38. Colonel William L. Hauser, USA, "Leadership for Tomorrow's Army: An American General Staff System," *Parameters, Journal of the US Army War College,* September 1978, pp. 2-9.

39. Sorley, "Turbulence at the Top."

40. See the concept of "uncertainty absorption" in March and Simon, *Organizations,* p. 165.

41. An excellent conceptual treatment of these nuances is to be found in: Colonel William O. Staudenmaier, USA, *Strategic Concepts for the 1980s* (Carlisle Barracks, PA: Strategic Studies Institute, US Army War College, 1 May 1981).

42. Noel M. Tichy, "Problem Cycles in Organizations and the Management of Change," in John R. Kimberly et al., *The Organizational Life Cycle: Issues in the Creation, Transformation, and Decline of Organizations* (San Francisco: Jossey-Bass, 1980), chap. 6.

43. Charles M. Mottley, "Strategic Planning," in Fremont J. Lyden and Ernest G. Miller, eds., *Planning, Programming, Budgeting: A Systems Approach to Management,* 2d ed. (Chicago: Markham, 1972), chap. 6.

44. Roberta Wohlstetter, *Pearl Harbor: Warning and Decision* (Stanford: Stanford University Press, 1962), pp. 12-13.

45. Richard K. Betts, "Analysis, War, and Decision: Why Intelligence Failures Are Inevitable," *World Politics,* October 1978, p. 75.

46. Ibid.

47. Wilensky, *Organizational Intelligence,* p. 62.

48. Ibid., p. 80.

49. Richard K. Betts, "Surprise Despite Warning: Why Sudden Attacks Succeed," *Political Science Quarterly,* Winter 1980/81, p. 570.

50. William H. Kincade, "Over the Technological Horizon," *Daedalus,* Winter 1981, p. 125.

51. Harvey Brooks, "Notes on Some Issues on Technology and National Defense," *Daedalus,* Winter 1981, p. 130.

52. Aaron Wildavsky, *Speaking Truth to Power: The Art and Craft of Policy Analysis* (Boston: Little, Brown, 1979).

53. Maxwell D. Taylor, "Tell the Military Exactly What You Want," *Washington Post,* 11 March 1981, p. A23.

DEPARTMENT OF DEFENSE ORGANIZATION: PLANNING FOR PLANNING

6

ARCHIE D. BARRETT
Professional Staff, House Armed Services Committee

The mission of the Department of Defense (DOD), above the operating levels actually engaged in dealing with the physical environment, is planning. This statement, although subject to a plethora of caveats, is nevertheless more true than false. After all, planning addresses the future activities of an organization, whether in the next hour, week, year, or decade. Planning is concerned with proposals for the future, the methods by which these proposals may be achieved, and the evaluation of both proposals and methods.[1] Whether the responsibility of a functional unit is personnel, acquisition, research and development, testing, manpower, military advice, command and control, or program evaluation, its principal activity is planning the ultimate behavior of other individuals or groups.

Planning is not discrete; it is a composite activity of the entire organization. The plans of any unit depend on the plans of many, if not all, other parts of the organization. The general plans developed by top management, if the plans are realistic, reflect the participative efforts of all organizational levels. These plans are based on inputs from throughout the organization detailing such items as personnel and equipment capabilities and limitations, resources on hand, shortages, the state of present and future technology, and the competition (or threat) faced by the organization. By the same token, lower level plans, if they are responsive, consist of courses of action that will contribute to the achievement of goals established in the general plans approved by top management.[2]

It follows that planning and organization are intimately related. The structure, processes, and functional units of an organization establish, among other things, the way in which it will go about planning; that is, the plan for planning of the organization.

How well does the organization of the Department of Defense measure up in terms of its ability to plan? What, if any, changes are needed? Although these are important questions, they cannot be answered directly. No comprehensive studies of the Department of Defense (DOD) as a planning mechanism have been accomplished. Because planning and organization are inextricably related, however, this paper provides an indirect answer based on the Defense Organization Study of 1977-80 (DOS 77-80).* Almost without exception, the findings and recommendations of these studies either implicitly or explicitly address the capability of the Department of Defense to plan.[3] The second section of this paper provides an integrated critique of DOD organization that synthesizes the findings of the studies. The third section recommends changes in the present structure which respond to the critique. The final section discusses the advantages offered by the proposed revised organizational structure.**

---

*The Defense Organization Study of 1977-80 (DOS 77-80) was established by Secretary of Defense Harold Brown in response to a memorandum of 20 September 1977 from President Carter which called for a searching organizational review of the Department of Defense. The Study eventually included five separate, independently prepared and published study reports which are cited fully in the endnotes. They address: departmental headquarters, the national military command structure, resource management (the planning, programming, and budgeting system; acquisition; logistics; personnel career mix; and medical care), defense agencies, and training. The DOS 77-80 effort consisted of more than the production of these five reports, however. All five final study reports were circulated among senior decisionmakers in the Office of the Secretary of Defense; the Departments of the Army, Navy, and Air Force; the Joint Chiefs of Staff; the defense agencies; the Office of Management and Budget; and the National Security Council. Extensive comments were exchanged as a result of these reviews.

**A full treatment of the subject would include the rationale supporting the integrated critique and consideration of alternative proposals for correcting identified weaknesses. However, the scope of the subject, the organization of the entire Department of Defense, is simply too broad to include this material in a chapter of modest length. The reader must judge the validity of the critique. Possibly, having considered the discussion here, he will envision more suitable alternatives than the proposals advanced. In any case, the subject will be examined more thoroughly in the author's forthcoming book.

CRITIQUE OF DOD ORGANIZATION:
THE INDICTMENT

Considered in its most abstract form, the organization of the Department of Defense consists of four basic elements that are responsible for the two principal functions of the Department, as depicted in figure 1. Each element contains one or more large subelements of the Department; for example, the four services are a part of the military department element. Also, the two functions, *maintaining* and *employing,* subsume a large number of subsidiary functions. The *maintaining* functions include recruiting, training, research and development, procurement, administration, logistical support, maintenance, and medical care. The *employing* functions are performed consequent to providing military advice to civilian authorities and directing the operations of combat forces in peacetime and wartime. These functions include assessments of enemy threat and friendly warfighting capability, strategic, operational, and logistical planning, and command and control arrangements.

If the basic "neutral" model is rearranged to reflect the findings and criticisms of the DOS 77-80 concerning the existing relationships among the elements, the concept of current DOD organization depicted in figure 2 emerges. This critique model is based on all the studies and cannot be attributed to any one; it is an interpretation that results from integrating their work and manipulating the basic organization model to depict the composite result.

The critique model indicates that the dominating organizations in the Department of Defense are the central management (the Secretary and Office of the Secretary of Defense (OSD)) and the services. The latter exercise preponderant influence over the joint structure. As a result, the relationship between central management and the services is the anvil on which the major decisions concerning both *maintaining* and *employing* functions are hammered out in the Department of Defense.

The service secretaries have little influence, relatively. They are not participants in top management and are not in a position to act as the actual leaders of their departments. They represent an intervening layer of management between the Secretary of Defense and the services which is subject to challenge in the absence of more meaningful contributions.

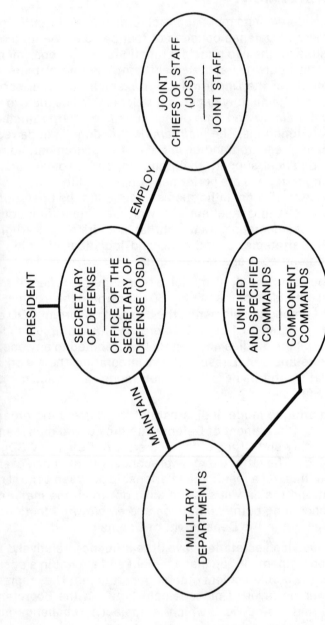

BASIC ORGANIZATION MODEL DEPARTMENT OF DEFENSE

PRESIDENT

SECRETARY OF DEFENSE
OFFICE OF THE SECRETARY OF DEFENSE (OSD)

JOINT CHIEFS OF STAFF (JCS)
JOINT STAFF

EMPLOY

MAINTAIN

MILITARY DEPARTMENTS

UNIFIED AND SPECIFIED COMMANDS
COMPONENT COMMANDS

FIGURE 1: BASIC ORGANIZATION MODEL OF THE DEPARTMENT OF DEFENSE

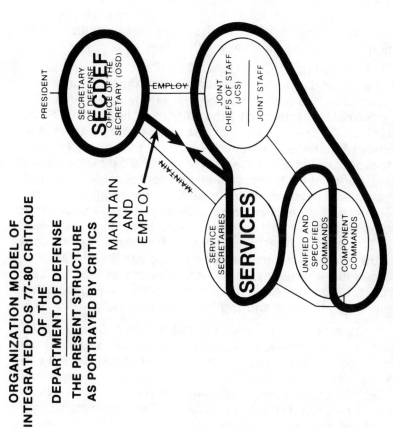

ORGANIZATION MODEL OF
INTEGRATED DOS 77-80 CRITIQUE
OF THE
DEPARTMENT OF DEFENSE

THE PRESENT STRUCTURE
AS PORTRAYED BY CRITICS

PRESIDENT

SECDEF
SECRETARY
OF DEFENSE
OFFICE OF THE
SECRETARY (OSD)

EMPLOY

JOINT
CHIEFS OF STAFF
(JCS)

JOINT STAFF

MAINTAIN
AND
EMPLOY

MAINTAIN

SERVICES

SERVICE
SECRETARIES

UNIFIED AND
SPECIFIED
COMMANDS

COMPONENT
COMMANDS

FIGURE 2: INTEGRATED DOS 77-80 CRITIQUE MODEL OF THE
ORGANIZATION OF THE DEPARTMENT OF DEFENSE

115

The joint organizations are far too weak. The two primary functions of the joint system, military advice and employment of forces in the field, are compromised. Military advice, the principal function of the Joint Chiefs of Staff (JCS), is flawed by the inability of the chiefs, also imbued with service responsibilities, to address a broad range of contentious issues as a corporate entity. The JCS acts as a forum for arriving at conjoint service positions through negotiations in which each service seeks to maximize its position through bargaining at multiple levels.

By this reading, however, the JCS fails to approximate fulfilling its raison d'etre for two reasons. First, the JCS bargaining approach produces military advice that is fundamentally different from what was intended by the authors of the National Security Act—and, more important, of less value to the President and Secretary of Defense. The framers of the act sought an organization to produce military advice derived from the deliberations of a corporate body of the highest military leaders considering issues from a national perspective detached from, but cognizant of, service interests. Second, because bargaining is unable to produce compromises acceptable to the services in contentious areas, the JCS finesses a broad range of issues that shape the very core of the US defense posture. These issues include the allocation of resources, basic strategy, roles and missions of the services, joint doctrine, and the functions, responsibilities, and geographic assignments of unified and specified commands.

The Joint Staff is fashioned to assist the Joint Chiefs of Staff in the bargaining process. Its procedures establish rules of the game for consultation that maximize service influence and preclude an independent Joint Staff voice. Its analytical capability has been systematically weakened. Furthermore, the services control its personnel structure and have no interest in developing a Joint Staff whose talent rivals service staffs.

The commanders in chief of the unified and specified commands (CINCs) have neither the influence nor the clear-cut, durable links with higher authority commensurate with their responsibilities as theater commanders of US forces in the field. In crucial decisions determining the composition and warfighting capability of theater forces, subordinate component commanders and, by extension, the services overshadow the CINCs. No overarching joint readiness assessment system exists to analyze the preparedness of each unified theater force and subsequently relate this assessment through joint channels to re-source allocation decisions intended to correct deficiencies. Instead, readiness evaluations are conducted by the component commands, controlled by the services, and linked to service budget proposals. In contrast, the CINCs have no spokesman in Washington to represent their collective views. Consequently, the joint influence on resource allocation decisions that ultimately determines the structure and readiness of forces is almost nil or irrelevant, despite the obvious fundamental importance of these decisions to the accomplishment of the basic joint function, *employing* US forces. Finally, the CINCs' chain of command from and to the Secretary of Defense is rendered potentially indecisive by its routing through the Joint Chiefs of Staff, a committee, as opposed to a single military official acting as the agent of the Secretary of Defense in supervising the CINCs.

By inference, the component commands are too independent of the unified commanders. These commands have dual designations as major service commands. This latter identity is far more influential than the joint, or unified, nature of their assignment. The services train and equip as well as control "the flow of men, money, and material to the CINCs' components. The Services (and the components) thus have the major influence on both the structure and the readiness of the forces for which the CINC is responsible."[4] The configuration of each component in a theater as a self-sufficient fighting force with a full range of support possibly results in costly redundancies in areas such as supply, maintenance, administration, and discipline. Consolidating some functions deserves serious consideration, particularly in the logistics areas where control by the theater commander could possibly increase warfighting capability as well as save dollars.

The preeminence of the four services in the DOD organizational structure is completely disporportionate to the services' legally assigned and limited formal responsibilities for the *maintaining* function—in essence, organizing, training, and equipping forces. The interests of the services in maintaining organizational independence and ensuring their capability to accomplish service missions provide continuing incentives to influence as many decisions affecting them as possible. In effect, the services have co-opted the joint structure through the dual roles of the service chiefs, overweening influence on the Joint Staff, participation in CINC selection, and predominant control over the component commands. As a result, the underlying framework for making and implementing decisions in the Department of Defense, whether on *maintaining* or *employing* issues, is dialogue between the Secretary of Defense/Office of the Secretary of Defense and the services.

This finding does not mean that the military is unresponsive. On the contrary, the adherence of the services to civilian control is beyond question. It does mean that the military input into decisionmaking, whether through service secretaries, the Joint Chiefs of Staff, Joint Staff, CINCs, or components, is predominantly service-oriented. On a broad range of contentious issues, military advice from a national perspective is unavailable to civilian decisionmakers who are forced to provide this perspective themselves, whether or not they are qualified to do so.

Given that the basic DOD relationship is between the Office of the Secretary of Defense (OSD) and the services, with the unfortunate absence of a truly joint military voice, are other aspects of the relationship in balance? Definitely not. In each of the functional resource management areas examined by the studies the services are allowed too much latitude.

In the acquisition process the tendency of each service to favor alternatives that will enhance its organization and to rush into production with inadequate test and evaluation is not sufficiently offset by a broader OSD perspective. In the area of health care, excessive service autonomy results in inconsistent planning that makes it impossible to ascertain medical readiness needs despite convincing evidence of serious shortfalls. Although some evidence suggests service logistics concepts may be outdated and should be challenged, progress in this direction is unlikely in the absence of OSD action. The services are unable to address many training problems effectively. More vigorous OSD involvement is needed, even though this would diminish traditional service autonomy in training. A similar situation exists in personnel management with respect to developing a uniform methodology and DOD-wide data bank as prerequisites to optimizing the mix of experienced and inexperienced personnel in various career fields.

Despite these management shortcomings in specific functional areas, the Office of the Secretary of Defense is endowed with sufficient authority, responsibilities, control mechanisms, and talent to make it a formidable counterpoise to the services. The Secretary of Defense ultimately controls defense policy, strategy, resource allocation, and manpower decisions within the Department. Although the studies that compose the DOS 77-80 fault the Office of the Secretary for failing to provide stronger leadership in several areas, they do not call for expanding OSD power. In fact, offsetting the foregoing criticisms to some extent are charges of OSD overmanagement in the acquisition review process, overly detailed program guidance, and imprudent step-by-step direction of complex military operations during crises.

The underlying theme of the studies relative to the Office of the Secretary of Defense (OSD) is that a change in management approach is needed. The Office of the Secretary slights the broad policy function; it fails to define the linkages between national objectives and military planning, to evaluate alternative approaches to military requirements, and to ensure that decisions, once made, are implemented and the results assessed for needed adjustments. Effecting the needed change to a management approach in which broad policy is the central focus will require correction of a number of weaknesses: ineffectual military participation in OSD policy formulation; insufficient delegation to operating levels of the Department; imprecise delineation of authority between the Office of the Secretary of Defense and the military departments; weak OSD evaluation capability; inattention to output measures such as joint warfighting or readiness capabilities in resource allocation decisions; and absence of cohesion and teamwork among constituent elements of the Department.

A PROPOSAL FOR REORGANIZING THE DEPARTMENT OF DEFENSE

The preceding section was titled an "indictment" of DOD organization. In terms of the legal analogy, this section skips the trial, assumes a guilty verdict, and turns to a proposed "sentence." Within the confines of a relatively short chapter it is sufficient to state that the conclusions of a number of previous studies over the last two decades, as well as comments from throughout the defense community, support the general thrust of the DOS 77-80 critique.[5] Furthermore, although other alternative organizational structures are conceivable, the one discussed here is most consistent with the study proposals when they are considered in light of comments on the studies from throughout the defense community.*

OVERVIEW

Figure 3 depicts the principal aspects of the proposed reorganization of the Department of Defense. The restructured organization features a streamlined *maintaining* arm, stronger *employing* arm, explicit delineation of the roles of central management (the Secretary of Defense *and* Office of the Secretary of Defense), and increased emphasis on higher administration by the Secretary. Thus, each service secretary strengthens his cognizance of the *maintaining* functions by consolidating his relatively small secretariat with the large military headquarters staff and assuming control, in tandem with the service chief, of the resulting integrated headquarters staff.** The unified and specified commands appear closer to the other joint elements; together with the chairman, they form the nucleus of a joint institution within the *employing* arm. The chairman is more independent of the Joint Chiefs of Staff (JCS), but nevertheless maintains his corporate identity as a member of the JCS. The Joint Staff is less dependent on service staff influence. Depicting the Secretary of Defense not only within the element containing the Office of the Secretary of Defense, but also outside of it indicates added emphasis on senior-level administration—concern

---

*It is important that a clear distinction be made between the sources of this and the last section. The *critique,* although admittedly the author's interpretation, is derived exclusively from the five studies and seeks to portray their conclusions faithfully. The *proposal* has a more diverse lineage. It is based on the recommendations of the five studies plus comments (criticisms and counterproposals) from throughout the defense community (including the JCS, services, and OSD offices). While the *proposal* in general follows the study recommendations, this is not always the case. It is best considered as a representation of the author's judgment on the merits of the arguments concerning the issues and his interpretation of the organizational implications of the various recommendations.

**The service secretariats are large in absolute terms; at the beginning of Fiscal Year 1980 their strengths were: Army, 378; Navy, 852; Air Force, 320. But they are small relative to the service headquarters staffs whose strengths as of the same date were: Army, 3,381; Navy/Marine, 2,228; Air Force, 2,930. Thus, the service secretariats average less than one-sixth the size of the service headquarters staffs. Source: Budget data submitted to the Executive Secretary, Defense Organization Study, 1979.

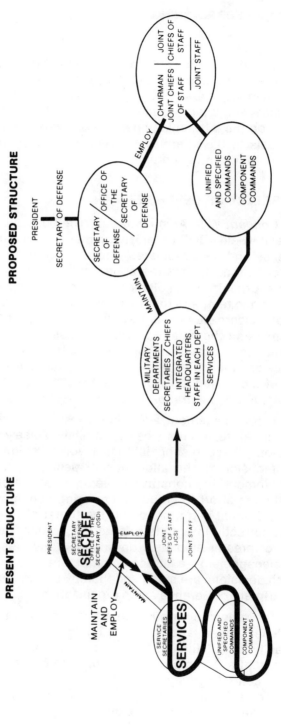

ORGANIZATION MODELS
BASED ON DOS 77-80 INTEGRATED CRITIQUE
PRESENT AND PROPOSED STRUCTURES
DEPARTMENT OF DEFENSE

PROPOSED STRUCTURE

PRESIDENT

SECRETARY OF DEFENSE

SECRETARY OF DEFENSE / OFFICE OF THE SECRETARY OF DEFENSE

EMPLOY

CHAIRMAN JOINT CHIEFS OF STAFF | JOINT CHIEFS OF STAFF

JOINT STAFF

MAINTAIN

UNIFIED AND SPECIFIED COMMANDS

COMPONENT COMMANDS

MILITARY DEPARTMENTS SECRETARIES / CHIEFS INTEGRATED HEADQUARTERS STAFF IN EACH DEPT.

SERVICES

PRESENT STRUCTURE

PRESIDENT

SECRETARY OF DEFENSE OFFICE OF THE SECRETARY (OSD)

SECDEF

EMPLOY

JOINT CHIEFS OF STAFF (JCS) JOINT STAFF

MAINTAIN AND EMPLOY

MAINTAIN

SERVICE SECRETARIES

SERVICES

UNIFIED AND SPECIFIED COMMANDS

COMPONENT COMMANDS

FIGURE 3: MODELS OF PRESENT AND PROPOSED ORGANIZATIONS OF THE DEPARTMENT OF DEFENSE BASED ON THE DOS 77-80

121

with the performance of the Department of Defense as an organization—as well as the usual attention, as the principal OSD executive, to substantive policy issues. Taken together, the changes would remove the bipolar axis depicted in the critique model on the left, replacing it with an organization balanced on the basis of the interplay between *employing* and *maintaining* considerations and interests.

SECRETARY OF DEFENSE

Concern With Administration. The burden of managing the large, unwieldy DOD organization may overwhelm a Secretary of Defense and his associates who lack an adequate, systematic approach that defines the appropriate relationships among the several organizational elements and continuously undertakes to sustain and reinforce them. All Secretaries would agree that their major concern should be the objectives and purposes of national defense and the means to achieve these ends. What they may not recognize is that to avoid being distracted by relatively minor issues and inundated with details they must devote a significant part of their attention, outside the realm of substantive defense issues, to *administration* in the broadest sense of that word.

Top management administrative responsibilities cannot— and, therefore, will not—be accomplished elsewhere in the organization. These responsibilities involve designing, evaluating, and redesigning the allocation of decisions (that is, relationships) among the constituent elements of the organization in a continuing effort to adjust to changing conditions and improve organizational performance.[6] If the thrust of the DOS 77-80 has been correctly interpreted, the studies sound an unmistakable call for greater emphasis on administrative responsibilities by top management—a lasting commitment to refine the manner in which decisions are made and thereby continuously improve the Department of Defense as an organization.

The rationale for such an effort is not altruistic. It is an enlightened understanding of the limits of central management's capacity to "do" things. And it is a corresponding appreciation of the potential for improved performance of Departmental activities, if central management accords greater priority to ensuring that the decisions which determine "how" things will be accomplished are as optimally allocated among the "doers" as possible.

Shouldering these administrative/organizational responsibilities would require that the Secretary simultaneously play the part of an observer of, and a participant in, DOD activities. In figure 3 he appears separate from the Department and again as a part of the central management element becuase he must be capable of disengaging from day-to-day concerns to examine the organization from a detached vantage point; consider changes designed to improve the substantive, issue-oriented, day-to-day performance; and devise strategies to effect the changes he determines necessary.

Guidelines for Top Management Administration. It follows from the above that administration of the Department of Defense (DOD) requires (1) an operative concept of the organization, such as the proposal advanced here, and (2) guidelines (the rudiments of a strategy) for realizing and continually adjusting the concept. The two propositions below, together with their subelements, constitute a set of guidelines derived from the study materials to achieve the proposed DOD organization.

1. *Place more emphasis on ensuring that DOD activities are successfully accomplished and less on accomplishing them.*

(a) *Impose a decentralizing bias through continuous review of OSD activities to identify circumstances which justify delegation.* Decentralization will not naturally arise as an alternative from within a bureaucracy such as the Office of the Secretary of Defense (OSD). This bias must be imparted as a matter of policy through the strong, continuous, personal efforts of the Secretary of Defense and his politically responsible assistants whose objective is effective operation of the Department, unconstrained by particular bureaucratic interests.

(b) *Pursue, as a matter of principle, the proposition that any activity in the Department of Defense is subject to the most detailed scrutiny and supervision of the Secretary of Defense.** Until this *centralization proposition* becomes operative, large portions of major areas, such as training, personnel, Joint Staff practices and procedures, logistics, military planning, health

---

*On first reading, propositions (a) and (b) may appear contradictory. They are compatible, however, because different circumstances surround DOD activities. Any specific activity may require, under certain circumstances, close central management scrutiny as is the case with training today, according to one of the studies. But in the absence of compelling reasons for centralization, activities should be decentralized.

care, and command, control, and communications, are effectively fenced off from the Secretary of Defense's oversight. As a result, subordinate elements have less reason to be responsive to overall DOD objectives, especially when they conflict with more particular interests. Just as harmful, in circumstances where delegation jeopardizes higher control, central management is reluctant to decentralize activities.

(c) *Strengthen and expand activities which central management is uniquely capable of performing within the Department and which are inadequately performed today:* developing management information systems; challenging the status quo; developing additional systems similar to the planning, programming, and budgeting system (PPBS).

2. *Configure the inherent patterns of conflict and cooperation in the Department to achieve overall defense objectives.* Adopt the following sets of working hypotheses and corresponding operative principles:

—The constituent elements of the Department are likely at times to pursue their conflicting interests to extremes detrimental to the organization as a whole. Consequently, *configure relationships within the Department to ensure that competing interests check and balance each other.*

—An incipient basis for agreement and cooperation exists in every conflict situation because the members of each constituent element (for example, the Army and Navy) are also members of the Department of Defense and other groups (for example, the Infantry, naval air, the Air Staff). An individual's membership in a group is almost invariably accompanied by sensitivity to its claims and objectives. Multiple memberships result in responsiveness to overlapping, sometimes conflicting, claims and a corresponding disposition toward conciliation.[7] Consequently, *in structuring decisions, ensure that the claims of all relevant interests are operative on all participants responsible for deciding.*

The following types of action stem from applying the operative principles.

(a) *Mobilize all significant interests whose perspectives are germane to decisions on Departmental activities.* Strengthen relatively unorganized interests, such as the joint military perspective, and weak institutions, such as service secretaries.

(b) *Structure conflict to insure that all relevant interests figure in decisions.* Channel conflicts into adversary relationships that delineate the differing positions, alternative solutions, and their implications.

(c) *Structure conflict resolution to encourage cooperation and legitimize, as a last resort, the exercise of authority.* Cooperation can be fostered in a number of ways: First, improve the quality, consistency, and flow of communications, thereby reducing conflict based on inadequate or erroneous information. Improve management information systems, military advice, readiness evaluation, and feedback channels. Second, structure conflict to include the participation of all relevant interests and automatically promote cooperation. Increase the certainty that opposing positions will be revealed and challenged in forums with authority to make decisions and thus encourage the cooperation of participants reluctant to face such exposure. Third, intensify the latent claims for accommodation by unorganized or weak interests on participants. Finally, in addition to voluntary cooperation, encourage negotiated cooperation through bargaining and compromise by reinforcing participants' anticipation that central management intends to exercise its authority to decide an issue in the absence of agreement.

OFFICE OF THE SECRETARY OF DEFENSE

The Roles of the Secretary/OSD Element in the Department of Defense. At the conceptual level, the DOS 77-80 materials reveal agreement that the central management should provide policy direction for the Department of Defense, but refrain from involvement in the details of implementation. A different picture emerges from examining the recommendations the studies advance to overcome specific problems. Rather than have the Secretary/Office of the Secretary of Defense maintain a rather detached, aloof stance that guides the Department through the development, articulation, and adjustment of policy, the recommendations suggest the legitimacy of a broad range of central management responsibilities and activities. This suggestion is noteworthy because the Office of the Secretary of Defense has been sharply criticized for more than two decades for not adhering to the general policy concept. It is not necessary to agree with each study finding and recommendation to conclude that it would be impossible for the central management to hew to the general concept and accomplish what is expected.

The following is a brief description of five central management roles "legitimized" by the study findings and recommendations.

1. *Source of Policy Direction.* This is the widely accepted, general concept of the role of the Secretary/Office of the Secretary of Defense (OSD). Policy planning, analysis, development, formulation, evaluation, and adjustment are agreed Secretary/OSD provinces. The remaining roles, however, are also legitimate, in fact essential, if the Department of Defense is to function as an integrated organization.

2. *Complement to Other DOD Elements.* The Secretary/Office of the Secretary of Defense act as a complement to the other parts of the Department. Whatever the shortcomings of the other elements, it is expected that they will somehow be balanced or offset by central management. Three types of complementary relationships are identifiable. They portray the Secretary/Office of the Secretary (1) challenging the status quo—for example, sponsoring consideration of alternative concepts for logistics support, personnel management, and life-cycle equipment support costing; (2) performing activities the other elements are incapable of accomplishing—for example, developing DOD-wide health care and personnel management information systems and representing the Department in external relationships; and (3) offsetting parochial interests of the other elements—for example, in budget proposals, military requirements planning, weapons testing and acquisition, and defense agency policies.

3. *Principal Source of DOD Organizational Integration.* The central management is responsible for integrating the Department. This involves much more than achieving agreement on policy objectives, difficult as that may be. The DOS 77-80 recommendations propose that the Secretary/Office of the Secretary of Defense (1) sponsor "systems" analogous to the Planning, Programming, Budgeting System in other areas, such as training and medical care to provide a DOD-wide perspective and a vehicle for evaluating performance which would complement the present decentralized, loosely coordinated approach; (2) consciously relate input to output, and vice versa, across DOD organizations —for example, initiate joint (output) readiness evaluations; (3) coordinate the efforts of diverse subordinate elements; and (4) pursue the unique position of central management to foster cooperation throughout the Department.

4. *Line Manager.* Central management acts as a line manager in performing some tasks relevant to the Department as a whole. Examples include OSD supervision of the defense agencies and dependent health care programs.

5. *Source of Authority.* This role exists by virtue of the Secretary's authority to impose decisions on the other elements as a result of the broad comprehensive legislative powers vested in him. A great deal of evidence indicates that the Secretary who attempts to "rule" the Department of Defense or any other bureaucracy by fiat is doomed to failure. Inevitably, his other roles, such as coordination and fostering cooperation, are sabotaged and the Secretary's accomplishments extend only as far as his individual resources can carry him. However, when acting in accordance with the other roles fails to resolve issues satisfactorily, the Secretary must resort to explicit exercise of his authority.

MAINTAINING ARM—THE MILITARY DEPARTMENTS

The service secretaries pose a dilemma. If the position were abolished, the costly service secretariats (combined payroll approximately $50 million a year) and a cumbersome administrative layer would be eliminated. However, the Department of Defense would lose the potential they represent for improved management, as well as their valuable, if intermittent, present contributions.[8] The following recommendation avoids both horns of the dilemma and places the secretaries in an organizational context that encourages realization of their potential.

Streamline the *maintaining* arm by integrating the military department headquarters staffs. Provide each service secretary and service chief with a small, generalist personal staff (40-60 individuals). Below the service secretary/chief level, consolidate the existing service secretariats and military staffs into a single staff for each department headquarters with major functional areas headed by appointive assistant service secretaries and their military deputies (the present deputy chiefs of staff).

EMPLOYING ARM—THE JOINT CHIEFS OF STAFF AND THE COMBATANT COMMANDS

Through a separately instituted US Army, the existing DOD organization ensures that national security problems are examined from the standpoint of their implications for land warfare. An effective way to ensure promotion of a cause is to create an institution which recognizes that cause as an organizational interest. The principal purpose of the following recommendations is to establish a joint military institution *within* the present *employing* arm, at its core consisting of the chairman of the Joint Chiefs of Staff and the commanders of the unified and specified commands (CINCs), with an organizational interest in propounding and seeking acceptance of joint military positions. Such an institution would act as a counterpoise to service military viewpoints. Other recommendations would create a more independent Joint Staff. Although leaving the responsibilities of the Joint Chiefs of Staff unchanged, except with respect to the chain of command, the realigned *employing* arm would increase the challenge within the Joint Chiefs of Staff to service-oriented policy positions.

Strengthen the Chairman, Joint Chiefs of Staff. Increasing the chairman's independence and influence is the key element in establishing an institutional proponent for the unified, or joint, interest.

—By direction of the Secretary of Defense, formally designate the chairman an independent source of military advice (without prejudice to his traditional duties as JCS spokesman). In particular, make the chairman responsible for review of service and defense agency budget proposals and submission of his recommended priorities to the Secretary of Defense.

—Enhance the chairman's role as the joint military link to the Office of the Secretary of Defense through memberships on senior advisory bodies, such as the Defense Resources Board (DRB) and the Defense Systems Acquisition Review Council (DSARC); ties with the under secretary for policy and his planning office; and formal participation in developing defense policy guidance.*

—Establish the chairman as the principal military link between the Secretary of Defense and the commanders in chief of the unified and specified commands (CINCs), to include replacing the Joint Chiefs of Staff in the chain of command (see related CINC recommendations below).

—Assign a dedicated staff to assist the chairman in the performance of his additional responsibilities.

Strengthen the Commanders in Chief of the Unified and Specified Commands. Increase the influence of the joint perspective within each unified and specified command, and in Washington.

—Designate the chairman as the single military superior of the CINCs, responsible for action as their supervisor under the

---

*The chairman has become a member of the DRB and the DSARC since publication of the studies.

aegis of the Secretary of Defense, and as their spokesman at the seat of government.

—Assign the CINCs a coordinate role with that of their component commanders in a revised readiness evaluation system. CINC assessments would be integrated by the chairman into a consolidated joint position that would challenge or complement the proposals emerging from component-to-parent-service channels.*

Increase the Independence of the Joint Staff. Eliminate practices that subordinate the Joint Staff to the service staffs.

—Terminate procedures that require service coordination and thereby give service military staffs predominant influence over the content of Joint Staff position papers—and consequently, the substance of JCS advice.

—Ensure that the JCS provides initial high-level guidance on contentious issues to the Joint Staff; require that formal position papers conveying military advice to civilian authorities include alternatives developed by the Joint Staff and considered by the Joint Chiefs of Staff.

—Revise Joint Staff personnel procedures to ensure assignment of the best qualified officers by creating a referral system under the direction of the chairman which is sensitive to legitimate service and joint personnel considerations.

WEIGHING THE PROPOSED REORGANIZATION

How would a Department of Defense realigned according to the proposal function? This section gazes into the crystal ball and presents a favorable assessment.

INSTITUTIONALIZED JOINT PERSPECTIVE

Creation of strong chairman-CINC ties would provide the joint military perspective with an institutional base. The chairman-CINC axis would defend joint interests just as the Army now defends land-warfare interests. Freeing the Joint Staff from inordinate service influence would allow it to serve a more dispassionate, integrative role, assisting the Joint Chiefs of Staff in synthesizing the service and emergent chairman-CINC joint military positions, where possible, and clearly delineating differences, when necessary. Maintaining the chairman as a member of the JCS would recast its terms of reference without changing

---

*For a listing of measures that would further strengthen the unified commands vis-a-vis the components and services, see footnote at the beginning of the next section.

the nature of that body as a conflict arena; the joint military perspective would gain an institutional proponent and compete with service viewpoints.

But the Joint Chiefs of Staff would also continue to act as a device for conflict resolution, the outcome being more biased in favor of joint perspectives than at present. The changed circumstances would contribute to revitalizing the JCS, a point further discussed later. When irreconcilable differences emerged, the civilian leadership would be better served by advice from two *military* viewpoints. This outcome would alleviate the present unhealthy tendency of the DOD structure to transform all controversies, even those based upon essentially military differences, into breaches between military and civilian authorities. Thus, limited reorganization would vest a legitimate, but presently impotent, joint interest in accordance with the management guideline that calls for mobilizing all relevant viewpoints, bringing them to bear on decisions, and providing means for conflict resolution.*

INTEGRATED MILITARY DEPARTMENT STAFFS

Merging the two headquarters staffs in each military department would provide an opportunity for the service secretaries to become authentic managers of their departments. Secretariats, by simply existing, create a separate institutional status for service secretaries that has the unfortunate effect of isolating them from their departments. Ending structural isolation by integrating the secretariat and military staff would place the secretary at the center of military department action. Thus, integration would overcome the principal organizational causes of weak ser-

---

*Establishing a strong joint interest would require additional measures. Although the proposals for strengthening the chairman and the Joint Staff would be sufficient, those involving the CINCs would hardly leave them capable of rivaling the service components. At a minimum, CINC staffs would require augmentation in order to accomplish integrated theater readiness assessments. Other measures should be considered in terms of their contribution to shifting the balance of influence toward the CINCs, as well as on their merits. These include consolidating theater support at the unified command level; making CINC selection more contingent on qualification for joint command and less on service affiliation; reassigning the principal responsibility for joint training and doctrine from the services to the Readiness Command; creating a unified strategic command consisting of land, air, and sea components; and reorganizing the unified commands by integrating the component and unified headquarters into a single staff headed by land, sea, and air deputies, as appropriate, reporting to the CINC.

vice secretaries. First, they do not enjoy sufficient first-hand access to balanced, accurate, thorough, comprehensive, and timely information crucial to civilian participation in defense policy decisions.[9] Second, service secretaries are unable to participate significantly in the initial stages of Departmental military policy formulation which establish the framework and, in large part, the substance of the final product—and which are necessarily conducted by the service staffs.[10] A resolute service secretary, in establishing a genuine civil-military managerial partnership with the service chief through integration of the headquarters staffs, would end the present structural isolation. That would thereby terminate the tailoring of issues before they reach the secretary and guarantee his ascendancy over the channels of access between the service(s) and the Secretary/Office of the Secretary of Defense.

Revitalizing the service secretary position in this fashion could yield greater delegation and decentralization of DOD activities. Provided they roughly agree on objectives and means, a Secretary of Defense could reasonably place greater reliance on service secretaries, who in fact (as well as by law) manage their military departments. With integrated military department staffs, the Secretary of Defense could depend on the service secretary, acting as an intermediary, to bring to bear the Secretary's appreciation of broad diplomatic, political, economic, and defense policy factors when military staffs first consider an issue. By the same token, the Secretary could be more confident that a service secretary, acting as an intermediary in behalf of his department, represented a position developed with his personal involvement by staff members cognizant of its broader implications.

In addition to his roles as manager and intermediary, this type of service secretary would serve as a unique counselor to the Secretary of Defense. With his "hands on" knowledge of the activities, strengths, problems, and peculiar requirements of his service(s), the service secretary would be a valuable source of advice to the Secretary, as changing internal and external conditions caused modifications in the broader aspects of policy. In sum, a strong service secretary with an integrated staff would increase, rather than decrease, DOD central management's ultimate control of his military department, thus offering an attractive alternative to centralization.

But integration of the two military department staffs would result in a stronger service secretary *position,* not necessarily in stronger service secretaries. It would merely increase the available opportunities for highly qualified and motivated civilians to contribute. That in itself would possibly encourage recruitment of talented individuals and dissuade less endowed persons from accepting the position. In any case, the performance of weak secretaries would not be appreciably worse with integrated staffs and the opportunities for strong managers would be expanded significantly. Consequently, in organizational terms, the case for integrating the military department headquarters staffs is very strong.

STATUS OF THE SERVICE CHIEFS

The major changes in the *employing* and *maintaining* arms would leave the service chiefs' formal status almost completely intact. This result would have the advantage of avoiding some of the acrimony that inevitably attends reshuffling the organizational accoutrements of a powerful position. Nevertheless, the chiefs' *de facto* status would change as a result of vesting the chairman and CINCs as an institution, and more favorably positioning the service secretaries. Although a service chief's status might not diminish, his standing would depend to a greater extent on his ability to perform in a more complex, competitive, and challenging environment than simply on the authority of his office. The cogency of his positions, his skill in building coalitions, and the coincidence of his objectives with those of the politically accountable service secretary would figure more prominently in determining his stature.

These changed circumstances would undoubtedly influence the evolution of the Joint Chiefs of Staff and military departments. The outcome cannot be predicted, but the directions in which they would be influenced are discernible. If the service secretaries were sufficiently demanding, the changes might force the service chiefs to shift their focus, to a degree, away from military operations, the principal mission of the joint elements, to the relatively unattended principal military department responsibilities: recruiting, training, equipping, and supporting combatant command forces. In addition to strengthening the position of the commanders in chief of the unified and specified commands (CINCs) and making it more attractive, this eventuality would increase emphasis on defense problems that are at once among the most significant facing the nation and the least glamorous.

Certainly, the resource-management weaknesses identified in the DOS 77-80, and certified in recent defense history, confirm the need for unremitting, high-level attention to the problems of securing and retaining manpower; providing effective, yet economical, military training; acquiring high-quality, affordable, reliable, and maintainable weapon systems in sufficient quantity; and transporting and supporting forces throughout the world on short notice. A reordering of priorities to ensure that military department leaders concentrate on these principal service concerns would constitute an achievement well worth adopting the reorganization proposals.

The emergence of this pattern in the military departments would favor, perhaps decisively, revivification of the Joint Chiefs of Staff, transforming it from a body criticized for its lethargy and cumbersomeness to a valued source of military advice which gives effective expression to conflicting military viewpoints. The chiefs would be freed of the responsibility of equally representing conflicting, sometimes contradictory, service and joint/national interests. Reflecting service "input" concerns as the framework for the positions they favor in the Joint Chiefs of Staff, the chiefs would face the considerations of military commanders in the field synthesized by the chairman.

Thus the JCS, as a conflict arena, would foster more straightforward competition of a broader spectrum of *military* interests arising from both the *maintaining* and *employing* arms. Irreconcilable differences would be elevated to the Secretary of Defense. But a number of factors, including the recognized strength of a united military position, would bias the Joint Chiefs of Staff toward conflict resolution which accommodated joint as well as service military perspectives. And the broad prior experience of all participants at this level, in both the services and joint commands, would add the leavening that makes compromise and cooperation palatable. This method of arriving at military positions would be more balanced and would more nearly coincide with the expectations of the framers of the National Security Act.

If the *maintaining* and *employing* institutions evolved as conjectured above, it might be possible to reduce the large planning, operations, and intelligence components of the service headquarters staffs. In the four service headquarters the combined total of personnel assigned to these functions numbers in the thousands. Staff contingents of such size are not justifiable if the services are in fact *maintaining,* or input, organizations.[11] Reducing these operations-oriented parts of the service staffs could supply the personnel needed to man a dedicated staff for the chairman, increase Joint Staff operations, planning, and command and control capabilities, and provide the unified commands with the wherewithal to assume new operational readiness evaluation responsibilites.*

SECRETARY/OSD FOCUS ON ALLOCATING DECISIONS

Unlike the *maintenance* and *employing* arms of the Department of Defense, the central management would not change structurally. But central management's approach to its responsibilities, including structural change, would alter significantly. The *form* of the decisionmaking processes would become more important to top managers. Although they would by no means relinquish interest in the *substance* of decisions, they would eschew, when possible, devoting their limited resources to supplying that substance. Rather, senior executives would concentrate on developing and maintaining well-ordered decision structures and relying on the substantive products which they yield.

---

*It would not be prudent, however, to eliminate the operations-oriented parts of service staffs. It is true that the National Security Act, as amended through 1958, appears to make a rigid distinction between *employing* and *maintaining* organizations. It directs that military missions be performed by the combatant commands, "under the full operational command" of the unified and specified commanders. The military departments are to assign forces to the combatant commands as determined by the President and are thereafter only responsible for administration and support. But the services are also responsible beforehand for organizing, training, equipping, and otherwise preparing forces for combatant assignments. Obviously, these latter responsibilities require intimate knowledge of ultimate employment. Consequently, there is a legitimate need for service staff expertise in military operations. (See relevant citations at endnote 11.)

The DOS 77-80 critique, and the proposal advanced here, however, reflect the view that each arm of the DOD organization has a vital concern with the activities of the other. As opposed to the rigid separation between the *maintaining* and *employing* arms apparently intended by the National Security Act, on the one hand, and the alleged present dominance of both arms by the services, on the other, this proposition requires (1) a genuinely joint institution within the *employing* arm, (2) preponderant attention by each arm to its principal responsibilities, and (3) interaction of each arm with the other from the perspective of its assigned responsibilities.

Many controversies, now inaccurately couched in terms of "vertical" civil-military conflicts, would assume their genuine dimensions as disagreements between competing military perspectives. The reorganized Department of Defense would resolve a large proportion of these issues at levels below the Secretary, or at least transform them into broad questions more suitable for his attention.

The position of the Secretary of Defense would be strengthened in several ways. The Secretary could remain detached from many controversies, particularly in their initial stages, confident that the service secretaries and JCS chairman in the realigned organization would factor his concerns into the lower level deliberations. The Secretary could be certain of a modicum of support when he chose a course of action from among the alternatives provided by the organization, thus enhancing his ability to achieve acceptance of his policies within the military establishment and by Congress. Also, as a result of his confidence that the internal organization would automatically produce substantive approaches to issues consistent with his objectives, the Secretary could devote more time to the usual concerns of top managers, considering ways to adjust Departmental objectives and activities to the challenges posed by an evolving external environment. Thus, the Secretary would be in a better position to lead the Department in defining national defense objectives and selecting the means to achieve them. That is, the capability of the Department of Defense to *plan* from an overall organizational perspective would improve as a result of the Secretary's attention to both administration and substance.

At the outset, this chapter emphasized that planning, as an organizational technique, is a *composite* decisionmaking process in which the skills of a variety of specialists are brought to bear on a problem before a formal decision is reached.[12] Composite decisions depend on the contributions of many specialist components. Development of the Rapid Deployment Force (RDF), for example, depends on the planning contributions of air, sea, and land-warfare specialists. Perhaps in an ideal world these contributions would be made cooperatively with few disagreements. In this case, with OSD, service, and Joint Staff experts working in harmony across the spectrum of issues from policy, objectives, and strategy to training, transport, and military operations, the contribution of the Secretary, who makes the formal decisions on RDF planning, might be relatively minor.[13] Because conflict is as much a part of the nature of organizations as is cooperation, however, and is particularly manifest in the Department of Defense, the role the Secretary must play is much more important in the real world. He must ensure that intramural conflict not distort planning—that decisions respond to overall DOD and national objectives. Under the proposal advanced here, the Secretary would place greater emphasis on administration to achieve that result. By devoting attention to designing, evaluating, and redesigning the allocation of decisions to ensure that all relevant interests (specialties) participate, the Secretary would ensure the substantive quality of DOD planning.

THE INTEREST OF THE SECRETARY OF DEFENSE

A large part of the behavior of organizations can be explained in terms of their interests. The Defense Organization Study of 1977-80 can be interpreted to recommend that the Secretary of Defense discover and assert his organizational interests. The most significant implication of the reorganization proposal is that through its acceptance the Secretary would recognize his interest in executive-level *administration*—the allocation of decisions throughout the Department of Defense.

An emergent JCS chairman-CINC axis, if it developed a strong institutional identification, would probably pursue joint interests. Moreover, a resolute service secretary heading an integrated staff would ensure that the positions taken by his military department adhere to his policy interests. Unfortunately, no basis exists for a corresponding expectation that DOD central management will undertake improved higher level administration as an interest. After all, administration in this context is not an inherent interest of the Office of the Secretary of Defense. Except for the high-ranking officials who compose the Secretary's political cadre, the Office of the Secretary is a continuing bureaucracy that would be as likely as any other DOD element to reallocate decisions in favor of its particular organizational interests. Good administration, then, in the sense of continually refining the allocation of decisions in the organization as a whole, is the unique interest of the Secretary of Defense. The key to improving the organization of the Department of Defense is first, the Secretary's appreciation of his interest in administration, and second, his success in imparting this interest as a matter of policy throughout the Department.

Most recent Secretaries have been inactive as administrators, passively accepting the existing structure, processes, and functional assignments, while devoting their attention to the substance of issues. Does this indicate that, although higher level administration is a particular interest of the Secretary of Defense, it does not warrant the priority traditionally reserved for substantive issues? The answer suggested by the DOS 77-80 is that the substance of an adequate national security posture, the ultimate concern of a Secretary of Defense, is directly related to, and can be little better than, the organization responsible for planning it. If the organization is unbalanced, giving too much influence to some interests and little or none to others, inundating top managers with inordinate detailed responsibilities while leaving military department managers weak and largely ineffective, and devoting consummate attention to some activities while leaving others relatively unattended, the resulting defense posture will inevitably reflect these imbalances and imperfections. Administration of the Department of Defense deserves to be embraced as a matter of unsurpassed concern by the Secretary of Defense.

NOTES

1.   Herbert A. Simon, Donald W. Smithburg, and Victor A. Thompson, *Public Administration* (New York: Alfred A. Knopf, 1950), p. 423.

2.   Ibid, pp. 423-50.

3.   Paul R. Ignatius, Department of Defense Reorganization Study Project, *Departmental Headquarters Study, A Report to the Secretary of Defense,* 1 June 1978; Richard C. Steadman, *Report to the Secretary of Defense on the National Military Command Structure,* July 1978; Donald B. Rice, *Defense Resource Management Study, Final Report,* February 1979; Major General Theodore Antonelli, USA (Ret.), *Report to the Secretary of Defense of the Defense Agency Review,* March 1979; Major General Donald E. Rosenblum, USA, *Combat Effective Training Management Study,* prepared for Assistant Secretary of Defense (MRA&L), July 1979.

4.   Steadman, *National Military Command Structure,* p. 33.

5.   Department of Defense Organization Studies. vol. 1: comments on *Departmental Headquarters Study* and *National Military Command Structure;* vol. 2: comments on *Defense Resource Management Study;*

vol. 3: comments on *Defense Agency Review.* Available from Office, Secretary of Defense, Deputy Assistant Secretary of Defense for Administration, Directorate for Organization and Management Planning.

6.   Herbert A. Simon, *Administrative Behavior* (New York: Macmillan Publishing Co., Inc., 1976), pp. 245-46.

7.   David B. Truman, *The Governmental Process* (New York: Alfred A. Knopf, 1962), pp. 506-16.

8.   Richard J. Daleski, *Defense Management in the 1980s: The Role of the Service Secretaries,* National Security Affairs Monograph Series 80-8 (Washington, DC: Government Printing Office, 1980).

9.   William A. Lucas and Raymond H. Dawson, *The Organizational Politics of Defense,* International Studies Occasional Paper No. 2 (Pittsburgh, PA: International Studies Association, 1974), p. 130.

10. Paul Y. Hammond, *Organizing for Defense: The American Military Establishment in the Twentieth Century* (Princeton: Princeton University Press, 1961), pp. 295-96.

11. US Department of Defense, Office of the Secretary of Defense Historical Office, *The Department of Defense, Documents on Establishment and Organization 1944-1978,* "Department of Defense Reorganization Act of 1958—6 August 1958" (Washington, DC: US Government Printing Office, 1978), pp. 188, 200, 207-9, 215.

12. Simon, *Administrative Behavior,* p. 228.

13. Ibid., p. 221.

ON MAKING THE SYSTEM WORK

7

LAWRENCE J. KORB
Assistant Secretary of Defense for Manpower,
Reserve Affairs, and Logistics

THE PROBLEMS

The major problems that decisionmakers face in planning our national security are largely inherent in our system of government and national character. These problems are also the result of the highly fragmented nature and problem-solving orientation of the present-day defense establishment.

In chapter 3, James Oliver and James Nathan note that the constitutional constraints on defense planning tend to favor the Madisonian view of limited executive power as opposed to the Hamiltonian bias toward the centralization of power. The fear of tyranny and the separation of powers, upon which the Constitution is based, have no doubt militated against an effective, coherent national security policy. While the Constitution makes a partial distinction between which foreign policy powers belong to the Executive and which are the domain of Congress, much is still left unclear. Although originally conceived to prevent the arbitrary and capricious exercise of power by the President, the diffusion of power and the ambiguous delegation of authority between the Executive and the Congress have inhibited the formulation of a consistent line of policy on an increasing number of occasions. This problem is further compounded by the fact that members of Congress, especially in the House, must constantly be concerned with reelection and, thus, often succumb to short-run political pressures rather than exercise a long-term view with regard to certain issues. The failure of Congress to lift the arms embargo against Turkey for almost five years is a recent example of this tendency.

I agree with Nathan and Oliver that the fragmentation of power basic to our democratic system of government goes deeper. Not only does the separation of powers between the Executive and the Congress often impair the effective formulation and implementation of foreign policy, but the various interest groups embodied in the electorate frequently hold numerous and conflicting views on any single policy issue. With increasing frequency, as President Carter noted in his farewell address, the President and members of Congress are forced to recognize the claims of a multitude of single-issue interest groups, all lobbying to make their views known and accepted. Many of these interest groups are able to mobilize public opinion effectively through the media and thus further complicate the decisionmaking process.

Finally, the Constitution impacts upon the formulation and implementation of national security policy in less direct but equally important ways. The government bureaucracy that exists today has evolved in response to the structural blueprint provided by the Founders and embodied in the Constitution. Bureaucratic organization was initially devised as a means of making the business of government more efficient, but it has reached the point where the sheer size of the government bureaucracy inhibits effective planning. In the words of I.M. Destler:

> It is a bureaucracy which can provide unbalanced or incomplete information, continue outmoded policies through its own inertial momentum and treat the needs of particular offices and bureaus as if they were sacred national interests.[1]

The number of people currently involved in the decisionmaking process not only has ceased to aid policymaking, but has, in fact, slowed the process. The creation of numerous departments within the government and a plurality of agencies, committees, and interdepartmental "coordinating groups" has "clogged the system" and made policy formulation more difficult. The issues that arise rarely affect only one group of people and cannot be considered the exclusive domain of one organization or department. The result is obvious; not only is there disagreement within an organization, but each organization holds different, often conflicting views on a single issue. For example, when the Department of Defense is involved in policy formulation, normally there is disagreement among the military services or other branches within the Department, as well as between the Department of Defense and the Department of State, Arms Control and Disarmament Agency, or other organizations involved in the policy process. The current disputes over the roles and missions and the organizational home of the Rapid Deployment Force and over whether the United States ought to attend the next meeting of the Standing Consultative Committee are reminders of this phenomenon.

The discussion in chapter 6 by Archie Barrett about the organizational structure of the Department of Defense expands upon this point and describes these interdepartmental power struggles and their effect on decisionmaking. In summarizing the findings of the Defense Organization Study of 1977-80, Barrett points out that the dominating organizations within the Department of Defense are central management (Office of the Secretary of Defense) and the military service staffs, and that most decisions are primarily made by these two groups. The basic conclusion of the study is that the components of the Department of Defense have power incommensurate with their responsibilities. Both the civilian service secretariats and the organization of the Joint Chiefs of Staff are weaker than they ought to be. The service secretariats lack the size and expertise to compete with the Office of the Secretary of Defense or the miliary service staffs. Within the joint arena, the Chiefs are primarily concerned with protecting service interests and their Joint Staff is hampered by its charter and lack of exceptional military officers. The obvious consequence is that military advice given by joint organizations is fragmented and compromised.

The commanders in chief of the unified and specified commands also have less power than their assigned responsibilities would indicate, and component commands are overly independent of the unified commands. Moreover, the Office of the Secretary of Defense has not provided the broad perspective or long-range orientation necessary to counteract the trend toward service independence. In Barrett's words, it "fails to define the linkage between national objectives and military planning," and the interdepartmental squabbles have an inordinate influence on defense planning. The effect of this uneven distribution of power is that the services are able to pursue policies which are favorable to their own organizations but which are not necessarily beneficial to the Department. Service autonomy has resulted in policy that is often inconsistent and shortsighted in areas ranging from acquisition to training to health care.

What Destler refers to as "inertial momentum" is a related consequence of bureaucratic organization. As both Kronenberg and Bobrow note in earlier chapters, because planning is such a complex process which has to involve numerous organizations and departments, there is a tendency to pursue past policies whether or not they are completely appropriate to a new situation. Planners ordinarily do not see alterations in policy as potentially beneficial to our national interests. Instead, they all too frequently see changes to the status quo as a threat to their competence or the relinquishment of power. It is clear that this mind-set is not conducive to effective long-term planning. The unfortunate consequence of this bureaucratic infighting is that questions of long-term strategic importance are often reduced to short-term victories or losses for the organizations and people involved. Therefore, it becomes impossible to maintain a future-oriented perspective when policy is increasingly dictated by organizational power struggles and confusion of priorities.

The problem of coordinating the groups and individuals who participate in the formulation of security policy can occasionally be improved by the creation of lateral interagency relationships. However, lateral relationships are clearly not the *definitive* solution to the need for coordination within the government. Although they are sometimes helpful, too often these groups merely reflect larger organizational problems. There appears to be a clear need for better direction from above; a greater degree of centralization is necessary for effective decisionmaking and the implementation of plans.

Because planning includes a number of people and organizations and is done largely in response to short-term contingencies, it is difficult if not impossible to employ individuals strictly as long-term planners. Nor are those who focus on long-term programs rewarded by their organizations. Again, one can see the tendency on the part of the decisionmakers to maintain policies they are familiar with, in large measure because it is so complicated to devise new plans. As Davis Bobrow argues in chapter 4, policymakers are not accustomed to planning around future contingencies, but would rather respond in an ad-hoc fashion when situations occur. Because of the multitude of uncertainties involved in long-range planning, there is a great temptation to stick to what is known, and, as such, this kind of long-term planning is not part of the policymaking process. A related problem is that in order to maintain a long-range perspective, planners must be somewhat detached from day-to-day concerns. However, if the planner is too far removed from the rest of the decisionmaking process, his recommendations might overlook important considerations and may not be realistic estimations of the future. Because of the orientation toward the present, decisionmakers are not willing to relinquish the people whose skills they value by placing them in the detached organization.

Just as the system does not reward long-range planners it similarly does not train individuals to make policy according to what Bobrow contends is a proper forecast of the future. Nor, as Luttwak notes in chapter 2, has our historical experience tended to produce long-range thinkers. Nor, as Kronenberg observes in chapter 5, does military training focus on long-range problems. Thus, it is not surprising that planners think in the short range and in terms of quantitative factors. The emphasis on cost efficiency can interfere with the formulation of an effectiveness strategy and further inhibit effective long-range planning.

THE SOLUTIONS

The other chapters in this book advocate various kinds of solutions to deal with these problems. The solutions range from changing the curricula in military schools to reorganizing the Department of Defense. It is difficult to analyze the impact of any of these solutions unless they are actually put into effect. In my view, it is more fruitful to take the system and its characteristics as given and work within it. Neither the separation of powers, frequent elections, nor intradepartmental conflict can be made to go away. Nor are major changes likely in defense organization or the service promotion or assignment systems.

However, as Henry Kissinger demonstrated in the first Nixon administration, an individual who understands the system can use it to produce effective mid- and long-range plans while simultaneously dealing with day-to-day crises. The problems of the Carter administration in the national security area were exacerbated by the fact that many of its members did not understand the system while some others spent too much time trying to change it. Moreover, there is no guarantee that some of the changes would not exacerbate the problem. For example, allowing more input into the process by unified and specified commanders could bias it even more toward short-term considerations.

This analysis is not meant to suggest that we should not try to change the system where it has obvious flaws. It is meant to indicate that awareness of the problems will militate against the most obvious pitfalls, and that any changes will be marginal at best. However, when these changes accrue over a considerable period of time, they often produce a significant alteration in the original model. For example, if one compares the US defense establishment of 1947 with that which exists today, the contrast is striking. The Secretary of Defense does have the tools to manage the Department; the services have lost so much power that their leaders, both civilian and military, claim that they can no longer adequately address even their reduced functions; a dozen defense agencies now exercise control over many defense functions for the Secretary of Defense; the specified commanders perform many of the key functions of the Department of Defense; and the Chairman of the Joint Chiefs of Staff in effect has become the primary military adviser to the National Security Council system and relies primarily on a reasonably effective and promotable Joint Staff. In fact some claim that in the 1977-81 period the Department of Defense was too centralized and diverse viewpoints were not given an adequate hearing to the detriment of policy outcomes.

It is also important to keep in mind that many of the problems noted by our authors and discussants are cyclical in nature. Fragmentation of the national security policy process by congressional overcontrol in the 1970s already seems to be receding in this decade. Similarly, a new consensus within the public on rebuilding our military strength has emerged over the last few years, replacing the divisiveness on this issue within the body politic of the last decade. Moreover, while it has been some time since the military has produced strategists of the stature of a Mahan or a Mitchell, the fact is that it has been capable of producing long-range strategic thinkers of consequence and may continue to do so. For example, the Army is now developing the concept of the extended battlefield as an antidote to the much criticized attrition strategy. Finally, the adviser to the President for National Security Affairs is currently criticized for not being forceful enough, while his immediate predecessors in that post were criticized for exercising too much control over the decision-making process.

While it certainly is not a justification for our flawed national security policy process, I do not find it any worse across the board than that of our adversaries or allies. The Soviet Union continues to pour the bulk of its strategic resources into fixed, land-based missiles in spite of the fact that these will soon become vulnerable to a preemptive first strike. Similarly, France's national character impels it toward a "force de frappe," while the recent histories of West Germany and Japan prevent them from procuring the military strength appropriate to the threat that they face.

Nevertheless, for those who feel that the system must be restructured, I propose another Hoover Commission to examine how we are organized for national security (as well as other areas). With two living, vigorous former Presidents, it would be appropriate to create a Carter or Ford Commission or a joint Carter-Ford enterprise. The prestige of either or both of these men may be needed to highlight the problems and legitimize the solutions explored elsewhere in this book. However, even if such a group could be created, progress would be slow and we would have to muddle through for another decade at least.

The real question, and perhaps the hidden agenda in our discussions, is whether a pluralist democracy can compete successfully with a determined oligarchy for influence in a fragmented international system when the resources of that democracy are shrinking. In the 1980 election, the American people provided the environment for this notion to compete. It is now up to our elected, appointed, and career officials to work within that environment to plan effectively for national security. If they allow the nature of our political and bureaucratic system or our national history to get in the way, they will have only themselves to blame.

NOTE

1. I. M. Destler, *Presidents, Bureaucrats, and Foreign Policy* (Princeton: Princeton University Press, 1972), p. 3.

PLANNING AND DEFENSE IN THE EIGHTIES

8

PHILIP S. KRONENBERG
Virginia Polytechnic Institute and State University

The preceding chapters are based on papers presented at each of the six monthly sessions of the Dinner Seminar Series on National Security Affairs. At each session, several hours of rather intense discussion of the evening's topic followed a summary presentation by the paper's author.

My intention in this final chapter is to capture the essence of that rich discussion among the seminar participants and to place it in what I hope will be a useful perspective for those working in the security and foreign policy community as well as for students. I pursue this objective in two stages. First, I summarize at length the discussion and recommendations relating to the topics for *each* session of the seminar. Then I identify several major themes that emerged over the course of the six sessions and interpret their meaning for national security planning.

PLANNING AND STRATEGY

The role of strategy stands necessarily at the center of any discussion of national security planning. That was certainly the case in the inaugural session of the seminar series which was sparked by the Luttwak paper's thesis that—in effect—strategic thought is bankrupt in the United States.

DIMENSIONS OF MEANING

Implicitly, all the seminar participants seemed to operate with roughly the same image of strategy and its relationship to planning. We shared the notion that strategy is a kind of broad plan of how to define and orchestrate the means needed to pursue national objectives. Presumably, this broad plan or strategy should be articulated with more detailed plans to acquire, prepare, deploy, and employ the means—organized human and material resources and weapons—that would adequately serve a full spectrum of national objectives.

Agreement was less obvious as we turned to examining the dimensions of meaning that need to be applied to the idea of strategy to improve security planning. One dimension reflected the distinction between military strategy and national strategy; the latter concerns the bringing to bear in peacetime and wartime of all sources of national power—not just the military—to achieve national objectives. National strategy is a much broader concept, yet the discussion moved easily between it and the more frequent object of discussion: military strategy. This shifting sense of definition could be accounted for by the view that acquisition and use of military means are heavily constrained by institutional, economic, and political factors. For this reason one would conclude that the focal point of discussion rested on considerations of "grand strategy": the plans to orchestrate all elements of a country's power on behalf of *security* objectives, not the larger scope involving all national objectives.

Related to this was the suggestion that strategy today is much more than merely the management of conflict. Given today's circumstances, one may have to fight "come as you are." Goals and resources must be managed to achieve desired ends.

This process is complex and fraught with systemic problems transcending the relatively simple projection of the military into conflict situations. The international system is unstable and subject to rapid, unpredictable changes. Our own political system is characterized by elements of instability, including rapid turnover of political leadership from the President on down. We have not had a two-term President since Eisenhower. A third systemic problem mentioned was the fragmentation of power in the United States. There is severe competition between the congressional and executive branches, with the latter further fragmented by the competition among bureaucratic agencies. A fourth systemic problem cited was the tendency at the highest level of governmental decisionmaking to deal with crises in an *ad hoc* manner. This tendency to centralize decisionmaking and to cling to an *ad hoc* approach is (1) *made necessary* by the unpredictability of conflict situations, the unfamiliarity with planned options of relatively inexperienced senior policymakers (owing to high turnover rates), and media pressure for instant answers and solutions, and (2) *made possible* by the dramatic improvements in command and control communications technology.

Another systemic problem, felt by some to affect the meaning of strategy in the United States, is fragmentation of the planning structure. This fragmentation was seen to be both vertical and horizontal. Vertical fragmentation is reflected in discontinuities between, for example, a grand strategy that orients US power toward the defense of NATO Europe and an emerging theater strategy in Southwest Asia that cannot plausibly support European requirements for Persian Gulf oil. Horizontal fragmentation exists where imbalances occur in planning the ostensibly complementary elements of strategy at any level—for example, the insufficiency of conventional or general purpose forces relative to strategic nuclear forces under the Eisenhower-Dulles strategy of massive retaliation. Or more currently, do strategic arms limitation concepts undermine deterrence, when one takes into account certain deficiencies in US general purpose forces? Both vertical and horizontal fragmentation produce what Luttwak's paper refers to as "substrategic perspective"; that is, orientations and planning judgments which make good sense when applied to *part* of our system of security, but which appear deficient when one takes the measure of the system as a *whole.*

While there seemed to be general agreement that fragmentation in strategic thought and the planning effort was a continuing problem, there was a paucity of suggestions for dealing with this. Several participants, however, suggested certain issues that would have to be addressed. One was the need to devise ways to select and relate objectives in framing strategy and the plans to support it. A comprehension of "the big picture" is not easily acquired; hard choices have to be made and priorities set that reduce their fragmenting or inconsistent elements or tendencies. This point was related to the observation that it is one thing to charge that US leaders lack a vision of strategy, and yet a different thing to determine whether or not a strategy can be sold to Congress and the people. If a strategy cannot be sold, "then you might as well not have one."

As ensuing discussion of the relationship of Congress to strategy and planning pointed out that congressional observers have noticed a lack of declaratory strategy coming from the Executive and the military. This may have been the reason for drawing Congress, during its assessment of SALT II, into a more global debate over the general US security posture, rather than limiting debate to strategic arms limitation policy. However, there seemed to be support in the seminar for the thesis that Congress is ill-suited to *develop* strategy; initiative in the formulation of strategy is done best by the executive branch. That point of consensus was coupled with another: Congress must endorse any strategic concept framed by the Executive. This means that any major strategic concept ultimately must stand up to critical scrutiny. The public and the Congress must understand and support such a concept if it is to lend meaning to the direction of US security planning. Of course, a key element of congressional support for a strategic concept is the willingness of Congress to appropriate money in support of the programs associated with the concept. With some apparent distress, one of our group expressed his view of the issue in these terms: "In the strategic area we are talking about national survival. Our choice is either to select the best strategy that money can buy or to base our strategy on the availability of funds." His judgment was that too often the latter prevailed.

Another dimension of how the meaning of strategy does or does not get incorporated into security planning concerned the *ad hoc* style of making security decisions. A consensus was apparent that far too many choices in the national security field were based on *ad hoc* decisions by military and civilian leaders. This reflected the limited strategic thinking which several in the seminar felt was a characteristic of American society. One person expressed the view that we do not think strategically in the Pentagon because so much of the intellectual energy and time of our very best people is consumed by the program review and budget process. To the extent that this assessment is correct, coupled with the incapacity of Congress to initiate strategic formulations, one can grasp why some key decisionmakers react to the crises of the moment on an *ad hoc* basis, uninformed by well-staffed strategic perspectives or plans rooted in carefully thought-out perspectives.

THE VIETNAM SYNDROME

Perceptions of the US experience in Indochina and the Vietnam conflict emerged throughout our deliberations in the session. The Vietnam experience provided an important vehicle for us to put a concrete face on some of the more abstract issues of strategy and planning under consideration. One underlying question seemed to animate the conversation: Why did the United States lose in Vietnam? Two partial answers competed for the attention of the group.

One answer consisted of variants derived from the position taken in the Luttwak paper that the US failure was due to the persistence of a bureaucratic approach to the war which was insensitive to the strategic realities of that conflict. This bureaucractic approach was seen to be the responsibility of the American officer corps as it pursued the ends of service parochialism and career advantage. While there was general agreement that the conduct of air, naval, and ground operations had not been well integrated—perhaps for reasons of service particularism—there was little support for the thesis laying blame at the door of the officer corps.

Far broader support emerged for the position that the United States failed in Vietnam because of deficiencies in the national policies and military strategies of the civilian leadership. One of our group concluded simply that the United States got involved in something that we had not expected and our military instruments were not adequate. He rejected the generalization that the military had failed. Instead, he argued that the military delivered what the public had paid for and—agreeing with the theme of Gelb and Betts in *The Irony of Vietnam*—the "system worked." That is, the decisionmaking system effectively pursued a policy for twenty-five years; that system worked even though the policy failed ultimately.

Vietnam did not see the United States limiting itself to one style of war. For example, firepower was not emphasized to the exclusion of maneuver. Further, many military leaders in the Vietnam era advocated various strategic and tactical approaches. But not all approaches were endorsed by their political superiors. One participant spoke of air attacks being limited to the largely ineffectual tactic of trying to bomb individual trucks at night on a road when Washington had denied them the opportunity to bomb trucks by the thousands as they were coming into harbors on boats. Only at the end of the Vietnam conflict was airpower used against such targets.

An interesting variation on the second answer to the question of why the United States failed in Vietnam was expressed by one participant's statement: "There might not have been any strategy that could win it." He was not interested in defending American political leaders concerning Vietnam or trying to determine whether the United States won or lost the war "politically." Instead, he felt there were more compelling questions: Was the military clear about its preferred strategy and did the civilians fail to accept it? Did the civilians deceive themselves about the level of effort required and whether it was sufficient at various stages of the conflict? Did the military give them that kind of information? Did the military persist in suggesting that the war needed to be widened and did the civilians say they would not accept this advice? Were the theater and tactical constraints well justified by grand strategy. An answer to some of these questions may be found in the remarks of another person:

> At the political level, we never thought through what we were doing. But, at one level, we were aware that we couldn't sustain this war for very long. Or was the leadershp afraid of being pushed too hard by the public? Were they afraid of a consensus or full support? There was always this conflict in the leadership in which they were concerned that the public would get too emotional and demand too harsh an outcome.

THE BUSINESS OF WAR

Assuming that there are elements of wisdom in both the answers to why the United States failed in Vietnam, how are we to explain these shortcomings of military and political leadership—and their institutions and policies? Do these shortcomings persist? The Luttwak paper indicts a bureaucratic, managerial process as a "fatal deformation that has overtaken the armed forces of the United States." This process is spawned by the merging within large bureaucratic structures of a managerial ideology with an efficiency-oriented decision technology of systems analysis. Thus, notions of civil efficiency and economies of scale—and the ethos of the manager—produce reliance on the production of firepower, organizational giantism, and careerism at the expense of maneuverable combat formations led by experienced officers with the skills and incentives to win in war rather than an obsession with "ticket punching" opportunities for promotion. The top of this perverse system produces, in Luttwak's judgment, politically astute bureaucrats, but few strategists.

Although there was a certain nodding agreement that bureaucractic defense organizations are perhaps too large and unwieldy, the group's concerns moved elsewhere to explore the idea of efficiency in a military context and the role of systems analysis as a tool in defense decisionmaking.

The uncertainty of decisionmakers about the kinds of conflict which forces will have to face were thought to compel the establishment of larger and more capable force structures and weapons systems. Presumably, their inherent flexibility would enhance their potential for success in uncertain future employments of military force. There is no "one best way" to fight in the abstract. In responding to the argument that American forces are preoccupied with firepower, one member stated that "the United States Army knows maneuver, but eventually you have to close with the enemy to destroy him. I would suggest that in grand strategy, ultimately, the control of land and people is your final objective."

A related point, which perhaps merited greater development at the time of our discussion, was the problem of measuring efficiency in a war setting. What measures do we use, who does the measuring, and who interprets the results in terms of "winning" and "losing." Different people define the reality differently. There is also the trap of letting the selection of measures undermine our capacity to ask useful evaluative questions. One person warned that "analytic processes may trivialize all the output measures. We need measurement tools but they may inhibit the ability of the system to ask interesting questions." The military definition of success is elusive.

A related point was raised by one member of the seminar who suggested that efficiency may be defined too narrowly; civil efficiency is not necessarily inimical to successful military strategy. A strategist must seek to accrue resources.

The notion of civil efficiency as a logic to make resource choices is at the heart of systems analysis. One of the members asserted that systems analysis is used for procurement, not for determining battlefield tactics, in the US military establishment. "Generals don't 'buy' systems analysis for fighting wars," as one general officer put it. That same officer complained that "the real problem of the service is *romanticism*: the idea that will and guts will prevail over the enemy. But we also need money, materiel, and the good people that one might be able to get from increased resources—or better use of existing resources." While not disagreeing with this last statement, another person raised a *caveat* about the seductions of systems analysis. His point was that the application of systems analysis has migrated from its original intended use as an aid in making *marginal* choices among comparable systems. In his opinion it has arrogated broader choices to itself, as a decision technology and as an institutional function.

CURING THE MALAISE OF STRATEGY

This session ended with general agreement that the health of national and grand strategies in the United States is feeble. But what to do?

Several within the group voiced the conviction that more serious study of military history would be helpful. It is a way to better understand the present and to develop expectations about the future. It is especially useful for defining the strategic equation.

Some concern was expressed, however, about the problem of how to extract correct strategic insights from historical experience and how to discern the limits of historical interpretation. The danger of drawing the wrong conclusions from history is always a possibility. One of the interesting ideas to emerge during this discussion was the view that the study of failure in war is particularly instructive for the development of strategic consciousness. This viewpoint was challenged by one of our members who argued that success or failure is always relative to the side one is on. "One-sided history is not very valuable; for each success there is a screw-up, or a failure, or a loss. There is always a problem of feedback; we look at the way in which German generals prepared for their campaigns." The point perhaps is that history is never complete nor is it ever macroscopic. The versions of history that we study may be too narrow to reveal the linkages and nuances that we need to understand.

The seminar ended its first session in a mood of some frustration about the absence of an integrating sense of strategy in this country which would provide clearer guidance for planning and action. The discussion around this point moved in two directions. One thrust concerned the failure of the uniformed services to propose an integrated strategy to the political leadership. The participation of the United States in the Vietnam conflict was characterized by several strategies and doctrines based upon different services, rather than a coordinated strategy. One person suggested that this is still a problem; the United States is currently pursuing separate approaches in each of the services and we have today no joint military doctrine and strategy and no integrative political leadership. It was suggested that reform of the Joint Chiefs of Staff system might be an appropriate step. There was some agreement that joint approaches would be an appropriate basis to draw on the strengths of the several services. However, it was thought that joint approaches posed special difficulties because they must move to interservice agreement on overall ends before there would be any hope for serious improvement in joint planning and action.

A second thrust in the closing discussion examined the linkages between strategy and programs. There was some criticism of what might be called the naive rationalism of those who lament the absence of serious strategic thinking in America as a basis for shaping plans and programs. One participant argued that it may be theoretically correct to first do strategic thinking and then build programs around it, but this is seldom the case in the "real world." Programs will determine the operational strategy in the short run. There was agreement with this observation but there persisted a conviction that a dialogue over strategy is urgently needed. It alone can provide a better framework to make planning and program decisions.

THE PLANNING ENVIRONMENT

The focus of our second seminar session, in December 1980, was on the factors in American institutions that constrain long-range security planning. The paper prepared for this session by James Oliver and James Nathan, "The American Environment for Security Planning," portrayed three elements that condition the planning effort: the evolving constitutional framework, the patterns of an open democratic political process, and the bureaucratic establishment which plans and executes security and foreign policy. They described an evolving system which has moved toward Madisonian concepts of decentralized government and competition for influence over public policy by countervailing forces within society—including our bureaucratic establishments.

DEMOCRACY AND DEFICIENT PLANNING

One of the early points made in our seminar discussion was that it may be inappropriate to characterize as *weaknesses* the many environmental factors that place stress on our effort to plan. The point made was that totalitarians do best at centralized planning because they are unfettered from restrictions placed on leaders in open societies. Yet, they tend to become captive of their own plans. Our abridged efforts to conduct planning of this type may represent a strength. Do we really need an efficiency orientation in our planning process? We may be better served by people who are able to handle rapidly changing situations requiring initiative and discretion and the challenge of public accountability. While there was some disagreement about the assertion that totalitarian planning is necessarily more efficient than the democratic variety, there was further support for an open planning structure. One of our group suggested a preference for the environmentally derived difficulties our planners face. "If we must err, I would err on the side of the problems we face in building a consensus in the society, rather than try to centralize choice."

These favorable impressions of the planning context were held by a minority of the seminar. The dominant view was that the environmental constraints within which planning must proceed were a deficiency of a democratic society. The problem confronting us was characterized by one person as "making planning better when you're operating in a fishbowl." He noted the consequences for the Nixon administration of the Cambodian secret bombing as a case in point: "They were trying to signal Hanoi that this new team was tougher than the Democrats had been. But the public reaction to the secrecy surrounding the bombing insured that the political value of the bombing to the administration would be self-destructive." A general officer disagreed with that assessment, arguing that secrecy is not all bad. "I would distinguish between secrecy in planning, where it belongs, versus secrecy in the execution, which is much more difficult." Several others picked up on the secrecy theme. Incident to a discussion of the domestic constraints on security planning, one person cautioned us about the appropriateness of the Cambodian bombing. He felt we must be aware of the international constraints at work as well as domestic constraints in order to put the secrecy decision in perspective. "The needs of the Cambodian Government were important and they did not want a formal Cambodian protest. The administration kept things secret in order to protect Sihanouk so he would not be forced to make a formal protest." Another participant agreed, indicating that the United States had been bombing the trail in Laos—which was also illegal—but Prince Souvanna Phouma, the Laotian leader, who had asked the United States to do so, wanted to keep it secret.

There was a discussion of the causes of the short-term bias that some have pointed to as a factor which undermines careful planning. Disappointment was expressed that more attention has not been given to what might be considered an American cultural bias: the assumption that all things can be "problem-solved." There was an assertion that our culture and our bureaucratic institutions have relatively short time horizons. "Even business tends to focus primarily on each year's 'bottom line.' " This position was challenged by one experienced planner who pointed to widespread planning in the civilian sector, especially long-range planning by large corporations.

The reactive nature of planning in response to public opinion polls and media coverage engendered lively discussion. One critic of current practice felt that things had changed—and not for the better—since the late 1940s and the Truman-Acheson efforts to mold public support for the premises of NSC 68 (a policy statement on US objectives and programs for long-range national security). His criticism was that policy seems to be adjusted to satisfy the newspapers and television, rather than having any long-range component aimed at the future. The executive branch appears unwilling to ride out "bad press" for a few days until a fresh event diverts attention elsewhere. "Rather than trying to shape the public mind, it seems the President and his staff are constantly watching the media to see whether they get a good score on a daily basis."

Another view of the reactive character of planning emphasized the structure within which choices are made. This discussion of the constitutional basis of our structure recognized that the designers of our constitutional system were ambivalent about the role of the mass public and believed that planning should come from the leaders of the government. The constitutional system was designed for a relatively small population, a small society with limited landmass. Our first President cautioned his countrymen to avoid foreign entanglements. "How can the United States Government after World War II try to plan its national security within a set of institutional constraints set up under very different circumstances?" This question prompted one of the participants to challenge the premise that there are too many impediments to making significant changes in this constitutional arrangement.

Oliver and Nathan cite a litany of sources suggesting the growing problems in the national security arena that have emerged from our system. Recognizing that the Constitution will not be modified overnight, isn't it time to consider how to redress the American constitutional order and suggest approaches that might work in the future. We are trying to deal with late twentieth century problems with creaking machinery set up in the late eighteenth century to deal with a very different kind of world.

POLITICAL LEADERSHIP AND BUREAUCRATIC PLANNING

Our discussion of the contextual deficiencies that constrain planning led one member to express his frustration at hearing no solutions other than improbable constitutional reforms. He was particularly concerned about the effect of bureaucratic practices on efforts to plan. "I question whether planning even takes place! Have the programmers captured the world?" The institutional environment in which planning is attempted is not congenial to planning. A strong Executive is crucial to planning and must give high priority to the planner's role. There was some sympathy for the view that effective planning cannot be done within the current system.

Others felt that planning was alive and well—and should be held in less bad repute. "Are we not confusing planning with what the bureaucracy does?" A planner does not provide the rules for making final decisions. These are done politically. There may be two levels or kinds of planning contexts. One is operational and concerned with more narrowly defined planning of immediate military means and ends. This may be very susceptible to institutional reforms within agencies. The second kind of planning is longer term in character and is heavily constrained by the institutional factors discussed here. Efforts to improve planning thus constrained require a clearer view of the interactions between planning within the bureaucracy and planning at the highest level of the government. "We must alway ask, who informs whom?" Is the bureaucracy setting the premises or are the decisionmakers making choices and informing the bureaucracy? One policy-level participant was of the opinion that planning efforts had changed many of President Carter's choices. The influence patterns worked in both directions. Plans require action to bear fruit.

One comment that relates to the political-bureaucratic interface was that, in our system, the overall concept behind a plan should come from a high government level but also should be coming up from "the people" to that level. This observation evoked the comment that there may be a failure at times to distinguish between the bureaucracy and the people; advice to political principals in the executive branch comes primarily from bureaucratic staffs. One member expressed the view that perhaps the government relies too much on the military to do its national security planning. There is, in his opinion, very little civilian guidance to the military on fundamental assumptions, risks, or objectives. He suggested that we should look for more options from other agencies; in crises, nonmilitary options are rarely presented because prior planning has not been accomplished by other federal agencies outside of the Pentagon. A related point was that events frequently drive decisions and that plans often become futile—irrespective of who drafted the plans. He rejected the swivel chair image of contingency planning where the decisionmaker during a crisis merely reaches around to make a selection from a great cafeteria of plans. However, he did not wish to diminish the importance of having planning because force structure choices require very long lead times given our modern technology.

The dynamic processes associated with relations between bureaucratic planners and political principals at the highest level depart from the usual mechanistic view of planning held by many. For example, a wry question was raised about NSC 68—which many view as the first comprehensive statement of US national strategy of the Cold War: "Was it planning or was it bureaucratic infighting?" One opinion was that Secretary of State Acheson was looking for a simple statement that could be used to bludgeon the mass mind of the top bureaucrats so they would implement President Truman's decisions. The Kissinger era also was examined for insights into the dynamics of high-level planning. One view was that Dr. Kissinger seemed to exploit secrecy in the decision process in order to circumvent and ignore the bureaucracy. Another person responded by recalling that Kissinger had established a process in which the bureaucratic players could engage in serious policy studies and bring their views to the attention of the President. A further point made was that Kissinger also was very skilled at articulating his goals and plans. The observation that the Central Intelligence Agency and State Department were barred from key involvement by Kissinger, and that he seemed to manage SALT as a separate process, precipitated the following comment:

> No Secretary of State could think like Kissinger as a planner; none was as able. However, his ability to rely on others to implement policies was very erratic. Acheson was much less a

planner, but much better able to move the bureaucracy in the direction he wished.

The necessity for involving representatives of all agency positions in the development of a plan may not be compelling. Strong support was expressed for the view that decisionmakers must look instead at what objectives are to be achieved. Working out the details of a plan is much less important than ensuring a consensus about the plan. For that matter, redesigning the structure for planning may not make that much difference. As one broadly experienced policymaker asked:

> Will it fix it if we readjust the organizational boxes? We have a people problem and they may be more important. Our system is very adept at accommodating these shifting demands. The machinery is okay. We are suffering from Vietnam, Watergate, and the traumas they caused.

TO SHAPE THE ENVIRONMENT

Our larger problem of conducting successful security planning within the constraints of a complex society may turn on our understanding of the different types of planning we need and how these relate to different facets of our environment. Either we change the environment or we must adjust our expectations of planning. A major theme that emerged toward the end of our second seminar session concerned the lack of public understanding of defense needs and the logic of our policies.

One experienced observer of the defense budget process felt that the public is basically not knowledgeable about national security. But there is competition for the mind of the public on defense issues. Different groups seek to build support for their preferences; the budget is where this competition is joined. The satisfactory resolution of outstanding defense problems cannot be accomplished solely by initiatives within the Executive and Congress. The public must be persuaded of the importance of policy and planning. One participant concluded that a major failure of the Carter administration had been in the education function necessary to planning. It had neglected to reach out to the public and to educate Americans in a convincing way about why the administration should be supported in pursuing certain courses of action. This concern suggested that the implicit question for the policymaker and the top-level planner should be: "Will it play in Peoria?" For those who take the additional position that government should listen, as well as market policy, to the public, there is another question: *Should* it play in Peoria?

The need for education would seem to extend to the Congress and the Fourth Estate. One seminar member observed that in his policy-level experience, Congress—as well as the general public—is not at all clear about what is going on. Furthermore, he judged that many columnists are usually several months behind what is taking place within the government. Long-range trends are not discernible to them or to the public. This last observation evoked strong disagreement: "Decisionmakers don't have a monopoly on information. But unless the public becomes engaged, then the media will focus on issues other than those in which the government is interested."

One participant suggested that reliance on educating the public about security needs from one authoritative source might be inadequate. The long-term integrity of the system dictates the use of all the major institutions to build a broad base of support. While granting that the initiative should lie with the Executive, the Congress was proposed as the best location for planning itself. This legislative orientation was challenged by pointing to NSC 68 as a classic example of significant security planning and policy development that had its genesis in the narrow base of the Executive.

The seminar closed with general agreement that the executive branch must involve Congress in the making of choices so that there is less opposition from that quarter. This would entail a bipartisan, consensual approach. Furthermore, the lesson to be learned from the Carter administration's failure to garner popular support for its plans indicates that a President must do more than make policy choices based on the bureaucratic politics of his government.

> The President can't simply make choices and then let them go. He must push issues—just a few. If he is singing the wrong notes, he'll get shot down. But it is important that he be out front leading.

FORECASTING AND PLANNING

Planning has its basis in expectations of the future. In his paper "Security Futures: INTELLIGENCE and intelligence," Davis B. Bobrow provided the third session of the seminar, in January 1981, with a sweeping view of the factors which deny an adequate informational base to long-range planning. Despite the extraordinary efforts, at times, of defense planning and intelligence-related organizations to prepare for extraordinary problems, the results are unremarkable. The seminar participants examined certain root causes of the forecasting deficiencies endemic in the defense community and explored some of their implications for planning.

KNOWING THE FUTURE

That which has not yet happened is not easily known. Yet, in concept, planning rests on knowing the future and therefore becomes a necessary consumer of the evidence, inferences, and hunches of organizations dealing with information in order to produce expectations of the future.

The conceptual and empirical difficulties of bringing planning into a useful relationship with information about futures captured the attention of the seminar throughout the evening. One person commented that planning may well be an impossible task, given the forecasting problems. He offered as an example the impossibility of foreseeing or taking reasonable precautions against events in Iran in the past two years. Also, it would have been impossible for the Soviets to foresee the full scope of the crisis in Poland or the results of their involvement in Afghanistan. Given the conclusion that foreseeing the future as a precondition for successful planning is impossible, he recommended increasing our capability to exploit hindsight. One reaction to this suggestion was the view that there is an inherent American antipathy to examining the past. For example, seldom does a new administration find it advisable to heed lessons learned by past administrations—even when they are of the same political party.

One person separated the forecasting problem into two different problems. First, one finds efforts to make long-term determinations of the defense capabilities—tanks, aircraft, ships—that will be needed in, say, Fiscal Year 2000. We may not have the information and brainpower to succeed here. The second forecasting problem is more tractable: forecasts of current trends which —if continued—have certain implications for the force structure that will be needed. These trends provide a necessary base case against which one can plan. An example of this second type was suggested: we could have—but did not—forecast and plan to deal with the rising costs of weapons systems. "The United States should have long ago devised a plan to serve the Turkeys and

Somalias. If we had taken seriously our policy of reinforcing security throughout the world we would have done so. The post-World War II equipment surplus is no longer available for these sorts of uses. Today, generally we can provide only the least expensive of our weapons. Therefore, we may be unable to intervene when and where our interests dictate." We should have anticipated such problems; the data and the forecasting techniques were available.

ORGANIZATIONAL CLIMATE

The pathologies of large organizations were seen to play a major role in the climate in which planning and intelligence organizations operate and interact. Turf defense, uncertainty avoidance, undue optimism about one's own capabilities, and shaky assumptions about the stability of current realities were among the general factors our group found troubling.

In this context one tendency noted was the inclination for those engaged in intelligence work to measure military-related things. Because it is relatively easy to do and productive of "hard" results, even when remote facilities or objectives are involved, this type of intelligence occupies most of what is published within the decisionmaking network, at the expense of nonmilitary information. This skews the information base of the planner.

The intelligence community has also experienced a reduction in the public acceptance of and its capability for HUMINT, the use of human resources for intelligence collection. The resources that allow intelligence organizations to bring a sense of touch and judgment to their work have been downgraded. One experienced intelligence officer put it this way:

> HUMINT has been collectively undermined as a result of the view of some people that "opening mail" is immoral. It is also undermined by the corresponding—and mistaken—presumption of some intelligence experts that the United States can achieve our objectives with national technical means of collection.

Concern was expressed that too often we acquire a certain technology-based capability which is only, say, 80 percent effective. We badly need the other 20 percent, but the HUMINT is not available to fill this gap. Nevertheless, the view was that intelligence collection is adequate; it is analysis that usually falters.

Analysis is not considered "sexy" within the intelligence community. The field of analysis needs to be promoted; first-rate people need to be attracted to analysis, not collection.

Considerable enthusiasm was expressed for the Bobrow proposal to build the capability for a surge capacity in intelligence and planning to deal with urgent contingencies. There is some evidence of joint effort among several parts of the intelligence community but its prospects are not well understood. Increased surge capability was thought to be of crucial importance. One important reservation was raised about the establishment of an International Affairs Reserve to bring language, foreign area, and international topic expertise rapidly to bear on sudden information processing and analysis requirements. While the use of civilian reservists to surge the intelligence capability seemed good in principle, the nature of intelligence work poses severe practical limitations on the feasibility of their employment.

DISINCENTIVES FOR PLANNERS

The organizational climate of the Pentagon and other bureaucracies concerned with intelligence and security planning frustrates efforts to deal with the future. The Bobrow paper profiles several sources of this syndrome. Others were discussed in the seminar. The problem is so fundamental to these organizations that one person suggested that we cannot even mobilize the capacity to anticipate our short-range problems, our next crisis. Several reasons were discussed.

First, this sort of work is simply not much "fun." Therefore, it fails to attract the required interest or talent—the best people want to be in policy, not contingency planning. Second, a sense of urgency is missing. People tend to view this type of endeavor as a distraction and put it aside. Third, there are many bureaucratic problems of an interorganizational character. Military planning at a technical level is easy to do. It is quite another matter to elicit the cooperation in planning of the Departments of State and Treasury, for example, and to integrate the sorts of questions they pose into military planning issues. Fourth, there are also bureaucratic problems that are intraorganizational in nature. Within the Defense Department the Joint Chiefs of Staff still control contingency planning, but have little interest in allowing planning problems to surface in a visible way. To do so would incur the risk by the Joint Chiefs of being required to share control over planning in this area. Finally, there are security problems. The mere act of deciding to plan for a likely contingency can be compromising. If the fact that we are engaged in a certain planning effort—much less the plan itself—should leak, we stand to endanger our relations with friends and allies. One can but speculate about the British reaction to the discovery that imaginative US planners in the 1920s had produced Plan ORANGE-RED to handle the contingency of a wartime coalition of Japan and Great Britain against the Americans.

Some of these disincentives to planning were thought to be illustrated by the aftermath of Exercise NIFTY NUGGET, conducted in 1978. NIFTY NUGGET was the first simulated government-wide mobilization since the actual experience of World War II. This exercise revealed serious problems in military planning, munitions, equipment, and manpower under a currently plausible short-warning mobilization. Despite the revelation over two years ago of significant problems during the exercise, not much progress has been made in correcting the difficulties.

FOCUSING THE PRODUCT

An issue that threaded itself throughout this session was how to focus the attention of decisionmakers, overburdened with day-to-day responsibilities, on long-range objectives, intelligence, and planning. A subsidiary issue—related to the preceding comments about organizational climate—was how the organizations responsible for long-range planning in a complex bureaucracy can be situated best to gain access to key decisionmakers and to focus their attention over the planning horizon.

While accepting the notion that the intelligence product of the Central Intelligence Agency and other parts of the intelligence community could be improved, there was broad support for the view that the intelligence product is usually adequate. For example, in the case of the energy crisis, the problem was not that intelligence on energy failed. The problem was that decisionmakers did not accept the analyses that were available and do something about them in time. This was not a problem of intelligence, as such, but of causing the key people to focus on the information and to act on its implications.

The related problems of bringing intelligence organizations into effective institutional relationship with decisionmakers and getting those who ultimately must make choices to focus their attention on the intelligence product may well depend on the ability of intelligence to claim relevance. Relevance in the view of a policymaker means that intelligence or plans people can tell where the future crisis will come and what needs to be done about it today. It was noted that senior Air Force generals have at times criticized the long-range planning unit in the Air Staff because its product did not focus on actions that should be taken at present to equip that service to meet challenges in the future. Even when the future is being considered, decisionmakers are properly concerned with the present action implications.

The problem of focusing the attention of decisionmakers on information and plans that are relevant for them applies not just to principals. Other actors must become better focused. The forecasting of trends and the identification of potential crisis environments necessitate that both planners and the intelligence community overlap their responsibilities. Is the intelligence community focusing on the right issues? Planners should have a stake in this answer. How are planners using the intelligence product? The intelligence community should be concerned with the orientation of the planners and the areas they are staffing.

Another suggestion was that the problem of lending focus to the intelligence product and planning involves concern with form as well as substance. Dissemination becomes of some importance. The product must be read. Therefore, the intelligence people must assess what they have to offer and tailor it to the intended recipients. Further thought on the format used in the planning process was stimulated by the Bobrow proposal for a modular concept of planning. This concept would allow planners to determine what relevant contingency planning tasks can be performed well in advance of a crisis situation. Parallel support emerged in our discussion for meeting the needs of requirements planning. Bobrow's proposal for updating decisions about long lead-time investments provides a way to use adjustments in the acquisition format to improve the development and procurement of high technology systems.

Another approach to enhancing a sense of relevance around longer term thinking arose during the discussion of NIFTY NUGGET, mentioned earlier. Several policymakers and general officers praised the value of exercises. "Nothing attracts people like exercises. Exercises are valuable methods for exposing deficiencies as well as focusing the attention of senior decisionmakers." There was general agreement in the seminar on this point. One planner indicated that good exercises are the objective of planning. Another value seen for exercises is in their ability to integrate disparate units.

MAKING UNCERTAINTY RELEVANT

Once the attention of interacting groups and their principals has been focused on the planning future by exercises and various organizational techniques, the problem of *followup* remains. Several participants expressed reservations about the tenacity with which hard planning choices would be enforced by the senior political leadership. One said: "How much national will do we have? If we bother to make a plan for the next five years, what hope is there that anyone will work to bring it about? The basic problem is our philosophical conflict over objectives." A second view, reacting to the then controversy over sending US military advisers to El Salvador, asserted that "the issue in Latin America is whether or not we should try to influence events with our resources, whether or not we will support an autocratic regime and try to bend it ultimately to pursue some other alternatives." A third person reacted to the followup issue with this observation: "There are not a lot of clearly defined national objectives, like the US Apollo program for a manned lunar landing or the Soviets' drive for nuclear superiority, where you commit large resources over the time horizon."

The problem of followup may be more tied to the long-term problem of force structure planning. But there are other compelling issues. Our group was reminded by one of its members that an underlying proposition is that we are dealing with a world where force structure is not enough. We must learn to deal with a world in which our ability to understand and cope with local situations is crucial. "We are not a society in the habit of doing this. We are a long way from getting it together."

The concluding comments by Davis Bobrow at the end of this session may have captured the mood of the evening. "Something can be done. Everything has been tried once. It is time to try again—to try to give future planning a chance." The difficulty of anticipating the future in impressing these expectations on doubting decisionmakers cannot deter us. The uncertain future must be confronted as relevant and as a significant responsibility of those who plan and lead.

THE PLANNING PROCESS

The Kronenberg paper, "National Security Planning: Images and Issues," served to initiate discussion at the fourth session in February. The agenda for this session was intended to focus on those factors that actually determine the characteristics of planning behavior and to explore possible general principles for guiding the planning process.

THE MEANING OF PLANNING

Planning as an idea conveys a notion of thoughtfulness, of attempting to reason from expectations of the future to those action imperatives which will produce desired results. This image is one of concern with the careful weighing of information and the design of actions that will shape events in the long term. Many have judged that there was a sore lack of this planful quality in the conduct of foreign and defense policy. Former Secretary of State Kissinger was quite critical in his early writings of the absence of long-range planning in government. Yet, some argue that he was captured to some degree by short-term concerns once he entered government.

Despite the complexity of the forces and machines that are the objects of planning and the sophisticated information systems which feed the planners, there was general agreement that planning is an art form depending, at least in part, on skill in dealing with the political process. In commenting on the three types of planner orientations toward politics developed in the Kronenberg paper, one participant commented that he knew of few people in the defense community who fit the apolitical technician type of planner who views his work as an ethically neutral science. As another member put it, "it's difficult to be apolitical when resource allocation is involved."

Several comments were prompted by Kronenberg's thesis that there exists in national security planning a two-culture problem that leads to tensions between reactive and contemplative orientations. One person found the distinction to be particularly apt but suggested that activist, short-term traits are not uniformly characteristic of the military. He felt it would be useful to further divide Kronenberg's categories into reactive and contemplative staff officers and reactive and contemplative military leaders. Another member of the seminar suggested that the two-culture argument could be interpreted to imply that civilians should be responsible for long-range planning (contemplative mode), and the military for current planning (reactive mode). He felt this would be in error because, in a sense, the active and contemplative categories are built into military staffs. At the lower ranks one finds younger, more activist officers. At the supervisory and senior ranks are the contemplative officers whose experience causes them to act with greater circumspection.

One perspective a participant offered to the seminar to better describe the nature of planning was derived from asking the question: "Compared with 1955, how did we arrive at our current strategic position?" His interpretation was that the United States has changed—and in retrospect—in an apparently systematic way. To accomplish this change little that was systematic was involved. Often, as the Kronenberg paper argued, there was action taken *before* the rationale for action was developed. What we see today, if one looks back, is an enormously complicated political system groping ahead. It did not follow an overall plan which would apply coherence and rationale before the fact of action. "From this perspective on our past we can observe that the United States does arrive at a certain coherence over a long period of time." Of course, the shifts in direction are multiple and complex. In fact, we have not yet arrived at the end point for this period. Nonetheless, historians will be able to look back and discern a coherence in this entire period.

There was broad support for this retrospective analysis of the planning process. One person, in stating that the analysis was correct and that matters had worked out well over time, cautioned that the shifts and turns which describe this process were nonetheless very costly.

> I could cite several examples—the prematurely cancelled Navajo ramjet intercontinental missile project, in particular, comes to mind. We could have saved billions in our subsequent cruise missile programs by refining the Navajo concept. The point is that we no longer have the resources to accommodate as comfortably the groping process described in your retrospective analysis.

One should be sensitive to the influence of the time dimension and the specificity of goals on the planning process. Long-range planning must first develop a hierarchy of objectives, a set of priorities. Then planning can proceed. This is a different proposition from operational planning where the situation and objectives are specified. Here the problem is to select the means to achieve the given objectives. From the decisionmaker's standpoint, he wants to know what he needs to do today in order to reach a given long-range goal. A real challenge, according to an experienced planner, is to lay out the objectives and then debate the strategy to achieve the objectives. He was not sure that we can do long-range planning in the same sense that we do short-range planning because of the problem of scenario dependence—the specification of situation and objectives found in operational and crisis planning. "But we should have a debate on objectives and subsequently on strategy. And the debate on strategy should be iterative; there needs to be an extended series of discussions on these issues."

Many important choices are made during periods of crisis. This fact has significance for the meaning of planning. In times of crisis, planning, strategy, tactics, and all other aspects of preparation for action are limited to a very short timespan and a very few individuals. Consequently, these choices do not receive the scrutiny we normally associate with planning. This time compression effect was described by one of our seminar colleagues: "I participated in one such incident. Over a single weekend an entire military program for Israel was developed and provided to the President at his request for a Monday meeting with the Israeli Prime Minister."

Finally, planning acquired a particular meaning in the context of the seminar. The group did not interest itself at any session in the details of "paper" plans. Instead, we considered very general plans. One person expressed the view that such plans ideally would have enough specificity to preclude the Army from building tanks that the Air Force cannot carry in its aircraft. Nevertheless, we did not choose to treat plans as documents. We viewed a plan as a conceptual direction.

PLANNING GUIDANCE

Several factors were suggested as undermining the utility of long-range planning. One was that a bureaucratic context leads other actors to challenge the proposed actions of the long-range planners. Second, one can be confident that the future will not fully conform to plans. Finally, even supposing that a long-range plan were accepted as valid, who then would give planners the power to execute plans? "Coming out of an NSC experience I conclude that planners are uniformly undermined." This observation led us to explore planning problems associated with leadership and political guidance.

In general, it is difficult to get decisionmakers to focus on the long range. Decisionmakers are probably most comfortable with extrapolation of the present into the future. In fact, this may be the only type of long-range planning acceptable to decisionmakers, however inaccurate the results and, therefore, unfortunate this predisposition.

Guidance based on the activism of political leadership with a well-defined world view may give sharp definition to planning. One member of our group developed the thesis that the eight years of the Nixon-Ford administrations saw the United States pursuing a foreign policy based upon a particular world outlook. During this period the government was *proactive*: it planned, calculated, then acted. Before and since this period, in his judgment, the United States has been *reactive.*

> During the proactive period, which I favor, our planning and action derived from *goals.* Goals stem from an ideology which defines how things happen or ought to happen. To plan you have to have goals, and an ideology provides them.

This confident view of ideology acquires the flavor of a revolutionary concept when ideology is linked with the top political elite. The claimed effect would mobilize and transform the entire system.

> Good long-range planning, in the sense that we have been discussing, would mean that there would never have to be a long-range planning unit or document because the top leadership would agree on objectives. This is the role of ideology that provides the goal. President Reagan is the first President in a long time who does not mind being identified as an ideological President.

There was disagreement with this position on two counts. First, even when we have an agreed ideology, there are further problems. Especially difficult are the bureaucratic conflicts over who will lead the implementation and the arguments over the tactics involved. A second point of disagreement emphasized the incompatibility of an ideological approach within the American political culture. Ours is a subtle system with a diversity of values and a corresponding difficulty in achieving consensus across a broad policy field such as the whole of foreign and security policy.

STRUCTURAL PROBLEMS

Two structural problems were thought to be associated with planning. First, there is the problem of how long-range planners are compartmentalized within the bureaucracy. If they are separate from the rest of their own organization, their product may be suspect. But they need to be detached in order to take a long-range viewpoint. This automatically results in a disadvantage for the long-range planner in competition with other, more pressing, demands on the decisionmaker's time. The disadvantage is compounded if, as is often the case, the decisionmaker has refused to part with the services of his best people by placing them in the detached organization.

Two members of the seminar offered illustrations related to the compartmentalization problem. One concerned the National Defense University, which is an agency of the Joint Chiefs of Staff. Recently, the Chairman of the Joint Chiefs of Staff asked the University to establish a group to conduct a long-range planning study concerning the Persian Gulf area. The Chairman was seeking a detached perspective to accomplish something the Joint Staff was too busy to do. The problem illustrated here is that if the long-range planning staff is a part of an integrated staff, it quickly becomes submerged in day-to-day activities. On the other hand, if the long-range planning staff is detached, it incurs the risk of not being relevant—a risk encountered by the National Defense University in this instance. A second example concerned the Air Staff in the Air Force Headquarters. It took several of its most brilliant planners, installed them in the Forrestal Building in downtown Washington—away from the Pentagon—and instructed them to develop a proposed long-range plan for the Air Force. They came back with a series of broad objectives but found they could go no further than this. Their relative isolation from the mainstream of the Air Staff in the Pentagon precluded them from developing relevant scenarios. Scenarios about plausible futures were needed to provide a context in which they could move from general objectives toward more concrete plans.

A point related to the compartmentalization issue is that planners must stay in touch with the real world if they are to constitute a voice that will be heard. And—to quote another panel member—"more than staying in touch with reality is required; it is also necessary to stay in touch with the 'horses,' the officials who have the clout and who make the decisions."

The second structural problem thought to affect planning concerns "turf-sharing." The observation was made that varying initiatives had been taken by the National Security Council staff to encourage broader participation among several agencies in the development of policy plans. It proved to be very difficult to obtain the involvement of the Department of Defense in long-range planning in terms of defining various futures and the forces and other resources required to meet these futures. The Defense Department was concerned with its own turf and wished to discourage the National Security Council from becoming involved in these matters.

Obviously, the structural relations in national security planning at this level are complex. This is a difficult process of consensus building. One person wished us to take note that the things we as a nation agree on are really the most critical items because we disagree on so much as a people. Clearly, this widespread disagreement is a major source of frustration for those in the planning process.

WHAT SUCCEEDS?

One of the most experienced members of our seminar observed that progress in improving long-range planning in some comprehensive sense may be unachievable. Perhaps the best we can hope to do is "whittle around the edges."

Yet, we have examples of successful long-range planning in the United States. It was suggested that the major campaigns in World War II, particularly in the latter part of that conflict, were conducted in accordance with a strategy stemming from a long-range planning effort. The Manhattan District which developed the atomic bomb was a spectacular effort. Surely the Apollo program was a marvel of long-range planning; it achieved its awesome goal of a manned lunar landing, and on time.

Members of the seminar identified certain circumstances common to these successful planning efforts. Each program had highly centralized direction, a very few people in charge who enjoyed unquestioned authority. The planning was accomplished within a limited context. Obviously, in our society, it is difficult to achieve these conditions and, once achieved, to maintain them over the period of the plan. With respect to long-range planning in an area as broad as national security, furthermore, it is doubtful that the relatively narrow perspective of these three examples is applicable; except, perhaps, to indicate the difficulty involved in long-range planning of broad scope.

The planning success of Robert Strange McNamara also was raised in our discussion and can be interpreted with greater optimism as an example of broad-scope planning. It can be argued that Defense Secretary McNamara conducted long-range planning in the sense that he established the defense strategy that is still operative today. He marshalled greater authority than is usual and thus enjoyed freer reign. He chose to pursue politically and bureaucratically plausible initiatives and he was constrained by prior programs which eventually resulted in the strategic "triad." Nevertheless, within these constraints he was able to establish a general, long-term framework for national security.

The complexity of our institutions and some of the structural constraints discussed above prompted one in our group to propose the merits of decentralized planning as an alternative to continuing reliance on a highly centralized planning process. One theme in the Kronenberg paper was that the planning process involves many overlapping, loosely connected actors, many of whom may not be aware of their influence on planning. One person picked up on this theme and observed that in planning, certain people are doing very critical things at any given point in time; neither they nor anyone else is fully aware of their larger—perhaps unintended—significance at the time. This pattern suggests we should take a closer look at decentralized planning. Several years ago this was the subject of an intense debate among economists. "In retrospect, there is somewhat widespread agreement that the decentralized planners have done somewhat better than the central planners."

Another parallel that was raised between security planners and the economics profession is in the area of goals. Based on the economists' experience, we might be led to conclude that it is very difficult to enunciate realistic national goals. "We should be very modest about defining or attempting to achieve them. The fact is that they change very quickly." Exception was taken to this line of argument by one of our participants who insisted that economics and national security planning are very different. "Goals to economists depend upon multiple, myriad consumers. National security goals serve a single consumer."

As in some of our earlier sessions, the "people issue" was raised. The important contribution of good people to the quality of the planning effort was an unchallenged thesis. Late in this session one of our members suggested that maybe we should concentrate more of our attention on developing "excellent people who can cope with the immediate situation as it arises."

A facet of the people issue concerns how most effectively to involve good people in the planning effort. One person with National Security Council experience drew on his observations of attorneys and proposed that effective staffing of senior decision-makers must transcend detailed analysis and involve broad support. "Although lawyers deal with very specific briefs, the best attorneys seem to prepare themselves for the briefs by discussing the issues with other lawyers." This suggested to him an approach to planning at the highest levels: First, senior decision-makers should sit down and discuss overall objectives for fairly extended periods. Out of these intensive discussions would come objectives. From that point a more systematic approach could be followed; the next step becomes a more directive process. One would communicate with key subordinates throughout the system or the agency. This would provide a basis to insure understanding and build broader consensus within relevant sectors of the administration. Then the principal would turn to the political realm and actively promote the plan, finally obtaining a broad, government-wide consensus.

One wag in our group whispered "God must have loved the planners—he made so many of them!" The pervasiveness of the planner's contribution was testified to by one general officer with Joint Staff experience. He was confident that every campaign in the history of war someone was there at the commander's elbow who said, "Don't do this, because ... do that!"

> He was there then, they're there today. The difficulty for command choice is that there are always people who can make a cogent case for other courses of action.

Also, present conditions and political factors weigh in the balance. In the case of General Eisenhower at the end of World War II in Europe, the question may have been one of priorities, political objectives versus purely military objectives. Right or wrong, some planner-advisers prevailed, others (the advocates of incorporating Berlin) did not. But there was not an absence of long-range planners.

The general's comment about the difficulty of choosing seemed to precipitate one of the more interesting conclusions from one of our participants about the successful planner's role: "The role of the planner is not to predict. The planner's job is to choose. It requires a goal, self-confidence, and power."

The seminar session then closed. The final comment of the evening was offered by a distinguished foreign visitor to the February session who capped our discussion of how planning may succeed with this somber thought:

> I am disturbed and disillusioned that there is no long-range plan and one cannot appear to be developed. Despite a following throughout the world that looks to the United States for leadership, it does not have the ability to focus on a number of things that are extremely important.

ORGANIZING FOR PLANNING

Our fifth session was held in March and addressed the organization of national security affairs in the United States and explored suggestions for improving planning and policymaking within these institutional arrangements. A paper by Archie D. Barrett, "Department of Defense Organization: Planning for Planning," provided the heuristic grist for the seminar. The Barrett paper examined the Defense Organization Study of 1977-80 and developed a series of provocative proposals based on his analysis of the findings of the Study. (The Study comprises five separate, independently prepared and published study reports, and the extensive comments on them by senior decisionmakers in the defense community.)

INCENTIVES AND REORGANIZATION

The writ of proposals for reorganization should probably be viewed in their broadest context. The detailed implications of any reorganization effort touch many facets of organizational life in addition to planning. For this reason, the first comment in this session urged us not to judge reorganization on only one criterion, that of facilitating planning. Planners have a variety of needs and organizational design is not the only factor that drives the planning process. While it seems to be the case that we can plan with some success for our hardware needs, "the vision of a strategic future is very difficult to come by. It is important that planners get objectives and guidance. The Barrett paper should not stand or fall on its contribution to planning alone."

The incentives to use reorganization to improve the defense system in general and planning, more specifically, are unclear. One of our colleagues expressed the view that, at least in the case of the Steadman study on the National Military Command Structure, Steadman had never been optimistic that the proposals would accomplish much. There was strong disagreement from another participant who observed that Steadman had worked very hard on the study and initially believed that it could have a major effect. One reaction to this exchange was that perhaps the system was working well enough in a peacetime context, and that there were no incentives to support sweeping changes. He was not sure what would happen to these incentives in the stresses of wartime.

One response to the diagnosis and prescriptions of the Barrett paper prompted one person to question the difference between what is desirable and what is feasible. "Organizational issues are not problems but dilemmas; they have horns. No one solution is without problems." Putting together the various perspectives illuminated in the Defense Organization Study may achieve a useful compromise or it could produce paralysis.

The structure of incentives does not easily change. We will not change things by reorganization unless we change the way we allocate resources and reward careers. We must change the structure of incentives for individuals; then we can move to other kinds of organization with some effect.

> What is the basic premise of the paper? That the Secretary of Defense should run DOD? Is that really possible? But no one lets the Secretary of Defense alone. Everyone demands things from him; he can't run DOD! It is very normal for the services and DOD to compete. But when you reorganize DOD it comes out the same.

One view of what must be done to transform these incentives pointed directly to the professionalism of the officer corps. One of the general officers in the group argued that "we need an ethic to bail us out of our current difficulties. We must have a notion of service that transcends individual service interests."

The national climate of tolerance for the way we do business was discussed as a central issue in the incentives surrounding reorganization. How serious are the problems examined in the study? There seems to be consistency between the findings of the 1977-80 Study and all the other reorganization studies before it, at least in terms of several prominent issues. Either the public concludes these are chronic problems that can be dealt with only through gradual means or that these represent a scandalous mess. "If it is viewed as a scandalous mess and the public is serious about planning and military readiness, then they would not tolerate it!"

DYNAMICS OF THE KEY PLAYERS

The role of the civilian service secretaries has been questioned in many quarters recently. Should the service secretary position be abolished? Several in the seminar supported the Barrett proposal for revitalizing the role of the service secretaries. One person said he had once supported eliminating the service secretary position, but had changed his mind; sometimes the service secretaries have made important contributions and their potential will be greater if their role is enhanced. They can represent the services to the outside world and the outside world to the services. This presumably helps with civilian control of the military and brings the concerns of civilians to the military. One serving officer had strong reservations about integrating the service secretaries and their staffs with the military service staffs, feeling this would dilute the professional content of military advice.

A supporter of Barrett's service secretary proposals concluded that one result of the change would be to reduce somewhat the current degree of autonomy enjoyed by the service secretaries and to integrate them more completely into the Department of Defense under the Secretary of Defense. Another interpretation of the service secretary revitalization, however, was that the integration of military and civilian service staffs would enhance the influence of the service secretaries over DOD matters.

The commanders in chief (CINCs) of the unified and specified commands include the principal general and flag officers who command American armed forces in the potential theaters of war around the world. There was broad support for the Barrett proposal to give them a more important role in policy and planning. One point of caution raised, however, was that we need to better understand and coordinate the very different planning assumptions maintained among the CINCs. For example, CINCs have different time concepts of M-Day and D-Day. "We have a series of planning systems that don't necessarily work well together." This concern was shared by another person who wondered how the Secretary of Defense could set up a larger system to get the CINCs more involved and get better overall input from them.

The proposal to add vitality to joint institutions by strengthening the Chairman of the Joint Chiefs of Staff (CJCS) and enhancing the independence of the Joint Staff was generally viewed as desirable. The effort to get a more independent Joint Staff might, in the view of some, have to rest ultimately on the aforementioned ethic which transcends individual service interests. The proposal to have all personnel of the Joint Staff work for the Chairman would change some of the arithmetic of influence. Still, as one seminar member pointed out, nine thousand people in the Pentagon do peacetime planning and programming. Only about four hundred do employment planning in the Joint Staff structure.

One concern expressed was that if the entire Joint Staff worked for the CJCS, that would kill their chances for promotion. It is part of the conventional wisdom of the Pentagon that officers in so-called "purple suit" joint assignments run some risks with respect to promotion. At *best,* it has been thought, a joint assignment will not be held against an officer under promotion review or being considered for an important career assignment. Recent evidence suggests a different trend. Officers assigned to JCS staff organizations are promoted at the same rates as their contemporaries who did not hold joint assignments. "On the JCS, we need and have a two-track system which provides a mixture of the real world of service and joint assignments to the staffs. Promotion in the JCS arena has been okay recently."

A larger question posed but never satisfactorily answered is "how strong should the JCS or CJCS be?" Can the Joint Chiefs of Staff come to grips with significant problems on a level of high national policy? These are not just problems concerning the employment of forces but also issues of resource allocation among the services.

STEERING THE SYSTEM

The Secretary of Defense is in a unique position in the making and execution of national security policy and plans by virtue of his distinctive political role in the government and his executive position in the huge Department of Defense. The Secretary's influence is further enlarged by the enormous staff resources available to him in the cluster of agencies known as the Office of the Secretary of Defense. For these reasons, one of the participants felt it was perhaps a little naive for some to suggest that the Secretary of Defense will allocate certain of his responsibilities more routinely to constituent elements of the Department. It was felt that the Secretary would always want to make the big choices. Furthermore, one participant thought that so much at the Department of Defense depends upon the differing styles of the various Secretaries. The issues are broader than centralization and decentralization. In the view of one observer, the centralization controversy seems settled while there is now incremental movement under Secretary Weinberger to change the process. Under Weinberger the Chairman of the Joint Chiefs of Staff can act differently and make changes on the margin.

Another aspect of the problem transcending the centralization-decentralization issue is that a healthy system is one in which the consumers shape the product. Right now the CINCs as the DOD "consumers" are entirely too far removed from the important decisions, particularly on hardware, according to one observer. This point was disputed by the judgment that the CINCs may offer bad counsel on weapon system choices.

This last point was thought to raise another. We need to focus more on feedback and performance in the field. The programmers must become better tied in to the operators and forces that actually use these complex systems.

The discussion of how the CINCs should be more effectively incorporated into the overall process of steering the US security system recognized that "CINCs can make mistakes too. Personalities are very important to making it all work." This assessment of the CINCs concluded with the view that they are especially good at the larger and more difficult questions of policy formation. The view of some that CINCs are less able to advise on weapons choices may be moot since such choices seem to be easier to make back in the Pentagon than the tough policy choices to which the CINCs bring strong credentials.

> If CINCs have a special knowledge of a geographic region that others don't have, then we should get more out of them and they should have a larger role than they have now. The CINCs should especially help us in determining what our objectives should be in particular regions.

An important part of the Barrett proposal to enhance joint planning and operational capability was to make the Chairman of the Joint Chiefs of Staff the principal link and supervisor of the CINCs, replacing the Joint Chiefs of Staff in the chain of command. Also, the Chairman was to be able to recommend budget priorities directly to the Secretary of Defense and, of course, have a separate staff dedicated to his support apart from the service chiefs.

In addition to reservations mentioned earlier about a strengthened role for the joint level, there was a feeling in the seminar that any problems surrounding these recommendations may stem from some residual fears of a general staff concept. As one colleague asked: "Can we do decent planning with the system we have or do we have to make radical changes, such as integrating the service staffs?"

The concern with an enhanced joint staff agency, a "general" staff, goes back in our political history at least to World War II. One participant advised that the general staff question, if one would read the congressional testimony after World War II, reveals an antipathy toward the *German* General Staff. A close student of these matters suggested that we are all subject to an interesting—and erroneous—legislative myth. The German General Staff was not what our worried legislators thought it was. It was really an Army staff, not a joint staff of all services. Perhaps the relevant question is the one raised at the end of our penultimate session by author Archie Barrett: "Can we get a general staff without creating a General Staff?"

The key to steering the complex, organic national security system is the nature of its guidance. An enhanced Joint Staff may not be sufficient to provide critical military advice; one former NSC staff member had doubts about getting objective views from JCS people. If the advice continues to favor service parochialism or interservice log-rolling, the basis for the guidance will be flawed.

The Carter Doctrine created a mismatch between the new element of US strategy and the forces available for its successful execution, should our policy hand be forced in the Persian Gulf and Southwest Asia. One of our members raised a key question that bears on the quality of political guidance: "Did anybody challenge Carter on the Carter Doctrine?" Was he told that tactical nuclear weapons would have to be used because the United

States would otherwise be unable to stop the Soviets in Southwest Asia? Evidently, this was considered. And perhaps a strategy-force mismatch will be with us always; a policy officer argued that resources will always constrain our planning process and our objectives: "The Joint Strategic Planning Document says we need 33 divisions to conduct 1½ wars—and we will never get the 33 divisions."

Some larger issues about political guidance are suggested by these points. Maybe President Carter was questioned within the executive branch about the Middle East and Southwest Asia. But he was not questioned by the Congress. For the military planner, the problem that the planning process must express is: What do you need to meet your strategy and how do you get there? In one military planner's view we do not do very well in the programmatic steps from where we are now to how we should accomplish our strategy requirements.

The view from the Hill has a different perspective. Looking at the last four years from a congressional perspective reveals a fatal flaw in Carter's programs—the failure to make clear the goals that justified the programs. A participant argued that one must go to Congress with a set of goals; weapons systems tend to acquire life and a constituency of their own.

The last observation gets at the heart of the guidance problem. The military wants and needs civilian guidance in its top-level planning. Should the military raise strategic questions to civilian decisionmakers in a direct way? As one general officer in the seminar replied: "We tried, but nobody would engage the issues." Another officer wondered aloud if civilian political authorities will ever go much past the broad issues and begin to more narrowly define their objectives. He answered his own question: "They want to keep their options open."

A tentative answer to this difficult problem came from several sources as we brought the fifth seminar session to an end. "You *can* get around the problems of not getting specific guidance from political leadership. You must look for goals rather than guidance." This advice parallels the analysis of the problem that led to failure with Congress by the Carter administration. In requesting guidance from political leadership, it may be asking too much if the hope is to get a definitive set of "yes-no" answers about political objectives.

IMPROVING THE SYSTEM

The sixth and final session of the series convened in April. Our objective was to assess and sift through our probings of security planning during the life of the seminar and to articulate a set of recommendations for improving security policy and planning and the quality of its products. The free-ranging discussion of the evening was inaugurated by our consideration of a paper prepared by Lawrence J. Korb entitled "On Making the System Work."

One thing the careful reader will soon note is that not all the thoughtful diagnoses and prescriptions for improvement that emerged in the past five sessions have been repeated in the final session. Each session acquired a life of its own and accreted its own distinctive insights.

LIVING WITH INCREMENTAL CHANGE

There was broad agreement in this session about the merits of working with the system as it is and learning to put some of its deficiencies in a more favorable light. One of our colleagues even exhorted us to overcome our guilt feelings about not having better plans! All of this is not to suggest smugness; the group certainly felt a need to improve things more, to muddle successfully through. One person even suggested that incremental change strategies might facilitate more rapid progress over time than would dramatic shifts that unleash large forces of resistance. The one disquieting observation in this paean to incrementalism was the hypothesis of one person that perhaps our Soviet opponents are much better off than we think and that while we are asleep at the switch our incrementalist strategy will put us increasingly behind.

Although there was virtually no discussion of our basic system of government, two people did point to problems. One cited the limits of an electoral system that is geared to short-term approaches; the other called for some practical steps to reform our constitutional order and establish a two-party parliamentary democracy. The thinking behind the latter proposal was that it would facilitate more stable policy commitments by the governing party, thus enhancing opportunities for successful long-range planning.

RELIANCE ON GOOD PEOPLE

There was great sympathy for the notion that our main problems could be solved with better people, from the White House down. The specifications of several in the seminar called for wise leaders who can lead, who can manage organizations, who can understand the problems, and who know how to work within the existing system in order to solve them. A premium was placed on seasoned people who do not require on-the-job training to handle critical decisionmaking roles. There was also recognition that we have inadequate methods for finding the right people, determining our true goals, and selecting the criteria for picking the people who will work toward those goals. "We must think through the system that should produce people who can do good planning and insure that it is as good as we can make it."

There was not much support for aggressive programs of reorganization. We were discouraged from "getting fancy" in reorganizing. The view was that we are good at creating structures and good at making them accomplish particular ends, but that we do not well understand some of the unanticipated side effects which are produced as we try to pursue our purposes. There was a strong feeling that good people can make any organization work. Furthermore, there was emphasis on small staffs with a great deal of authority, clear assignment of roles as to who sets the agendas for action, and a priority given to individuals who can work with each other—not *on* each other (especially around the President). One person stated that the most immediate positive action we could take would be to reduce the size of the staffs in the Department of Defense. "This would produce greater accountability and responsibility on the part of those working on the problems."

TOWARD MORE THOUGHTFUL CHOICE

The interactions of complex decisionmaking among the major departments concerned with security planning was a continuing preoccupation of the seminar series. There was great sensitivity to the long-range implications of the way we set priorities, handle trade-offs, and make current choices in acquiring forces, weapons, and management systems. There was interest in trying to provide benchmarks for making choices about the future. At the joint level, there was willingness to examine the charter of the Joint Chiefs of Staff, the law, executive orders, and the desires of the Chairman of the Joint Chiefs of Staff and the Chiefs—all who shape the system. There was a concern that at this joint level no staff capability exists to make tough decisions about new technology which may lack clear sponsorship by one of the services. (An example given of one such technology, identified by the Defense Advanced Research Projects Agency, is a means for propelling projectiles that uses electromagnetic force rather than traditional chemical explosive reactions). Another choice, rarely dealt with but at the heart of many joint-service tensions, is what needs to be given up in turf or program resources by the separate military services?

Another kind of choice-related problem that surfaced was concerned with improving our skill in finding and preparing for knowable contingencies. This is a crucial issue in the relationship between planning and the intelligence community. Another recommendation was to enhance our *comparative* understanding of different institutions and their problems in planning. Each of the four services is functionally *different* in terms of the number of movable things commanders have to control in a battle, the quality of information available to commanders regarding the status of their forces during battle, and the ranks of those who control moving things in combat. These variable factors were thought to cause differences among the services during planning and to exacerbate the problems of interservice planning.

Problems surrounding the information base used by planners to choose also were discussed. To succeed in war one's planning has to be better than that of the adversary. Therefore, successful plans must be based on knowledge of the capabilities of both sides. It was suggested that the United States has trouble seeing events the way Soviet planners do. Sometimes this is due to turf problems between the Central Intelligence Agency and the Department of Defense. Concern was expressed that if the Central Intelligence Agency—responsible for assessing Red (adversary) capabilities—were to do comparative assessments of Blue (friendly-US) capabilities, then the Central Intelligence Agency would have a potential to influence some DOD program funding. There was one recommendation that if the Joint Chiefs of Staff or the Office of the Secretary of Defense did not do the Red-Blue net assessment, then the National Security Council should perform this function. More widespread support seemed to emerge for the idea that the National Security Council would referee Red-Blue assessment disputes between the Central Intelligence Agency and the Office of the Secretary of Defense.

BROKERING THE SYSTEM

The need to find ways to mediate conflict and to develop constructive cooperative relationships among the elements of the national security system was a lively topic. It was acknowledged that all programs come together in the Joint Chiefs of Staff and the Office of the Secretary of Defense. The problem is how to get the services to trade off programs and priorities in order to satisfy larger defense needs. Of the two interfacing agencies, the Office of the Secretary of Defense clearly has much more influence both on statutory grounds and because there is no other place in the system where the whole defense program is put together.

The Barrett paper essentially proposed to organize the less politically organized interests in the Defense Department: the CINCs, service secretaries, and to strengthen the Chairman of the Joint Chiefs of Staff as a counterpoise to the four service chiefs. There was broad support for strengthening the National Security Council and Joint Chiefs of Staff as key coordinating agencies. Several members of the seminar urged that the coordinating function of these agencies be accepted as an appropriate part of the decisionmaking process and that the guerrilla warfare of bureaucratic politics stop once decisions have been made by these agencies, the Office of the Secretary of Defense, or the President. Probably the strongest recommendations to come out of the final session concerned the crucial role of the National Security Council. There were several proposals, including: a call for the military services to take the NSC staff into their confidence and provide the Council with the information it needs; the concept that the President and the NSC staff should lay out issues, views, and facilitate decisions; and that the NSC staff should become the strong and unbiased arbiter of disputes in the security planning arena. It should enjoy an unqualified role as honest broker for the President within the national security community.

The seminar members broadly supported an enhanced Joint Chiefs of Staff structure, with, among others, the recommendation that the Chairman should be given five-star rank and perhaps his own staff. This enthusiasm for a stronger joint arrangement was characterized by several comments identifying deficiencies in the quality of JCS staffing, compared with the quantity and quality of service staffs. The strong—and some would add legitimate—efforts of the Chiefs to protect service interests was also fairly broadly recognized. One person called for a firm clarification, and limitation, of the services' role vis-a-vis the joint structure and the Office of the Secretary of Defense.

The need was expressed for long-range planning to serve a brokering function by offering a kind of heuristic opportunity to lay out points of dispute, agreement, and difference among competing players.

Another point where active brokering in the planning function was endorsed concerned the role of the services in strategy development.

> The most difficult problem is to build a consensus about national security strategy. The biggest deficiency has been the inadequate explanation of the problems and of the different answers to the problems provided by the services to the decisionmakers.

The leadership problems of building a strategy consensus are intimidating. One of the participants expressed the view that "recent Presidents have not had this sense of strategy." Beyond recommendations for more forceful strategy leadership by the President and the Secretary of State, one participant pointed the group toward Congress and a larger role for public debates on the great issues of security planning and national strategy.

The reaction of the seminar to the Korb proposal for a body like the Hoover Commission to examine our national security institutions was unenthusiastic. The general feeling was that commissions are not especially productive. One general officer held the view that it might be too political in its charactistics and conclusions. Another criticism was that bodies of this kind tend to report out predesigned conclusions.

PLANNING, RATIONALITY, AND POLITICS

Despite the seminar's commitment to limit our agenda to planning—or perhaps because of that commitment—the course of our six-month enterprise followed many paths. Two factors may account for the broad sweep of ideas that were addressed and are recorded in this volume. First, the life of the seminar spanned the dynamic period of change attending the last months of the outgoing Democratic administration of Jimmy Carter and the first months of the new Republican administration of Ronald Reagan. Second, a number of the seminar participants were senior military officers, senior staff members, or policy officials associated with the Carter administration, the Presidential transition staff, or the Reagan administration. Each of these participants brought significant experience, insight, and substantive concerns to our deliberations. These two factors provided us with an expansive concept of the nature of national security planning and its relationship to larger questions of national and international focus.

Due to the background of the participants and the events that formed a national and international context for our discussions, the reader may have discovered the threads of many important themes in the preceding pages. Four of these themes strike me as having particular significance as the United States confronts its global responsibilities in the eighties.

First is an assertion that the national security edifice rests on a foundation of fragmented constitutional arrangements, conflictive relations among institutional estates and bureaucratic fiefs, and a Congress and public that are ill-informed and perhaps undermotivated when addressing tough national security problems.

At the core of this particular theme is an uneasy sense that the multiple legal authorities and political power centers distributed among numerous decisionmaking structures produce great ambiguity in policy, strategy, and political guidance. This complex structure supports multiple advocates who may all be partially successful by maintaining coalitions among legislative, executive, and interest groups. As a result, influence over policy and planning is dispersed among several governmental bodies, including Congress, and extragovernmental or corporate entities.

This dispersal at a macroscopic level causes uncertainty about the relative shares of responsibility between Congress and the Executive regarding longer term policy and strategy choices. This is not to suggest that Congress intentionally takes an active role in defining the details of strategy and policy. But the collective disposition of Congress toward determining how the appropriation pie gets allocated between defense and social programs forces defense officials to make some important trade-off decisions among different defense policies and strategic concepts.

At a more narrow level, the tendency of Congress to fund weapons systems rather than purchase mission capabilities is significant.

Bureaucratic fiefs encourage and cooperate with the structural relations which blur the decisionmaking boundaries between Congress and the Executive (thus policy controversies are seldom "settled" nor decisions "made" with any finality), adjust the trade-offs between defense and social programs, and reinforce the focus on weapons systems. The resulting dispersed structure of influence inhibits efforts to establish sharp definitions of purpose, policy, and strategy that might enhance the clarity of guidance for the national security planner. Interestingly, two Army Chiefs of Staff who served over 20 years apart both expressed alarm about these issues, Maxwell Taylor in 1959[1] and Edward Meyer in 1981. General Meyer stated his concern in the following terms:

> I contend that the mechanisms used in the past have been vertical addressals to specific weapons systems or specific elements of the forces to decide whether or not their capabilities could be increased.
>
> No one has looked horizontally at the capabilities of the forces to carry out what it is that the command authorities demand. Just how capable are the national defense forces to carry out the defined missions?[2]

Thus, these "vertical addressals" by the various principal actors in the decisionmaking structure to specific weapons systems or force structure elements discourage the horizontal assessments that might otherwise be made of entire programs or the capabilities to support major strategic or policy thrusts. A major cause of this shortcoming would seem to be the dispersed power structure of proliferated legislative-executive–interest group coalitions. These coalitions appear to generate sufficient incentives within the US political economy to insure their self-maintenance during peacetime. One can but wonder if their inadequate performance would be tolerated in the stress of a wartime environment. A foretaste is provided by the "discovery" of a strategy-force mismatch after the pronouncement of the Carter Doctrine toward the Persian Gulf region and Southwest Asia in January 1980, and the subsequent problems associated with implementing the Rapid Deployment Force concept.

A second important theme found in this book is that no clear consensus exists among America's civilian leaders about the preferred role of this country in the contemporary world. We are largely reactive. There is an urgent need to foster a dialogue about these issues in many forums within government and more broadly throughout the society.

At this time, there is strong support among the American people for increased defense spending in response to evidence of growing Soviet military capability and assertiveness. But other than this sense of reaction to a perceived Soviet threat, it is not clear what foreign policy goals motivate the public, Congress, and the Reagan administration to justify these major resource commitments. It may indeed be the case that the Carter administration and the Democrats were punished at the polls in 1980 for a serious failure to clarify national security goals before the Congress and to educate the American people generally to these issues. The Reagan administration inherits a need to crystallize a new consensus around national objectives and strategy. If they fail to do so, the administration and congressional Republicans run the risk of electoral losses in 1982 and 1984. If the Soviets should ease their assertiveness, the Republicans may be hard pressed to justify continued higher military spending together with social program cuts without a compelling rationale for the former.

Military leadership also seems to need and want clearer, more stable civilian guidance.[3] This certainly seems to be one of the key lessons distilled from the experience of the Vietnam conflict by many professional soldiers. A related lesson is the need for a continuing high-quality debate *in camera* between civilian and military leaders about the ends and means of strategy. National security planners should make a useful contribution to this dialectical process. This debate would help national leaders develop a more realistic sense of what it costs to field an effective instrument of foreign policy. It might also educate key players about the limits of the military instrument and the relative efficacy of nonmilitary means for pursuing US interests in the world.

Third is the theme that, short of a major national crisis like a war—which would galvanize our politics around the strategic initiatives of our incumbent national leadership—there is little prospect that a reactive style of decisionmaking by *adhocracy* can be resisted. Thus, it is expected that coping and incremental-ism, rather than major reorganization or institutional reform, will characterize the conduct of national security policy and plan-ning. More good people with clearer mandates to act rather than structural tinkering seems to be the medication of preference. The one structural reform that appeared to earn general support in the seminar was to upgrade the status and institutional auton-omy of the Chairman of the Joint Chiefs of Staff.

A final, significant theme in our discussions was the notion that planning is trivialized when it is viewed as the preparation of specific designs for action and actual documents. The essense of planning is the development of an integrative sense of concep-tual direction. For this reason, the collection of information by the intelligence community and other institutions tends to play an important but less central role than the quality of analysis and its persuasiveness in the minds of senior decisionmakers. In this context, planning becomes a matter of shaping conceptual orien-tations and, as such, is immersed in the stream of politics.

Plans are not self-executing. The commitments embodied in planning concepts are fragile and are subject to decay or repudi-ation as coalitions of interested players realign their relationships in response to changing circumstances. There was considerable support in the seminar for the proposition that the successful brokering of policy formulation as well as the disciplining of policy implementation at the higher levels must depend on a strong National Security Council and an effective NSC staff.

A member of our group had earlier published a penetrating article on the NSC system. A key point he made was that the NSC staff must be more than a source of personal staff assistance for the President; it must also perform an institutional role by raising critical issues for review by the President and seeing to it that his policies are enforced by the departments:

> President Carter has put particular emphasis on the NSC's personal advisory function, requesting independent ideas and analyses from his staff. Nevertheless, the institu-tional function must not be neglected. In forging a strong insti-tutional role for the NSC, the responsibilities of policy develop-ment, of forcing decisions on major issues, of decision-process management, and of ensuring that decisions are implemented, will be devolved to that organization.[4]

These four themes reflect some of the cardinal problems we tried to address in this book and the seminar series on which it is based. I share with my seminar colleagues a sense of frustration about our difficulties in providing adequate solutions to many of the problems of national security planning. But perhaps we too often seek to frame answers to the wrong questions. The problems may not be so much in our planning as in our politics.

Some who would lead our principal institutions prefer slogans and simple solutions rather than confront the opportunities and hazards implicit in a complex world. They may be our greatest threat because they would draw us inexorably toward the ultimate surprises of self-deception. This is the challenge to our planning and our politics. As Thomas Schelling wrote in his foreword to Roberta Wohlstetter's splendid book about the US surprise at Pearl Harbor:

> The danger is not that we shall read the signals and indicators with too little skill; the danger is in a poverty of expectations—a routine obsession with a few dangers that may be familiar rather than likely.[5]

NOTES

1. Maxwell D. Taylor, *The Uncertain Trumpet* (New York: Harper, 1959), p. 123.

2. "Defense: In Dire Need of a Coherent, Clear National Policy," *Government Executive*, January 1981, p. 14.

3. A perspective on this issue is developed by General Maxwell D. Taylor in "Tell the Military Exactly What You Want," *Washington Post*, March 1981, p. A23.

4. Philip A. Odeen, "Organizing for National Security," *International Security*, Summer 1981, p. 114.

5. Foreword by Thomas C. Schelling in Roberta Wohlstetter, *Pearl Harbor: Warning and Decision* (Stanford: Stanford University Press, 1962), p. viii.

SELECTED REFERENCES

Ackoff, Russel L. *A Concept of Corporate Planning.* New York: John Wiley & Sons, 1970.

Allison, Graham T. *Essence of Decision: Explaining the Cuban Missile Crisis.* Boston: Little, Brown & Co., 1971.

Ansoff, H. Igor. *Strategic Management.* New York: John Wiley & Sons, 1979.

Antonelli, Theodore, Major General, USA (Ret.) Department of Defense Reorganization Study Project. *Report to the Secretary of Defense of the Defense Agency Review.* March 1979.

Arnold, R. Douglas. *Congress and the Bureaucracy: A Theory of Influence.* New Haven: Yale University Press, 1979.

Art, Robert. "Bureaucratic Politics and American Foreign Policy: A Critique," *Policy Sciences* 40 (1973).

Barnet, Richard J. *Roots of War.* New York: Atheneum Pubs., 1972.

Basiuk, Victor. *Technology, World Politics and American Policy.* New York: Columbia University Press, 1977.

Betts, Richard K. "Surprise Despite Warning: Why Sudden Attacks Succeed." *Political Science Quarterly,* Winter 1980/81.

Bobrow, Davis B.; Chan, Steve; and Kringen, John. *Understanding Foreign Policy Decisions.* New York: Free Press, 1979.

Choucri, Nazli and Robinson, Thomas W., eds. *Forecasting in International Relations.* San Franciso: W. H. Freeman & Co., 1978.

Clausewitz, Karl von. *On War.* Edited and translated by Michael Howard and Peter Paret. Princeton: Princeton University Press, 1976.

Collins, John M. *Grand Strategy: Principles and Practices.* Annapolis: Naval Institute Press, 1973.

Crabb, Cecil V., Jr., and Holt, Pat M. *Invitation to Struggle: Congress, the President and Foreign Policy.* Washington, DC: Congressional Quarterly Press, 1980.

SELECTED REFERENCES

Cyert, Richard M. and March, James G. *A Behavioral Theory of the Firm.* Englewood Cliffs, NJ: Prentice-Hall, 1963.

de Tocqueville, Alexis. *Democracy in America.* New York: Oxford University Press, 1953.

Destler, I. M. *Presidents, Bureaucrats, and Foreign Policy: The Politics of Organizational Reform.* Princeton: Princeton University Press, 1974.

Domhoff, G. William. *Who Rules America?* Englewood Cliffs, NJ: Prentice-Hall, 1967.

Enthoven, Alain C., and Smith, K. Wayne. *How Much is Enough? Shaping the Defense Program, 1961-1969.* New York: Harper & Row, 1971.

Gansler, Jacques S. *The Defense Industry.* Cambridge: MIT Press, 1980.

Gelb, Leslie H., with Betts, Richard K. *The Irony of Vietnam: The System Worked.* Washington, DC: Brookings Institution, 1979.

Halberstam, David. *The Best and the Brightest.* New York: Random House, 1972.

Halperin, Morton H. *Bureaucratic Politics and Foreign Policy.* Washington, DC: Brookings Institution, 1974.

Halperin, Morton H.; Berman, Jerry J.; Borosage, Robert L.; and Marwick, Christine M. *The Lawless State: The Crimes of the Intelligence Agencies.* New York: Penguin Books, 1976.

Hammond, Paul Y. *Organizing for Defense: The American Military Establishment in the Twentieth Century.* Princeton: Princeton University Press, 1961.

Head, Richard G.; Short, Frisco W.; and McFarlane, Robert C. *Crisis Resolution: Presidential Decision Making in the Mayaguez and Korean Confrontations.* Boulder, Colo.: Westview Press, 1978.

Heclo, Hugh. *A Government of Strangers: Executive Politics in Washington.* Washington, DC: Brookings Institution, 1977.

Hodgetts, Richard M. and Wortman, Max S., Jr. *Administrative Policy.* New York: John Wiley & Sons, 1980.

Huntington, Samuel P. *The Common Defense: Strategic Programs in National Politics.* New York: Columbia University Press, 1961.

_____. *The Soldier and the State.* Cambridge: Harvard University Press, 1957.

Ignatius, Paul R. Department of Defense Reorganization Study Project. *Departmental Headquarters Study. A Report to the Secretary of Defense.* 1 June 1978.

Janowitz, Morris. *The Professional Soldier: A Social and Political Portrait.* 2d ed. New York: Free Press, 1971.

Kanter, Arnold. *Defense Politics: A Budgetary Perspective.* Chicago: University of Chicago Press, 1979.

Kaufman, William W. *The McNamara Strategy.* New York: Harper & Row, 1964.

Kennan, George F. *American Diplomacy, 1900-1950.* New York: New American World Library, 1959.

Kincade, William H. "Over the Technological Horizon." *Daedalus.* Winter 1981.

Kinnard, Douglas. *President Eisenhower and Strategy Management.* Lexington, KY: University Press of Kentucky, 1975.

_____. *The War Managers.* Hanover: New Hampshire University Press of New England, 1977.

Kissinger, Henry. *White House Years.* Boston: Little, Brown & Co., 1979.

Knorr, Klaus E. *On the Uses of Military Power in the Nuclear Age.* Princeton: Princeton University Press, 1966.

_____. *The Power of Nations: The Political Economy of International Relations.* New York: Basic Books, 1975.

Korb, Lawrence J. *The Fall and Rise of the Pentagon: American Defense Policies in the 1970s.* Westport, Conn.: Greenwood Press, 1979.

_____. *The Joint Chiefs of Staff: The First Twenty-five Years.* Bloomington, Ind.: Indiana University Press, 1976.

Krone, Robert M. *Systems Analysis and Policy Sciences.* New York: John Wiley & Sons, 1980.

SELECTED REFERENCES

Kucera, Randolph P. *The Aerospace Industry and the Military: Structural and Political Relationships.* Beverly Hills, Calif.: Sage Publications, 1974.

Lerner, Max. *America as a Civilization: Life and Thought in the United States Today.* New York: Simon and Schuster, 1957.

Lorange, Peter and Vancil, Richard F., eds. *Strategic Planning Systems.* Englewood, Cliffs, NJ.: Prentice-Hall, 1977.

Lovell, John P. *Foreign Policy in Perspective.* New York: Holt, Rinehart & Winston, 1970.

Lovell, John P., and Kronenberg, Philip S., eds. *New Civil-Military Relations: The Agonies of Adjustment to Post-Vietnam Realities.* New Brunswick, NJ: Transaction Books, 1974.

Lowi, Theodore J. *The End of Liberalism: Ideology, Policy, and the Crisis of Public Authority.* New York: W. W. Norton & Co., 1969.

March, James G., and Simon, Herbert A. *Organizations.* New York: John Wiley & Sons, 1958.

Margiotta, Franklin D., ed. *The Changing World of the American Military.* Boulder, Colo.: Westview Press, 1978.

Melman, Seymour. *The Permanent War Economy: American Capitalism in Decline.* New York: Simon & Schuster, 1974.

Millis, Walter. *Arms and Men: A Study in American Military History.* New York: G. P. Putnam's Sons, 1956.

Morgenthau, Hans J. *Politics Among Nations: The Struggle for Power and Peace.* 5th ed. New York: Alfred A. Knopf, 1973.

Nathan, James A., and Oliver, James K. "Bureaucratic Politics: Academic Windfalls and Intellectual Pitfalls." *Journal of Political and Military Sociology* 6 (Spring 1978): 81-91.

Neustadt, Richard. *Presidential Power.* New York: John Wiley & Sons, 1960.

Odeen, Philip A. "Organizing for National Security." *International Security,* Summer 1980.

Ornstern, Norman and Elder, Shirley. *Interest Groups, Lobbying and Policymaking.* Washington, DC: Congressional Quarterly Press, 1978.

Palmer, Dave Richard. *Summons of the Trumpet: U.S.-Vietnam in Perspective.* San Rafael, Calif.: Presidio Press, 1978.

Perrow, Charles. *Organizational Analysis: A Sociological View.* Belmont, Calif.: Brooks/Cole Publishing Co., 1970.

Pfeffer, Jeffrey, *Organizational Design.* Arlington Heights, Ill.: AHM Publishing Corp., 1978.

Rice, Donald B. Department of Defense Reorganization Study Project. *Defense Resource Management Study, Final Report.* February 1979.

Roherty, James M. *Decisions of Robert S. McNamara: A Study of the Role of the Secretary of Defense.* Coral Gables, Fla.: University of Miami Press, 1970.

Rosenblum, Donald E., Major General. Department of Defense Reorganization Study Project. *Combat Effective Training Management Study.* Prepared for Assistant Secretary of Defense (MRA&L). July 1979.

Sanders, Ralph. *The Politics of Defense Analysis.* New York: Dunellen Publishing Co., 1973.

Sayles, Leonard R., and Chandler, Margaret K. *Managing Large Systems: Organizations for the Future.* New York: Harper & Row, 1971.

Schelling, Thomas C. *Arms and Influence.* New Haven: Yale University Press, 1966.

Schendel, Dan E., and Hofer, Charles W., eds. *Strategic Management: A New View of Business Policy and Planning.* Boston: Little, Brown & Co., 1979.

Schilling, Warner R.; Hammond, Paul Y.; and Snyder, Glenn H. *Strategy, Politics, and Defense Budgets.* New York: Columbia University Press, 1962.

Schlesinger, Arthur M., Jr. *The Imperial Presidency.* Boston: Houghton Mifflin Co., 1973.

Seidman, Harold. *Politics, Position, and Power: The Dynamics of Federal Organization.* 2d ed. New York: Oxford University Press, 1975.

SELECTED REFERENCES

Shirley, Robert C.; Peters, Michael H.; and El-Ansary, Adel I. *Strategy and Policy Formation.* New York: John Wiley & Sons, 1976.

Simon, Herbert A. *Models of Man, Social and Rational.* New York: John Wiley & Sons, 1957.

Smith, Perry McC. *The Air Force Plans for Peace 1943-1945.* Baltimore: Johns Hopkins University Press, 1970.

Sorley, Lewis. "Turbulence at the Top: Our Peripatetic Generals." *Army.* March 1981.

Staudenmaier, William O. *Strategic Concepts for the 1980s.* Carlisle Barracks, PA: Strategic Studies Institute, US Army War College, 1 May 1981.

Steadman, Richard C. Department of Defense Reorganization Study Project. *Report to the Secretary of Defense on the National Military Command Structure.* July 1978.

Steinbruner, John D. *The Cybernetic Theory of Decision: New Dimensions of Political Analysis.* Princeton: Princeton University Press, 1974.

Taylor, Maxwell D. *The Uncertain Trumpet.* New York: Harper, 1959.

Thompson, James D. *Organizations in Action.* New York: McGraw-Hill, 1967.

Thompson, W. Scott and Frizzell, Donaldson D., eds. *The Lessons of Vietnam.* New York: Crane, Russak & Co., 1977.

Truman, David B. *The Governmental Process.* New York: Alfred A. Knopf, 1962.

Vagts, Alfred. *A History of Militarism: Civilian and Military.* Rev. ed. New York: Meridian Books, 1959.

Van Creveld, Martin. *Supplying War: Logistics from Wallenstein to Patton.* Cambridge: Cambridge University Press, 1977.

Weick, Karl E. *The Social Psychology of Organizing.* Menlo Park, Calif.: Addison-Wesley Publishing Co., 1969.

Weigley, Russell F. *The American Way of War.* Bloomington, Ind.: Indiana University Press, 1977.

Westmoreland, William C. *A Soldier Reports.* New York: Double-day, 1976.

Wildavasky, Aaron. *Speaking Truth to Power: The Art and Craft of Policy Analysis.* Boston: Little, Brown & Co., 1979.

Wilensky, Harold L. *Organizational Intelligence.* New York: Basic Books, 1967.

Wohlstetter, Roberta. *Pearl Harbor: Warning and Decision.* Stanford: Stanford University Press, 1962.

SEMINAR PARTICIPANTS

THE SPONSORS

Lieutenant General John S. Pustay, United States Air Force, has been President of the National Defense University since 15 July 1981. Before assuming his present position, he was Assistant to the Chairman of the Joint Chiefs of Staff. General Pustay's previous military assignments include service as Commander, Keesler Technical Training Center, Keesler Air Force Base; Director, Doctrine, Concepts and Objectives, US Air Force Headquarters; Executive Assistant to the Secretary of the Air Force; and Executive to the Chief of Staff, Supreme Headquarters Allied Powers Europe. He is the author of *Counterinsurgency Warfare,* has been a contributing editor to *Encyclopedia Americana,* and has written extensively on national security issues, such as Communist insurgency warfare, Japanese rearmament, peaceful coexistence, deterrence, and defense and national resources. A graduate of the United States Naval Academy and the Industrial College of the Armed Forces, General Pustay received a doctoral degree in international politics from the University of Denver.

Lieutenant General Robert G. Gard, Jr., United States Army (Ret.), former President of the National Defense University. General Gard has commanded the US Army Military Personnel Center; the US Army Training Center and Fort Ord, California; and the 9th Infantry Division Artillery in Vietnam. He has served as the Army's Director of Human Resources Development; Military Assistant to the Secretary of Defense; and Army Fellow with the Council on Foreign Relations. He is the author of monographs and articles that appeared in the scholarly press. General Gard is a graduate of the United States Military Academy and The National War College, and received a doctoral degree from Harvard University.

The Honorable Fred C. Ikle has been Under Secretary of Defense for Policy since April 1981. Dr. Ikle is the former Director, US Arms Control and Disarmament Agency; a former head of the Social Science Department, the Rand Corporation; and a former Professor of Political Science, Massachusetts Institute of Technology. He has figured prominently in past SALT negotiations and has written extensively on the subject of arms control and international political issues. Dr. Ikle received a doctoral degree from the University of Chicago.

The Honorable David E. McGiffert was Assistant Secretary of Defense for International Security Affairs until January 1981. He formerly served as Assistant to the Secretary of Defense for Legislative Affairs and as Under Secretary of the Army. He was a lecturer in law at Harvard University and the Harvard Law School, and was the Lionel de Jersey Harvard Student at Cambridge University. Mr. McGiffert is a member of the Washington law firm of Covington and Burling.

THE CONFERENCE DIRECTOR

Colonel Franklin D. Margiotta, United States Air Force, is Director of Research, National Defense University; Director of the National Security Affairs Institute; and Publisher, National Defense University Press. He formerly served as Dean of Curriculum and Research Professor at the Air University, and has extensive operational experience as a B-52 Aircraft Commander, Strategic Air Command. He is the editor of and a contributor to *The Changing World of the American Military* and *Evolving Strategic Realities: Implications for US Policymakers,* and the author of chapters in other books, as well as journal articles. Colonel Margiotta received a doctoral degree in political science from the Massachusetts Institute of Technology.

THE EDITOR AND 1980-81 SEMINAR CHAIRMAN

Dr. Philip S. Kronenberg is Director of National Strategy Studies and Associate Professor in the Center for Public Administration and Policy, Virginia Polytechnic Institute and State University. During 1981-82, he is on sabbatical leave from Virginia Polytechnic to study long-range defense planning as Research Professor of Military Affairs in the Airpower Research Institute of the Air War College. He formerly served on political science faculties and directed public administration institutes at the University of Tennessee and Indiana University. He served on active duty with the US Air Force in the early 1960s. His current research interests focus on the strategic management of complex organizations, foreign and security policy, and interorganizational theory. His books are *National Security and American Society* (1973), *The New Civil-Military Relations* (1974), and *Program Evaluation Methodology* (1980). His writings outside of the defense area include studies of the politics of planning, public agency responses to civil disorder, organization dynamics, and emergency management. His work as a consultant in security-related areas includes studies for the Navy Department, the Federal Emergency Management Agency, and the President's Reorganization Project, Executive Office of the President. He is the Editor of the Defense Management Series of the quarterly journal *The Bureaucrat* and serves on several other editorial boards.

THE AUTHORS

Dr. Archie D. Barrett is a member of the Professional Staff, House Armed Services Committee. A retired Air Force Officer, he was formerly a Senior Research Fellow, National Defense University. Before joining the university Dr. Barrett was the military staff assistant to the Executive Secretary of the Defense Organization Study (the Defense Department portion of the President's Reorganization Project). He has extensive experience in NATO general defense, nuclear and logistics plans and policies; Air Staff long-range planning, concept and doctrine development; and flight operations, strategic and tactical. Dr. Barrett's book, *The Organizational Structure of the Department of Defense in the 1980s,* is forthcoming from the National Defense University Press. He has a bachelor's degree from the United States Military Academy and master's and doctoral degrees from Harvard University.

Dr. Davis B. Bobrow is Professor of Government and Politics, University of Maryland, and a member of the Defense Science Board. In the late 1960s, he was responsible for the social and behavioral science research and development activities of the Department of Defense and has since served as adviser and consultant to senior officials in the US national security community. He is the author, coauthor, or editor of *Components of Defense Policy; Computers and the Policy-Making Community: Applications to International Relations; Weapons System Decisions: Political and Psychological Perspectives on Continental Defense; International Relations: New Approaches;* and *Understanding Foreign Policy Decisions: The Chinese Case.*

The Honorable Lawrence J. Korb is Assistant Secretary of Defense for Manpower, Reserve Affairs, and Logistics. During the 1980-81 Seminar series and prior to assuming his present position, he was Director of Defense Policy Studies, American Enterprise Institute for Public Policy Research. Dr. Korb served in the US Navy during the 1960s, has had a distinguished career as a researcher and scholar, and has written extensively on such relevant issues as the manpower and readiness problems of our current force and the history of the Joint Chiefs of Staff and their present and future role in foreign policy. His long list of books and monographs includes *The Joint Chiefs of Staff; Pentagon Politics; The Price of Preparedness;* and *The Fall and Rise of the Pentagon.* He is a member of the Council on Foreign Relations, and has been a consultant to the Office of the Secretary of Defense, the Office of Education, the President's Reorganization Project, and the National Security Council. He has a master's degree from St. John's University and a doctoral degree from the State University of New York, Albany.

Dr. Edward N. Luttwak is a Senior Fellow, Center for Strategic and International Studies, Georgetown University, and a research professor, Georgetown University. A scholar and lecturer in international affairs and national security policy, Dr. Luttwak has served as SALT consultant to then Senate Minority Leader, Howard Baker; as a member of the National Security Group of the Office of the President-elect, 1980-81; and now serves as a consultant to the Department of Defense and other US Government agencies. He is the author of books and articles on strategic and military affairs. Dr. Luttwak received a bachelor's degree in economics from the London School of Economics and a doctoral degree in political science from The Johns Hopkins University.

Dr. James A. Nathan is Professor of Political Science, University of Delaware. He recently completed a term as Scholar-in-Residence at the Naval War College Center for Advanced Research. The coauthor of several books, including *International Education in a Global Age; United States Foreign Policy and World Order;* and *The Future of Sea Power,* his articles have appeared extensively in leading political and military journals. Dr. Nathan received his master's and doctoral degrees from The Johns Hopkins University.

Dr. James K. Oliver is Professor of Political Science, University of Delaware. He has written extensively on national security policy, foreign affairs, the United States Congress, and American naval policy, and is the coauthor of three books on United States foreign policy, American naval power, and world politics, including

A Decidedly Inferior Form? Foreign Policy Making in the American Political System. Dr. Oliver received his master's degree from Florida State University and his doctoral degree in international studies from the School of International Studies, American University.

THE PARTICIPANTS

Dr. Joseph Annunziata, Office of Management and Budget

Dr. Archie D. Barrett, Professional Staff, House Armed Services Committee

Mr. William Beecher, Washington Diplomatic Correspondent, *Boston Globe*

Dr. David S. C. Chu, Director, Program Analysis and Evaluation, Department of Defense

Major General James E. Dalton, United States Air Force, Commandant, Industrial College of the Armed Forces

Dr. I. M. Destler, Senior Associate, Carnegie Endowment for International Peace

Lieutenant General Paul F. Gorman, United States Army, Director of Plans and Policy (J-5), Joint Chiefs of Staff

Lieutenant General Ernest Graves, United States Army, Deputy Assistant Secretary of Defense (Security Assistance)

Mr. Stephen J. Hadley, Shea and Gardner, Attorneys at Law

Dr. Arnold Kanter, Director, Office of Policy Analysis, Department of State

Dr. Catherine M. Kelleher, Faculty, National War College

Dr. Lawrence J. Korb, Assistant Secretary of Defense (Manpower, Reserve Affairs, and Logistics)

Mr. Franklin D. Kramer, Acting Under Secretary of Defense for Policy

Dr. Edward N. Luttwak, Senior Fellow, Georgetown Center for Strategic and International Studies

Colonel Franklin D. Margiotta, United States Air Force, Director of Research, National Defense University

Mr. Andrew W. Marshall, Director, Net Assessment, Office of the Secretary of Defense

Colonel Richard W. Masson, United States Air Force, Faculty, National War College

Mr. Philip A. Odeen, Partner-in-Charge, Coopers and Lybrand, Management Consulting Group

Honorable Brent Scowcroft, Consultant

Honorable Monteagle Stearns, former Vice President, National Defense University

Dr. John Steinbruner, Director of Foreign Policy Studies, Brookings Institution

Major General Lee E. Surut, United States Army, Commandant, National War College

Mr. Peter Szanton, Executive Associate Director for Organization Studies, Office of Management and Budget

Dr. Victor A. Utgoff, Professional Staff, Institute for Defense Analyses

Dr. Samuel F. Wells, Jr., Secretary, International Security Studies Program, Woodrow Wilson International Center for Scholars, Smithsonian Institution

Dr. Paul Wolfowitz, Director, Policy Planning Staff, Department of State

INDEX